Leo M Goethert

Cervantes and the Material World

*Hispanisms*

Series Editor
Anne J. Cruz

# Cervantes
## *and the Material World*

Carroll B. Johnson

University of Illinois Press

Urbana and Chicago

Publication of this book was supported by a grant from the
Program for Cultural Cooperation between Spain's Ministry
of Education and Culture and United States Universities

Library of Congress Cataloging-in-Publication Data
Johnson, Carroll B.
Cervantes and the material world / Carroll B. Johnson.
p.   cm. — (Hispanisms)
Includes bibliographical references and index.
ISBN 0-252-02548-2
I. Title. II. Series. 1. Cervantes Saavedra, Miguel de, 1547–1616
    Don Quixote. 2. Economics in literature. 3. Materialism in
    literature.
PQ6353.J625    2000
863'.3—dc21    99-006849
CIP

C   5   4   3   2   1

To the memory of
Sallie Garriotte Johnson,
1910–91

# Contents

# Acknowledgments

Some of the chapters in this book are reworked and expanded versions of articles that were published elsewhere:

Chapter 2 is based on "The Old Order Passeth, or Does It? Some Thoughts on Community, Commerce and Alienation in *Rinconete y Cortadillo*," in *On Cervantes: Essays for Luis Murillo*, ed. James A. Parr (Newark, Del.: Juan de la Cuesta, 1991), 85–104.

Chapter 3 is based on "Ortodoxia y anticapitalismo en el siglo XVII: el caso del morisco Ricote," in *Hispanic Studies in Honor of Joseph H. Silverman*, ed. J. V. Ricapito (Newark, Del.: Juan de la Cuesta, 1988), 285–96.

An abbreviated version of chapter 5 appeared as "De economías y linajes en *La Gitanilla*," *Mester* 25.1 (Spring 1996): 31–48.

Chapter 7 was published as "*La española inglesa* and the Practice of Literary Production," *Viator* 19 (1988): 377–416.

I wish to thank Anne Cruz for sponsoring this project and for her many and detailed comments and suggestions. Thanks also to Emily Rogers, formerly of the University of Illinois Press, for her goodwill and support. Edward Friedman, Michael Gerli, Steven Hutchinson, James Iffland, Francisco Márquez, Michel Moner, James Parr, Augustin Redondo, and Harry Sieber have also reacted to various versions of the ideas presented here, and I am grateful for their comments and suggestions. Finally, my wife, Leslie, suffered patiently through all the visions and revisions and finally made this book possible, in the most literal and material sense, with the timely purchase of a new computer.

## Note on the Text

Throughout this book I have used Burton Raffel's translation of *Don Quijote* in the Norton Critical Edition edited by Diana de Armas Wilson (New York: W. W. Norton, 1999), which is the new standard in English.

Cervantes and the Material World

# Introduction

Over the last few years I have become increasingly aware, to a point somewhere between preoccupation and obsession, of the sheer presence in Cervantes's texts of the material world, especially materialist practices such as commodification, commerce, and exchange. These practices impinge actively upon the lives of the characters, their motivations, and their possibilities for action. It is possible, for example, to observe a recurrent preoccupation with the clash of two different economic systems, a reenergized feudalism and an incipient capitalism, and to observe furthermore that this clash engages Cervantes's sixteenth- and seventeenth-century characters both ethnically and estamentally. In the process, the human and institutional relationships between characters are placed in crisis, altered, or maintained, depending on the outcome of the economic struggle.

There is also the important but rather more obvious ideological dimension to the presence of all these materialist practices: raising to the level of consciousness the socioeconomic issues in flux in Cervantes's society during his lifetime, the resolution of which would determine the course of Spanish history, to say nothing of the material well-being of the Spanish people, for centuries.

We tend to skip over the specific mention of these materialist practices, thanks to habits of academic reading conditioned by centuries of genteel attention to "the great questions," "the finer things," and "the higher aspirations of Man"—philosophy, the nature of truth and reality, religion, ethics, the theory of love. Or again by attention to the classification of themes, motifs, plots, and the study of their transmission through time and space. Or to the intricacies and the endlessly fascinating paradoxes of form. Even in the age of the post-, where it is permissible to fixate on sexual desire and bodily functions, there is a general tendency to overlook, to purposely or unconsciously blot out all the fictional-textual representations of the material conditions of life, except for the newly fashionable bodily functions.

Insofar as materialist practices appear in critical discourse, they tend to be viewed through the lens of the aforementioned finer things and higher aspirations. The prevailing opinion, at least in the United States, distinguishes between a feudoagrarian-aristocratic order in Spain, and a protocapitalist system based on piracy and other forms of predation in the lands outside the sphere of Christian European civilization: in the Ottoman empire and in the savage subarctic regions of the *Persiles,* for example. The former system is linked to the aristocratic value of *liberalidad* (the disinterested exercise of largesse), to a patriarchal social system, to Christian matrimony where chastity and reproduction join hands, and to chivalric literature. The opposing system is seen to embody notions of exchange in the service of self-interest, greed, rapacity, and sexual desire out of control, and has been linked to the literary genre of Byzantine romance. Not surprisingly, although much recent academic discourse has been devoted to "discovering" and demonstrating it, Spanish texts of the sixteenth and seventeenth centuries tend to identify strongly with the Christian-European system and its values, and to stigmatize the latter as the Other, in what Edward Said would call the "Orientalist discourse."

What is truly surprising and not a little disconcerting is that so many of my compatriots and fellow Golden Age scholars, all products of American democracy and its bourgeois institutions, also identify with the aristocratic values that were de rigeur in the rigidly estamentarian society of early modern Spain. Robert ter Horst is perhaps the most ardent in his embrace of the aristocrat's studied avoidance of the economic dimension of life. According to ter Horst, Cervantes had "inherited from the picaresque writings a major new subject, economic woman and man. His response . . . is to . . . reconvert the economic order to moral rule, to ascend out of the labyrinth of greed to the firmament of beauty and virtue."[1]

I want to insist on the economic order ter Horst finds so distasteful. At the same time, I find myself unable to isolate the specifically material practices from the sociocultural milieu in which they occur and take on meaning. Questions of the distribution of wealth, or the ownership of means of production, or indeed of membership in one or another economic order, are invariably embedded in social relationships, as Raymond Williams and Pierre Bourdieu have shown. My analyses consequently address the dynamics of family life, both socioanthropologically as an institution and psychosexually as the site of more or less forbidden desire. Capitalism's master trope of investment as insemination, with material profit figured as biological increase, has compelled an exploration of the relations between phallic aggression (or its absence) and economic systems old and new. Finally, because as General Franco's Ministry of Tourism never tired of repeating and as Américo Castro taught us to understand why, "España es diferente," the dialectic of an old and a new economic system is assimilated to the ethnic tension between Old Christians (*cristianos viejos*) and New Christians (*cristianos nuevos*, or *conversos* and *moriscos*) and the traditional division of socioeconomic activity and status in Spanish society.

Américo Castro taught us to perceive the intercaste conflicts underlying behaviors as diverse as eating pork products and getting into the Order of Calatrava, and how an entire society was organized around those conflicts. Fernand Braudel has taught us to perceive the importance of commerce in spite of national antagonisms in early modern Europe, and José Antonio Maravall has produced and inspired massive documentation of the Spanish experience in particular. For reasons that differ in each case, none of these seminal thinkers has defined or even particularly affected the course of mainstream Cervantes studies in the United States. This is a pity and a disservice to scholarship, because their work places us in a position to identify the themes Cervantes deals with in terms of their relation to the socioeconomic and political problematics of his time.

The issues that will concern us are adumbrated in the picaresque *Lazarillo de Tormes*.[2] The episode of the *escudero* (squire) dramatizes the change from a feudal to a capitalist mentality and the subsequent failure of the new order to take hold and prosper in the mid-sixteenth-century Castilian environment.

The traditional basic fighting unit composed of a knight and his escudero (literally 'shield-bearer') had been rendered obsolete by the evolution of warfare. One possibility for those escuderos whose function within the economy of medieval warfare had disappeared, and who couldn't live off what their land could produce, was a kind of updated version of their traditional role of service to a *caballero* (knight). During the sixteenth century many caballeros as well as titled aristocrats were moving from the country into the city, where they used the income from their country property to maintain a townhouse (or palace) and as lavish a lifestyle as they could afford. They needed servants to supervise the other servants in their households, so some escuderos were able to enter the service of caballeros and other aristocrats in the new urban setting. Unfortunately, the market was unable to absorb all the escuderos who needed somebody to serve. Too many of them flocked to the cities and kept up a façade of respectability while they looked desperately for some higher-ranking aristocrat who would take them into his service and provide for their needs.

Lazarillo's third master is just such a man. He and Don Quixote are the two best-developed representations in literature of this painful social reality: an entire social class whose reason for being has disappeared, that finds itself in a kind of limbo waiting for new institutions and new social structures to develop where there will be a place and a role for them. Don Quixote stays on his land and barely hangs on; Lazarillo's nameless escudero moves to the big city and hopes for the best.

Everything the escudero does and says can be explained in terms of this particularly wrenching instance of social and economic evolution. He tells Lazarillo that he came from near Valladolid in Old Castile, and that he had left his home because he refused to raise his hat to a higher-ranking aristocrat who was his neighbor. In the discussion that follows he equates honor (*honra*) with the capital (*caudal*) of the aristocratic *hombres de bien*. He clarifies this by observing that his own capital, in the form of the property he owns near Valladolid, is not sufficient to support him and that he has come to Toledo to find a higher-ranking aristocrat who will take him into his service, thereby demonstrating that, indeed, his only capital is his aristocratic honor.

Geographically he makes the same kind of journey as Lazarillo, from Old Castile to Toledo, from the mythic heartland of the old order to the capital of the new. In the meantime he clings to all the outward and visible signs of his nobility: his ostentatious leisure, his cape and other clothing, and his sword. Only aristocrats were supposed to carry swords; this is why he fetishizes his so insistently. Although he never uses it for anything except to take it out and admire it and run his finger up and down it, the sword is public proof that he is an aristocrat. Everything the escudero does is a desperate attempt to hang on to the old order. He cannot conceive society and his place in it except in terms of the old feudoagrarian order that no longer has a place for him.

Lazarillo represents the possible new socioeconomic order, in direct contrast to the escudero. In *Tratado 6*, he works for a chaplain of the Toledo cathedral selling water. This relationship is significant in itself. For the first time Lazarillo is not a servant but a kind of employee. The relationship between him and the chaplain is built around and mediated by money; it is in fact a kind of protocapitalistic relation. The employer provides the tools; Lazarillo contributes the labor. The employer gets thirty *maravedís* off the top, and Lazarillo keeps whatever is left, except on Saturdays, when the employer doesn't take anything. These details, as George Shipley has observed, identify the chaplain as a *converso* as well as an entrepreneur.[3] This is not surprising, since in the plurireligious Spanish Middle Ages commerce was generally the province of Jews, and after 1492 it was their descendants, the conversos, who dominated business and finance. It is interesting that this converso entrepreneur is also a member of the Toledo cathedral, apparently blissfully unaware of the impending Statutes of Purity of Blood (*estatutos de limpieza de sangre*) of 1547 that were about to put him out of a job, if not out of business.

Lazarillo puts in four years in this arrangement with the chaplain, at the end of which he has saved up enough money to buy himself a suit of clothes and a sword and to come out looking just like the escudero. The appearance is the same, but the intention and meaning are very different. For the escudero, the clothes and the sword are his birthright, and they are the outward and visible sign of his noble blood. For Lazarillo, the same clothes and sword are his by purchase, and instead of representing a desperate clinging to the past, they are the keys to the future. The clothes and sword are in fact an investment from which Lazarillo expects to realize a profit in the form of upward social mobility. Lazarillo thinks like a capitalist. He works for four years and achieves the "primitive accumulation of capital" that is the essential precondition for the development of capitalism. He invests this capital in the clothes, and he's on his way. When he sees himself "'dressed as an *hombre de bien*,'" he leaves the chaplain and goes to work in an *oficio real* (government job). José Antonio Maravall considers the government bureaucracy, along with the professionalized army, to be the two pillars of the modern nation-state that arise in the sixteenth century, so that when Lázaro says "'you can't get ahead these days unless you work for the government'" (128), he is proclaiming his membership in the new order.[4]

Unfortunately, his exercise of capitalism, which has made him momentarily independent, is short-lived. At the end of the book Lazarillo is once again in a dependent relationship, to the Arcipreste de San Salvador, and his marriage is merely a façade of respectability for the Arcipreste's illicit sexual relationship with his housekeeper. It has always been observed that by entering into this arrangement Lazarillo trades his moral integrity and self-respect for material well-being. He also trades away his financial independence and the possibility of a new kind of socioeconomic order when he allows himself to become dependent on the Arcipreste, and he trades the possibility of adult psychic independence for the dependency of childhood.

Lazarillo's story demonstrates that you can win a battle but you can't win the war. The possibility for change is clearly present in the text, there is a power struggle, and the old order reasserts its supremacy in the end. Cervantes will return repeatedly to this same struggle, documenting its evolution and its shape around the turn of the seventeenth century.

As an introduction to some of these questions in Cervantes, I want to pass in review some instances of commerce and other material practices in *Don Quixote*, simply to call attention to their presence, either running alongside or actively undercutting the official feudochivalric rhetoric.

At the metafictional level, the text we read owes its existence to the Toledo silk industry and its requirements for paper. What might have become of Cide Hamete Benengeli's manuscript had it not been bundled up to sell to a silk manufacturer as food for worms, and been discovered there by the second author in part I, chapter 9?

Within the fiction, we tend to overlook the obvious fact that the windmills, the flocks of sheep, and the *batanes* (fulling mills) are physical manifestations of the rural economy of La Mancha, and that the network of roads and roadside inns, and the *arrieros* and other sojourners are testimony to the centrality of La Mancha to peninsular and international commerce.

More particularly, we tend to think of Don Quixote as the antithesis of materialism in any form, but in fact his very existence as a crazily idealistic knight errant called Don Quixote is grounded in a prosaic commercial transaction. The text tells us that he "sold acre after acre of good crop land in order to buy books of these tales" (I, 1, 13).[5] Don Quixote sells off arable land, the sign of his membership in the old feudoagrarian order, to buy books of chivalry. In one sense this act results in a further impoverishment of an already impoverished country hidalgo. The same act can also be read, however, as an investment. Don Quixote does what the escudero of *Lazarillo de Tormes* could not: he converts his old order credentials into a commodity, which he then converts into cash, which he then exchanges for another, more useful commodity. Books of chivalry, like all books, are a special kind of commodity. For one thing, the use-value of a book is not extinguished by reading; it is available for any other reader who comes along. Nor is the use-value of a book limited to the act of reading. As Américo Castro never tired of pointing out, the book continues to resonate in the life of the reader long after it has been finished. The books of chivalry furnish Don Quixote with the idea of his new self-fashioned identity and with a wealth of specific content to be incorporated into his daily experience. Don Quixote's investment in the books is an investment in himself, analogous to Lazarillo's investment in his clothes. This existentially fecund investment will be explicitly contrasted to the bloodless (but profitable) commercialization of literature toward the end on the novel, in part II, chapter 62.

At the beginning of his first sally Don Quixote is dubbed a knight by the innkeeper, who reads, or pretends to read, from "a book in which he recorded the straw and barley he supplied to the muleteers" (I, 3, 25). This account book replaces the Bible or any other authoritative chivalric text as the scriptural basis of the character's transformation. By grounding Don Quixote's knighthood in the details of the fodder consumed by the mule trains crisscrossing the country, the text subordinates chivalry itself to peninsular and international commerce. The plastic image of Don Quixote humbling himself before the innkeeper and his account book becomes emblematic of the new relation of feudalism to commerce.

Don Quixote's intervention on behalf of little Andrés in part I, chapter 4, casts him in the role of uninvited arbitrator of a labor dispute. Management has made certain commitments that it now appears unwilling to honor. In particular, wages have gone unpaid, and labor is owed seven reales per month for nine months. Don Quixote does the arithmetic (badly; he is a knight, not an accountant) and demands instant payment of the full amount. Management attempts to deduct the value of three pairs of shoes plus medical expenses the employee had incurred; Don Quixote negotiates.

In the same chapter the text evokes Don Quixote's encounter with the Toledo merchants on their way to buy silk in Murcia. Antonio Domínguez Ortiz and Bernard Vincent tell us that Granada had traditionally been the primary source for silk, but following an epidemic that decimated the mulberry trees and the expatriation of most of the morisco labor force to Castile following the unsuccessful revolt in the Alpujarra in 1568, Grenadine production suffered an abrupt decline and the Toledo merchants had to find another source. Special permission was given for the establishment of a silk industry in the hands of moriscos in Murcia. This is the economic base that determines the first challenge to Dulcinea's beauty, and leads to one of Don Quixote's first drubbings.[6]

In part I, chapter 10, Sancho fantasizes the commercialization of the famous balm of Fierabrás at a return of about two hundred to one on the cost of production.[7] In part I, chapter 29, he fantasizes the commercialization of human beings in the form of the black vassals he expects to acquire as a result of Don Quixote's marriage to Princesa Micomicona. Not only does Sancho offer precise calculations of the number and price of his human merchandise, he expects to take the profits and buy into a modified form of the aristocratic lifestyle. This little vignette rehearses the entire unfortunate trajectory of mercantile capitalism in Castile, with the assimilation of the merchant to the prestigious but economically sterile aristocracy.[8]

The flocks of sheep Don Quixote attacks in part I, chapter 18, are a manifestation of the tension between the powerful grazing industry and the farmers whose crops were routinely destroyed by transhumance. Their metamorphosis into two armies led by powerful warrior-princes contains an encoded reference to the names of principal Andalusian and Extremaduran sheepowners, especially the family of Cervantes's bête noir, the Duque de Medina Sidonia.[9]

In part I, chapter 25, Don Quixote formally transfers ownership of three donkeys from himself to Sancho. The document formalizing the transfer, which Luis Murillo identifies as a "humorous imitation of commercial bills of exchange," calls itself a "primera de pollinos," standing elliptically for the formula "primera [cédula] de cambio."[10] The text of the document is indeed a reworked version of the classic instrument of exchange known as *letra de cambio*. Moreover, what is comically reproduced is a fraudulent letra, because no real exchange occurred. Although Don Quixote makes reference to "'these three donkeys I deliver and pay in return for three others I have already received here, receipt of which I hereby acknowledge'" (I, 25, 158), there were in fact no "three others" received and given in exchange. This little vignette rehearses the evolution of the letra de cambio from an indispensable adjunct to the exchange of merchandise to an instrument of financial speculation that concealed illegal interest-bearing loans.

Ernest H. Templin has observed that Don Fernando "accepts Dorotea as his wife without any allusion to the disparity of rank which has obsessed her from the beginning."[11] This episode brings home with particular clarity the fact, too easy to overlook, that Cervantes's young lovers in the intercalated stories are not simply generic "lovers," free-floating bundles of desire colliding more or less randomly in a void, the physical analogue of the disembodied "soul," every one exactly alike. Every time two fictional people come into contact, two entire lives—that is, two histories and two contexts—are engaged. Each character exists as a member of a family, as a son or a daughter, with or without siblings. Each is a member of a social class (or *estado,* in the preferred sixteenth-century terminology). Each is inserted into an economic system within which he or she enjoys certain defined duties and prerogatives, which determines to a great extent how he or she conceives, constructs, and confronts the world.

A couple of significant throwaway references to Genoese commercial enterprises suggest that Captain Ruy Pérez de Viedma would have preferred to go into business instead of following in his father's footsteps as a soldier. He does not take up arms and enter the king's service immediately in Spain, but travels to Italy instead. And instead of taking the most direct route, from the mountains of León to Barcelona or Tortosa and thence by sea to Italy, he goes by way of Alicante, where he embarks on a Genoese merchant ship loaded with wool bound for Genoa (I, 39, 266). His brief narration also points to the colonialization of the Spanish economy in the form of export of raw materials to be reimported as manufactured products. Later in his narrative Ruy Pérez locates a military objective by its proximity to Genoese commercial activity (I, 39, 269).

Has anyone noticed that personal satisfaction and narrative closure of the "Mambrino's helmet" episode, for all its philosophical-metaphysical-perspectivist complexity, is finally achieved in part I, chapter 46, only by the prosaic material operation of quietly buying all the disputed objects in question from the barber?

In part II, chapter 10, Don Quixote promises Sancho all the foals dropped by his mares, which are grazing on the village common. The reference to the municipal pasture evokes the frequent practice of public lands, concretely the sort of communal pasture mentioned here, being taken over and privatized by the wealthy and powerful. The offhand reference to the village common remits to a pressing question of land ownership and utilization, and to the struggle between public benefit and private acquisitiveness. The phenomenon of *usurpación* was the subject of a series of treatises beginning with the Cortes of 1558.[12]

The name of Sancho's fictitious *ínsula* Barataria was defined by Sebastián de Covarrubias in 1611 as "bribing a judge with an especially low price" (*baratería*).[13] That is, the place is defined by a combination of corrupt government and mercantile practices. Also present are associations to the largesse (*barato*) bestowed by aristocratic gamblers on the kibbitzers present at the game. One of the cases Sancho is called upon to adjudicate involves a winning gambler and a kibbitzer (*mirón*) to whom the winner had given an insufficient barato. The mirón turns out to be a poor hidalgo, whose nobility in combination with his poverty transforms him into a parasite with no means of support, like the escudero of *Lazarillo de Tormes*. This man's situation was denounced as early as 1558 by Luis de Ortiz, who wanted everyone, of whatever status, to be required to learn a trade or be exiled. The idea recurs in other political economists well into the seventeenth century. Naturally, this antiaristocratic utopian fantasy did not prosper, even in fiction.

Sancho shares with a long series of political economists a reformist project to replace idleness with productive labor in his domains (II, 49). This policy is a mixture of tradition and reform. On the one hand Sancho would respect the existing social order, including aristocratic and ecclesiastical privilege; on the other hand he would put everyone else to work. Perhaps the most significant single reform is his creation of a poor people's constabulary to determine their eligibility for welfare (II, 51). This interventionist stance opposes the traditional practice of Christian charity encapsulated in the proverb "haz bien y no mires a quién" ("Let not your right hand know what your left hand is doing," or, "charity is blind"). Sancho lines up with a series of reformers running from Vives through Juan de Medina and Miguel Giginta to Cristóbal Pérez de Herrera, all of whom favored some form of state control to limit charity to the truly needy and replace idleness with full employment.[14] It is interesting although probably futile to observe how much more humanitarian and utilitarian were the projects of those preindustrial Catholic pipe dreamers than what we now call welfare "reform" and surround with a rhetoric of morality and family values in late-twentieth-century America. But I digress.

The episode of the morisco Ricote (II, 54), which obviously dramatizes religious and ethnic tensions and the human consequences of a failed government policy toward a large, unassimilated ethnic minority, also situates the moriscos in terms of their contribution to the economy, with particular reference to capital formation and the flight of capital to Europe.

And what can we say, finally, of the business of literature? The emergence of the book as one of the first mass-produced commodities of early modern Europe, studied recently by Lisa Jardine, created a tension between the integrity of artistic vision and the market economy.[15] Part II of *Don Quixote* begins with a discussion of the author's place within the new commercial order, which becomes the subject of Márquez Torres's *aprobación,* with its pathetic evocation of the disparity between Cervantes's talent and his material well-being. Cervantes's text dramatizes this tension first in chapter 4, where Sansón Carrasco is critical of the author's pursuit of "the money he can make, which interests him a lot more than whatever praise he'll receive," but where Sancho is more than willing to provide him with "so many adventures and all sorts of goings-on that he won't be able to write just a second part, but a hundred of them" (II, 4, 381). The question comes up finally in part II, chapter 62, where individual artistic vision is relentlessly subordinated to the pursuit of profit by the publisher-bookseller in Barcelona.

The foregoing series of vignettes has attempted to suggest not merely the pervasive presence of the material world and material practices in the *Quixote* and to assess Cervantes's attitudes toward the economic underpinnings of the society he inhabited, although these questions are important and will be considered in some detail in the chapters that follow. I have also attempted to suggest how this presence and these practices influence or determine the characters' character and the courses of action available to them. The economic infrastucture is placed at the service of the construction of the narrative fiction, as a powerful engine of characterization and plot.

In the pages that follow I want to call attention to the presence and function of economic systems and practices in the *Quixote* and the *Novelas Ejemplares,* ranging from subordinate-clause throwaways to full-blown thematized meditations on feudalism and capitalism, on capital and labor, and on the ownership of the means of production. I want to consider, for example, the gypsies and the aristocrats of *La Gitanilla,* and the *converso* merchant family whose fall from and restoration to material prosperity is the story of *La española inglesa.* The clash of opposing socioeconomic orders is surely as important as religious antagonism in the captive captain's story in *Don Quixote,* part I, chapters 39–41. Ideological barriers based on ethnicity, religion, and political rivalry are undone by commodification and exchange in *El amante liberal* and in *La española inglesa*. We shall also look at Monipodio's gang of pimps and tough guys, organized into an old-fashioned medieval guild within a system of tributary relationships, as against the entrepreneurial spirit personified by Rinconete and Cortadillo in the eponymous *novela ejemplar*. The same dialectic is played out in a different key in part II of the *Quixote*, between Don Quixote's devotion to the feudal underpinnings of chivalry and Sancho's advocacy of a different order based on a relationship mediated by money. Even the ethnic and religious issues surrounding Ricote and the expulsion of the moriscos are subordinated to economic questions in *Don Quixote*, part II, chapter 54.

The specific textual analyses are organized around three broad categories. Part I deals with the uneasy coexistence of feudalism and capitalism in *Rinconete y Cortadillo* and two episodes of *Don Quixote*. Part II takes up questions of the relation among gender, class, and modes of production, first looking at Christians and Muslims in the captive captain's story (*Don Quixote*, I, 39–41) and then contrasting aristocrats and gypsies in *La Gitanilla*. Part III considers the paradoxical relation between ideological antagonism and international commerce, first with relation to the Ottoman empire in *El amante liberal* and then to Protestant England in *La española inglesa*.

My method in every chapter has been to attempt to identify the socioeconomic issues present in Cervantes's text, and then to provide enough "thick description" of the relevant historical context to enable a discussion of the fictional text within the context. In many cases this has resulted in lengthy narrations of certain events, of longer than thumbnail biographies of certain personages, and of descriptions of business practices and relevant legal codes. I have tried to keep the descriptions of the context subordinate to the elucidation of the text.

# Part 1

## Feudalism and Stillborn Capitalism

~ 1

# The Drama of Sancho's Salary

We *cervantistas* tend to consider the relationship of Sancho and Don Quixote in terms of various cultural contexts and structural oppositions such as the universal-poetic and the particular-historical, idealism and practicality, spirituality and materialism, Lent and Carnival, literate high culture and oral popular culture, (occasionally) nobles and commoners, and even Laurel and Hardy.[1] Américo Castro suggested the socially relevant categories of Old and New Christian, but this potentially fecund hypothesis fell victim to the prevailing critical orthodoxy, and was probably experienced as irrelevant or slightly embarrassing by mainstream Cervantes scholars.[2] We are even less accustomed to pondering Don Quixote's and Sancho's relationship in socioeconomic terms. Furthermore, our expertise in pastoral literature in combination with our general ignorance of real history leads us to assume that the characters' relationship exists in a timeless social context, that life in the country is the same in 1600 as at any other time in the preindustrial age. In fact, Sancho and Don Quixote exist in a precise space at a precise moment in history, inserted imaginatively by their author into the flow of time. They experience and are shaped by the particular events and crises of their immediate historical context.

Thanks to the work of Vicente Llorens, Noël Salomon, and other European hispanists we are reasonably familiar with Don Quixote's situation as a rural *hidalgo* living precariously on his modest estate and being slowly squeezed by the inflation induced by the influx of precious metals from America.[3] The parsimonious lifestyle imposed by his genteel poverty is evoked in part I, chapter 1, with specific reference to his two suits of clothes and his modest and invariable diet. We know that his status as hidalgo does not entitle him to be called *don,* and if we are of a mind to, we can construct the meaning of his self-promotion to *caballero* (with *don*) accordingly. His socioeconomic situation has been compared to that of the *escudero* in *Lazarillo de Tormes*. I remarked in the introduction that these two characters are the best-developed literary representations of the effects of the changing socioeconomic environment on the lowest rank of the old feudal aristocracy. We tend to pay less attention to Sancho, probably in part because the title of the book orients us toward Don Quixote and prompts us to attend to him first. I think we also consider Sancho less interesting than Don Quixote simply because he is a poor peasant, and we would rather identify imaginatively with an aristocrat. Finally, there is no tradition of poor peasants as heroes in literature. Behind this attitude is the assumption that Sancho's situation as a poor peasant is part of a timeless continuity of country life in the preindustrial era. But Sancho exists in the same historical moment, as well as the same rural Manchegan space, as Don Quixote. Simple logic suggests that he is affected by the same economic dynamics.

Eduardo Urbina seeks Sancho's antecedents in medieval chivalric literature, with particular reference to Amadís's squire Gandalín.[4] Closer to my focus is the work of Francisco Márquez Villanueva, which situates Sancho in relation to the socially relevant sixteenth-century theatrical rustic, and of Mauricio Molho, who worked out with mathematical precision the paradoxical coexistence within Sancho of the folkloric types Juan Tonto and María Lista.[5] The most concise overview of this historical moment and its relation to the fictional lives of Cervantes's characters is Augustin Redondo's "Acercamiento al *Quijote* desde una perspectiva histórico-social."[6] The value of Redondo's study is enhanced by his bibliographic thoroughness, especially with respect to recent works of social and economic history. In another extraordinarily useful study, Javier Salazar Rincón locates Sancho in the specific context of the economics of country life toward the end of the sixteenth century, as a "Manchegan *labrador* or agricultural day-laborer, poor, married and burdened with children, who lives out his chivalresque adventure in the hope of escaping from the poverty in which his humble birth has imprisoned him."[7] The social class to which Sancho belongs was the largest in the society—some 80 percent of the total population—and also the poorest, the least empowered, and most exploited. The ironically titled treatise of Fray Benito Peñalosa de Mondragón, *The Spaniards' Five Excellences, which Depopulate Spain for its Greater Power and Expansion* (1629), offers a graphic description of the life of country people.

> "The labradores in Spain are today the poorest, the most wretched, miserable, and downtrodden of all the social classes. You would almost think that everyone else had conspired to ruin and destroy them, to the point where the word 'labrador' has come to mean everything gross, malicious, and lowly. Their diet is the poorest: garlic and onions, bread crumbs, hard jerked beef, the flesh of unslaughtered animals, bread made from barley and rye. Their clothing is no better: sandals, smocks hanging in

shreds, fool's caps, homespun collars, burlap shirts, provision bags, and jackets made of rough animal skins. Their houses and huts are plastered with dung, with a little poorly cultivated land and a few skinny animals, always hungry for lack of a common pasture, and everything they have is burdened with mortgages, general and per-capita taxes, *censos,* and other forms of tribute. Their household goods and their wedding dowries are the objects of city people's amusement, and they are depicted on the stage in a way that makes them seem even more unfit for society, with their coarse mannerisms exaggerated for the amusement of the audience. When a labra-dor comes to the city, and especially if he comes on a lawsuit, who can imagine the calamities he suffers? Everyone cheats him, and everyone ridicules his speech and his appearance."[8]

This sympathetic description of country people's lot is complemented from the urban-aristocratic point of view in Covarrubias's dictionary (1611), s.v. *villa:* "Those who live there are properly called *villanos,* and since they have few dealings with city folk, they are very rustic and unpleasant. . . . Villanos normally kill with sticks and stones, showing no pity, and besides the fact of death it is considered a great dishonor for an hidalgo and man of means to die at the hands of these vile and treacherous people. From the word *villano* comes *villanía,* in the sense of something gross and discourteous." This brief entry contains an encapsulated overview of Cervantes's society, with its rigid estamentary distinctions, its automatic and official identification with the hidalgo class and its values, its opposition of city and country, and the dominant groups' barely-concealed terror of the underclass.

Noël Salomon calls attention to the official (i.e. urban-aristocratic) attitude toward country people as reported in other entries in Covarrubias's dictionary. Under *conejo* (rabbit) we find the proverb "Al conejo y al villano, despedázale con la mano" (Use your hand to break apart a rabbit and a villano). The lexicographer's gloss is particularly violent and hostile: "meaning that you don't speak to a rustic with courtly witticisms, but plainly, as when we disjoint a rabbit by grasping its legs and pulling its little arms and neck to break its back, instead of waiting for the master carver to find its joints and slice it in the air." A *pulla* is "a witty although somewhat obscene remark, like those that travelers make when they come upon villanos working the land, especially at harvest time." The definition of *pata* contains the following clarification: "this is why we call the villano who makes his big feet look even clumsier with his rough shoes a *patán.*"[9]

Javier Salazar Rincón gives an excellent summary of the rural crisis of around 1600, drawn from various sources, contemporary and modern.[10] The first symptoms of rural economic debility had already surfaced during the reign of Felipe II: the adverse effects on farmers of the price controls on wheat, the slackening of domestic demand for products, a slowdown of exports to America as the colonies moved toward self-sufficiency, and the devaluation of land that had been artificially inflated by the American-induced price revolution. In the 1590s the situation became much more serious, and poor country people were subjected to a series of crushing increases in fiscal obligations. Their traditional obligations, as vassals to their masters and as parishioners to their church, formed the foundation on which the new burdens arose. The government was "lost in a fiscal labyrinth," forcing a general tax increase. In addition, at about this time somebody discovered, invented, or reinvented the censo on property, and suddenly the countryside itself was tranformed into an investment vehicle for the already wealthy. Land was mortgaged and the burden of debt service was passed on to the tenant farmer. Interest charged on censos often amounted to 50 percent. Of course the new burdens of increased taxation and what has been described as "la carcoma de los censos" (the woodworm effect of the censos) fell hardest on those least able to pay. After a few lean harvests prices skyrocketed, and the already poor were further impoverished. Hamilton notes a six-fold increase in the price of a fanega of wheat in four years, from 204 maravedís in 1602 to 1,301 in 1605. This is coincident with a drop in the wages of rural day laborers of some 12 percent between 1551 and 1600, producing a disastrous loss of real purchasing power.[11] And to all this must be added the epidemics of 1596 and 1599, which decimated the rural population, reducing the productive capability of the land and adding another spiral to the vicious cycle of impoverishment.[12]

But the "carcoma de los censos" has another face. Sancho expresses a desire to purchase one himself in part II, chapter 13. In view of this it seems reasonable to investigate the institution of the censo in more detail. Carmelo Viñas Mey and David Vassberg offer excellent summaries.[13] An investor would buy a censo on a piece of property for a specified sum which was paid to the farmer who actually worked the land. The farmer would now have the necessary cash to place the land under cultivation. In return, the investor was entitled to a specified sum from the farmer, not only until the debt was repaid with interest, but forever.

Censos were purchased not only by powerful aristocrats, wealthy religious orders, and fat-cat foreigners, people who had serious money to invest, but by everybody who could get a few ducados together. What was unhealthy, and what the sixteenth- and seventeenth-century political economists denounced, was the spread of the aristocratic *rentier* mentality: invest in censos; do nothing; live off your rentas, in that aristocratic *otium cum dignitate* (*ocio*, in Spanish), or *descansadamente*, as the literature never tires of repeating. This meant that nobody who had any money was willing to work and that money was invested in vehicles that didn't produce any wealth, as agricultural or manufactured products would. It is in fact uncomfortably similar to the craze for stock speculation in 1920s America.

Political economists were harsh in their criticism of this mentality, which gave rise to what Viñas Mey calls a "gilded idleness" and the abandonment of productive activity. Pedro de Valencia has a long treatise denouncing *ocio*. Miguel Caja de Leruela calls censos and *juros* "'a couch for sloth to recline on: the cause, and not the effect, of idleness.'"[14] The proliferation of modern sedentary investment vehicles such as censos is considered contrary to nature, part of an artificial economy where wealth is really "funny money," generated principally by the sale of interest-bearing investment vehicles such as censos. This is strikingly similar to what happened to the American economy in the 1980s under Reagan, with similar results for those who came after. "This is what has so clearly destroyed this country and those who use these censos, because, fixated on the unearned income, they have abandoned the virtuous exercise of the professions, of commerce, of farming and grazing, and of everything that man naturally lives by," writes Martín González de Cellorigo in 1600.[15]

The proliferation of censos led to owner absenteeism and the abandonment of the land by the agricultural labor force. This inevitably resulted in less land under cultivation and diminishing productivity, creating shortages and driving up prices, leading to the exodus of impoverished country people into the cities. Writing in 1626, Pedro Fernández Navarrete describes the effects of this absenteeism, voluntary for the wealthy and imposed on the poor: "When the poor (who are the ones left to till the land) hold it so encumbered with different censos they have taken from wealthy capitalists, . . . [they] come to understand that without the participation of the wealthy and powerful they have no hope of remedying their situation, they do not hesitate to abandon the land and come flocking to the city," where the lucky ones were absorbed into the service sector of the urban labor force, as lackeys, coachmen, and porters, and the rest became part of the growing unemployed underclass.[16]

Fernández Navarrete also notes that the absenteeism of the wealthy "has taken hold mostly in those kingdoms where private holdings have been reduced to censos and juros, because those who own property, seeing that the greatest part of the taxes and other tributes are levied against land, while the income from censos and juros is tax-exempt, do not hesitate to throw off the shackles of farming and grazing and come to enjoy the income from their investments in comfort in the city."[17]

A word about juros, which appear so frequently linked to censos in this literature. Juros are bonds issued by the government to raise revenue. Investment in juros, as in censos, does not contribute to the creation of new wealth, and income from censos and juros, as Fernández Navarrete points out, was tax-exempt. The tax-exempt status of the income from censos and juros was an important consideration in 1626, as it is today. When he was running for president in 1992 it was reported that Ross Perot, who never tired of telling us how the government needs to get out of debt, had his entire fortune of two billion dollars invested in juros, or tax-free government bonds.

So when Sancho Panza fantasizes finding another purse with a hundred ducados—"'and I'll hug it like a baby, and I'll carry it home, and I'll use it to make loans [censos] and collect rent and live like a prince'" (II, 13, 423–24)—he is right in line with the prevailing mentality.

The Cortes of 1593 complained of "'the poor harvests of wheat this year in Castile and Andalucía, and how the labradores, who are the people who sustain this kingdom, have been destroyed as we all know, and how few are left with any possessions of their own or any flour left from previous years, and how burdened they are with the pecho [per-capita tax], the ordinary and extraordinary service, sales tax, quartering and maintenance of soldiers, provisioning the armadas and frontiers, the galleys and galleons, and the other forms of oppression they suffer.'"[18]

Martín González de Cellorigo offers the most dramatic, as well as the most frequently cited summary of the situation in 1600:

> Those who can, won't; and those who would, can't, and so the land remains unworked. By this I mean that those who have the means to bear the costs of farming and enjoy the profits refuse to invest, and on the other hand, the poor tenants who lack the necessary capital are unable to bear any cost, no matter how willing they might be. . . . Because, after they pay the tithe they owe to God they pay a much greater sum to the owners of the land, after which follow the innumerable taxes, impositions, censos, and tributes, besides the pechos and all the other obligations they are subject to. And if the harvest is bad, or if the animals die, everything is lost and the only recourse is to mendicancy.[19]

Writing in 1631, Miguel Caja de Leruela observes that country people, "when they are old, and broken by the labor of farming, are forced to leave their villages and beg in order not to starve."[20]

The Relaciones topográficas commissioned by Felipe II in 1575 and 1578 document with pitiless clarity the grinding poverty in which country people lived. In the town of Arroba (Toledo), the houses are described as "poor, made of oak and madrone and roofed with tile and straw." The labradores in the villages "have no idea what it is to sleep in a bed at night, or to eat under a roof during the day." In many places society was divided into those who have enough to eat and the pobres, defined as "those who do not." In Cervantes's wife's home town of Esquivias, for example, "a hundred households have enough to eat, and the rest are poor day laborers." In Carabaña (Madrid), witnesses declared that "there are people who have enough food to live on, and there are also poor people."[21]

The lean years were literally insufferable. In Getafe (Madrid), there was "a very great hunger, when it was impossible to find wheat, and people ate bread made out of grass they cut and dried and ground into flour, and many people got by in this way until there was bread again." Even in times of relative abundance the diet of country people was insufficient: "in winter they live on bread crumbs and oil, and in summer on bread crumbs with oil and vinegar, in which they cook their vegetables and pass their miserable lives."[22] Sancho declares he would rather "'stuff myself with plain ordinary gazpacho than fall victim to the stinginess of an arrogant doctor who'd just as soon kill me with hunger'" (II, 53, 643). Covarrubias defines *gazpacho* as "a certain kind of crumbs made with toasted bread and oil and vinegar, and a few other things they put in and grind up together. This is food for farm laborers and other gross people."

Salazar Rincón interprets Don Quixote's housekeeper's instruction to Sancho to "'go govern your own house and till your *pegujares*'" (II, 2, 371) to mean that Sancho is a landowner, although his holdings are miniscule.[23] In fact, Sancho is not a property owner. Covarrubias defines *pegujar* (s.v. *peculio*) as "the same as *pegujal,* which the father permits his son to hold, or the master his servant, as though the servants had a few animals among the master's flocks." The *Diccionario de Autoridades* says: "the same as *peculio,* or what the father permits his unemancipated son to hold, and the master his servant or slave, to cultivate for his own profit a portion of land, or to graze a few animals along with those of the father or master." This definition makes it clear that Sancho's *pegujar* is not a piece of property that belongs to him, but part of one that belongs to some unspecified master, possibly Don Quixote, who allows him to cultivate it. In other words, it is part of the feudal environment Sancho exists in, and there is a clear analogy between the authority of the master and that of the father. Everyone, Salazar Rincón included, has noted correctly that Sancho has always had to hire out his labor for a wage. What seems to be lurking underneath all this is some combination of "precapitalist" features such as the salaried laborer, and "feudal" features such as a relationship permanent enough to warrant the owner's permitting his servant to cultivate a portion of the master's lands for his own benefit. The individual in question, Sancho in this case, is simultaneously an employee and a servant.

And in fact Sancho had been an employee, a day laborer ( *jornalero* ), long before he entered Don Quixote's service. Here are some facts about his wages and what they would buy. The jornaleros were the largest and poorest social group in rural Castile; Salomon reports that over half the population of La Mancha were jornaleros. As a jornalero, Sancho has grown up in a culture of poverty. He is introduced in terms of his poverty, as "a good man / man with goods— if we can use that term for anyone who's poor" (I, 7, 41). His first jobs were in animal husbandry, taking care of someone else's livestock. As a boy he worked as a goatherd (II, 41), as a swineherd (II, 42), and "'afterwards, when I had grown up a little, I took care of geese instead of pigs'" (II, 42, 580). Graduating to adulthood meant moving into agriculture, in the most demanding and least remunerative jobs. The *Relaciones topográficas* observe that in Lucillos (Toledo): "most of the people are poor, and their occupation is to plow and cultivate the vineyards."[24] Before entering Don Quixote's service, Sancho had labored in "'plowing and digging, pruning and tending the vines'" (II, 53, 643).

His wages were inadequate to the basic necessities of life: "'When I worked for Tomé Carrasco, the Bachelor Sansón Carrasco's father, whom your grace knows well, I was paid two ducats a month, plus my food'" (II, 28, 511). Two ducados per month are twenty-two reales, which Charles V. Aubrun computes at twenty-two maravedís per day.[25] Fortunately, Sancho's *rucio* is also a source of income, as he reminds the animal: "'sustainer of half my person, because with twenty-six maravedís that you brought in every day I filled half my larder'" (I, 23, 139). Adding Sancho's salary of twenty-two to the twenty-six provided by his donkey gives a total of forty-eight maravedís (fifty-one if we take the phrase "la mitad de mi persona" literally and multiply the rucio's twenty-six by two), or about 1.5 reales per day. For comparison, Hamilton reports that a carpenter earned about two hundred maravedís per day in Castile, and 250 in inflation-ridden Andalucía. A jornalero in Castilla la Nueva earned eighty-five maravedís per day in 1600, or about four times what Tomé Carrasco was paying Sancho.[26] According to the fictional but verisimilar *arbitrista* in the *Coloquio de los perros*, the cost of feeding a single individual for a day worked out to 1.5 reales, or exactly the daily income of the four-member Panza family. Seasonal employment at harvest time paid approximately twice the normal daily wage, but the disparity between supply and demand for labor forced many rural day laborers to migrate from place to place. Sancho recalls being absent from home when something important happened because "'just then I'd had to go do some mowing in Tembleque'" (II, 31, 525).

Finally, the Panza family economy is bolstered by the labor of Sancho's wife and daughter in manufacturing. Teresa Panza is presented "combing out a bundle of flax" (II, 25, 496) or "spinning a tuft of cotton" (II, 50, 623). Her daughter, Sanchica, contributes to her own commodification on the marriage market as she is "'making needlepoint lace; she's clearing about eight maravedís a day, and locking it up in a box to help with her dowry'" (II, 52, 639).

Charles Aubrun notes that Sancho enters into three different contracts: he works for Tomé Carrasco for twenty-two maravedís per day, and he then works for Don Quixote under a totally different kind of arrangement. As Aubrun observes, the contract with Tomé joins an employer and an employee, while the contract with Don Quixote joins a lord and a vassal.[27] In exchange for the vassal's loyal service, the master has the obligation to feed and clothe, to house and defend him, and to reward him from time to time with special *mercedes,* as the vassal's service warrants and the master's possibilities permit. Sancho's arrangement with Don Quixote is the essence of feudalism. Aubrun goes on to observe that two economic systems coexisted in Spain in 1600. One is founded upon service, the other on a salary, and frequently the two overlap. We have already noted how Sancho is at once a salaried day laborer and a servant whose master allows him to cultivate a *pegujar.* The third contract to which Aubrun refers is the unspoken agreement that governs the relationship during the third sally. Sancho wants a written document, which Don Quixote refuses to provide. Sancho wants a salary; Don Quixote insists on *mercedes.* Aubrun's interest lies in demonstrating Sancho's unwillingness to choose between the seigneurial régime based on homage and service and the mercantile system mediated by money. He'll take the salary, but he also refuses to renounce the *ínsula,* should one be forthcoming. Aubrun concludes, correctly, that Sancho is too poor to permit himself the luxury of choosing.[28]

Aubrun notes something else important: the term *escudero* is ambiguous, as *caballero* is. It functions simultaneously in chivalric literature, where it denotes a knight's squire, and in contemporary society, where it means "the poorest of the poor hidalgos." We have noted this meaning in *Lazarillo de Tormes,* and it reappears at the beginning of *Don Quixote,* part II, where the neighbors stigmatize Don Quixote as an *hidalgo escuderil.* This kind of escudero frequently serves a wealthier, higher-ranking aristocrat, and often accompanies his wife, as Doña Rodríguez's late husband did before his death (II, 48), or the escudero in the home of the *teniente* and his wife, Doña Clara, in *La Gitanilla.* In any case, for Sancho Panza to assume the social standing of escudero is analogous to Don Quixote promoting himself from hidalgo to caballero. Aubrun observes that here we see the fundamental equivocation. Sancho understands the term *escudero* to mean the valet who accompanies his master or, more frequently, his mistress, in their comings and goings. Don Quixote, on the other hand, takes *escudero* in the archaic sense found only in chivalric fiction. From the purely economic point of view, these acceptations of the term are the same, in the sense that both kinds of escudero serve *a mercedes* and not on salary. Both exist within the old, feudoaristocratic order.[29]

I am unwilling to abandon the psychological reasons I adduced in 1983 to explain why Sancho chooses to leave home and sign on with Don Quixote as his escudero in the first place, namely that his household is charged with a forbidden eroticism, just as Don Quixote's is, and he needs to escape.[30] Nevertheless, it is clear that this action, like all human behavior, is overdetermined and therefore cannot be explained as the result of any one motivation. Sancho is poor at the beginning of part I, and he is still poor when he announces his decision to accompany Don Quixote again in part II, chapter 5. At this time Sancho explains his decision quite simply, in economic terms: "'I've made up my mind to go back into my master Don Quijote's service . . . because I need the money and also because I'm hoping . . . I might be able to find another hundred gold pieces just like the ones we've already spent'" (II, 5, 384). It is clear that behind this overt expression of economic necessity lies a psychological motivation stemming from the human relationship he has built up with Don Quixote over the course of their previous sally, but the fact of imperious economic need, especially now that we understand the Panza family's chronic, structurally induced poverty, simply cannot be ignored.

Sancho attempts to get himself out of poverty by all the means available to him. As Aubrun has observed, two economic systems coexist in the Spain of 1600. We might think of them as the old order (founded on direct reciprocal relationships of service and obligations) and the new (based on a human relationship mediated by money). In the old order one is a vassal; in the new he is an employee. And as Aubrun also notes, Sancho refuses to renounce either; his poverty will not permit him to.[31] In part I, Sancho had already fantasized about getting out of poverty by either the new or the old route.

There is first the proposed commercialization of Don Quixote's *bálsamo de Fierabrás*, in part I, chapter 10. This is a modern mercantile operation based on manufacturing and marketing in quantity. Augustin Redondo works out the cost-to-profit ratio with his customary precision. Sancho believes the balm could be sold for more than two reales per *onza,* while Don Quixote estimates its cost to manufacture at less than one real per *azumbre* ("'you could make three azumbres for less than three reales'" [I, 10, 55]). The *azumbre,* a measure of wine, is approximately two litres. The *onza* is a measure of weight used mainly for spices, and amounts to about twenty-eight grams. This means that three azumbres would yield at least 215 onzas, which would be sold for some 430 reales. With a manufacturing cost of only three reales, the profit would be an astronomical 427 reales. For perspective, Redondo notes that a pound of mutton sold for less than one real, a pound of beef or an azumbre of wine half a real, and a fanega of wheat (some fifty-five litres) less than two reales. Redondo considers this episode a kind of indirect mini-satire of the obscene profits being made by Genoese and Portuguese businessmen. It certainly demonstrates Sancho's ability to think like one.[32]

Later on, Sancho fantasizes the commercialization of human beings, the black vassals he expects to receive as his share of Don Quixote's exploits (I, 29). Redondo has twice studied this fantasy in relation to the real economic situation.[33] The trade in black slaves was held to be legitimate by Fray Tomás de Mercado, among other theologians. The legitimacy derives ultimately from the diabolical associations of the color black, although the practice was not without moral risks, as Mercado explains: "With respect to the law, I draw two conclusions: first, that the purchase and sale of Negroes is in itself licit and just; second, it is a mortal sin, and the Sevillian merchants who deal in slaves from Cape Verde are living in great danger."[34] The slave trade to America was in the hands of Portuguese businessmen, who had been granted a monopolistic *asiento* by the Spanish government in 1595. During this period, when Portugal was part of Spain, many Portuguese conversos moved to Spain to escape the newly militant Portuguese Inquisition. Many of these settled in the southern part of La Mancha, where Don Quixote and Sancho find themselves during the episode in question. Contraband trade in black slaves, also in the hands of Portuguese marranos, was big business in Sevilla during the same period.

It is more than reasonable conjecture to say that Sancho was acquainted with this trade. He employs the technical vocabulary of the professional *mercader* (*vender, pagar de contado, comprar*), and when he says "'however black they are, I'll make them white or yellow,'" he is punning on two levels. The first involves the metaphorical-alchemical transformation of the black bodies into silver and gold coins. The second is an insider's reference to slaves of various colors: *esclavos blancos,* or 'white slaves,' are generally moriscos who became abundant following the failure of the Alpujarras insurrection of 1568; *esclavos loros* are defined as "of a darkish color tending toward yellow."

But the material enrichment isn't the real end. The ultimate goal is the aristocratization of the businessman. Sancho makes the transition in fantasy: "'What difference does it make to me if my vassals are black? Do I have to do any more than load them up and bring them to Spain, where I can sell them and get paid in cash, and then I can use the money to buy myself a title or some post that'll support me happily ever after?'" (I, 29, 193). Aubrun explains that in Spain the merchant class, even those engaged in overseas trade, was ashamed of its wealth, which it invested in titles of nobility and public offices, kept its children out of business, and renounced political power.[35] Redondo observes: "What the escudero wants is to acquire a title or a public office in order to 'live easy.' The idea is not to invest the money to generate income but to let it sit idle, a mentality which will lead to the economic ruin of the country."[36]

Redondo also offers an ingenious reconstruction of Sancho's apparently capricious and unbusinesslike reference to "treinta o diez mil vasallos" (thirty or ten thousand vassals), which depends implicitly on Cervantes's own experience in business and accounting. The documents reveal that the number of slaves involved in any particular transaction at Sevilla was small, since the business was illegal. Thirty or forty individuals would be an average sale. At an average price per slave of one hundred ducados this yields a total of three to four thousand ducados. At the wage Tomé Carrasco was paying him plus what the rucio was bringing in, a total of forty-eight ducados per year, this is more money than Sancho could have earned in a lifetime. It is certainly enough, Redondo observes, to purchase a government job (*oficio*) or a public position (*título*). In view of the economics of the contraband trade in slaves and Sancho's personal finances it is reasonable to conclude that thirty or forty is the number of vassals Sancho projects. The printed text, however, refers to "thirty or ten thousand." Most likely, Cervantes wrote the figures in sixteenth-century accountants' notation, which would look like "XXX o XL vasallos." Redondo conjectures that the L of XL, elided with the V of vasallos as was customary, could have looked to the typesetter like U, the conventional sign for one thousand. It would be the typesetter, not Sancho, who jumps illogically from thirty to ten thousand. If this is in fact the case, then Sancho's fantasy about the number of vassals he can sell, and the mental arithmetic he performs to conclude that this deal will yield enough to set him up in a título or oficio, are right on target in terms of the economic realities of the period.

In contrast, Salazar Rincón considers only Sancho's ambitions to enter the old order: "The dreams of Sancho and his family . . . constitute a complete and precise portrait of the Spaniard of 1600 and his useless obsessions: to become wealthy; to govern *ínsulas;* to become a Count on the basis of having been born a labrador, with no trace of Jew, Moor or heretic; to live well and in idleness."[37] All this is true. Like Don Quixote, Sancho really does think in terms of the categories of the old feudoaristocratic socioeconomic order. It is also true that his ambitions to enrich and empower himself within those categories are thwarted. But in part II he simultaneously pursues a new order approach to prosperity, by means of a fixed salary.

It may be this unwillingness to renounce any economic strategy that identifies Sancho most effectively with the new order. Fernand Braudel observes that, contrary to a widespread assumption, the capitalists of the sixteenth century did not evolve from one type of enterprise to another, but rather engaged in all simultaneously, or as the economic conjuncture was propitious or not.

It would be a mistake to imagine capitalism as something that developed in a series of stages or leaps—from mercantile capitalism to industrial capitalism to finance capitalism, . . . with "true" capitalism appearing only at the late stage when it took over production, and the only permissible term for the early period being mercantile capitalism or even "pre-capitalism." In fact . . . the great "merchants" of the past never specialized: they went in indiscriminately, simultaneously or successively, for trade, banking, finance, speculation on the Stock Exchange, "industrial" production, whether under the putting-out system or more rarely in manufactures. The whole panoply of forms of capitalism—commercial, industrial, banking—was already deployed in thirteenth-century Florence, in seventeenth-century Amsterdam, in London before the eighteenth century.[38]

Sancho is ready to manufacture and market the *bálsamo de Fierabrás* at an enormous profit (I, 10). He is ready to engage in the profitable commodification of human beings and invest the profits in a title or office (I, 29). He is ready to invest any found wealth such as the bag of coins in the purchase of a censo or other investment vehicle (II, 13). His fantasies reproduce the cycle of new order capitalistic investment doubled back on itself and transformed into the vehicle for entry into the improductive old order that in fact obtained in Castilian society to the detriment of the economy, as so many commentators, from González de Cellorigo to Redondo, have observed. In part II he moves beyond fantasy; he demands a fixed salary and simultaneously refuses to renounce any mercedes that might be forthcoming.

This strategy pits him against Don Quixote, who rejects the salary and insists instead on the feudal system of mercedes. José Antonio Maravall has observed that "Don Quixote rejects capitalism, and holds instead to a distant world," where "all its specific elements proceed from medieval tradition," and that Sancho is "acting in accordance with the new mentality of commoners whose interests are closer to those of the modern political regimen."[39] This opposition occurs long before the Duques use the disenchantment of Dulcinea as a wedge to separate them. In fact, it begins even before the enchantment of Dulcinea.

Those aspects of the economic interaction between the two protagonists that are based on the old order are novelistically infecund because they don't generate any conflict. I want to pursue the salary-mercedes controversy precisely because it generates conflict in and of itself, and because it reverberates off the two men's respective relations to Dulcinea and to each other. This particular economic controversy, in other words, is a principal motor of plot and characterization.

Although the system of mercedes is presented in the text as part of the old order, in fact it was an aspect of the seigneurial reaction of the seventeenth century. Antonio Domínguez Ortiz observes: "Since war, the traditional source of enrichment in former times, was no longer profitable, and few dared to take up commerce and industry because of the well-known prejudices [i.e. the taint of Jewishness] as well as lack of aptitude, the high-ranking aristocracy trusted above all else in royal *mercedes* to obtain the funds necessary to sustain their rank. . . . Our aristocrats did not request money, but lucrative positions, commissions and reimbursement for expenses."[40] All this suggests that the old-new dialectic contains an additional irony, namely that lurking underneath Don Quixote's traditional and bookish feudalism is the seventeenth-century aristocratic reaction to the rise of a new class of bourgeois merchants or mercaderes, documented by Maravall and others.[41]

In part II, chapter 7, Sancho approaches Don Quixote, presumably on orders from his wife, to ask for a *salario conocido*, or 'established salary.' It is worth pondering the close phonic similarity between Sancho's formulation *salario conocido* and the feudal technical term *solar conocido*, the property that legitimized a family's claim to nobility.

From the start the question of salary and mercedes is bound up with the personal, affective relationship the two men have developed over the course of their first sally together. The overt text is about financial security and two competing economic systems; the subtext is about the strength or fragility of the emotional bond between two human beings. These two aspects of the question, initiated here, will continue to reappear throughout part II. The all-important question of Dulcinea's disenchantment will come to depend on the confluence of the personal and the economic relationships between the two protagonists.

Before he ever starts, Sancho demonstrates how difficult it is for him to make this request, first by attributing it to his wife and then by enveloping it in a comforting body-wrap of proverbs. His insecurity stems, I think, from his awareness of the economic novelty of what he is proposing, and simultaneously from his realization that the economic request has the potential to undo the human relationship. Unfortunately, his long preamble has the effect of making Don Quixote impatient and predisposing him negatively.

"Where I'm heading . . . is for your grace to tell me exactly how much I'm supposed to get paid every month, for just as long as I'm in your service, and to tell your estate it has to pay me that much salary, because I don't want *mercedes* that come too late or not at all—and let God help me have what I'm supposed to. . . . Now it's true that if it happens—and I say this because I don't expect or believe it will—but if it happens your grace finally gives me that island you've been promising, I'm not so ungrateful and I wouldn't carry things so far that I wouldn't want to figure out how much the island brings in, and then let my salary be discounted that much, *pro gata*." (II, 7, 394)

Sancho clearly manifests his preference for the security of a salary when he states simply that he does not believe in nor expect the ínsula. The request has a profound effect on Don Quixote. In the course of his answer Don Quixote evolves from a reasonable reliance on precedent and the authority of the books of chivalry to a more intransigent position, telling Sancho in effect to take the job as it is offered or leave it. This trajectory mirrors his gradual realization that Sancho's request poses a threat to his personal authority and to the old order on which it is based. It has a revolutionary potential to destabilize and then transform the entire relationship between the two men. And indeed, Don Quixote declares the relationship in crisis.

> "Look here, Sancho: I'd be happy to set you some precise salary, if only I were able to find one single precedent anywhere in all the histories of knight errantry, even strictly in passing, something to let me know, to show me, just how much you ought to earn each month, but I've read every one of those books, or at least most of them, and I can't remember reading where any knight errant told his squire just how much he was going to be paid. All I know is that every single one of them served at his master's will, and then, when they least expected it, if Fortune happened to favor their masters, they'd suddenly find themselves rewarded with an island, or something just as good, or at least would come out of it with land and a title." (II, 7, 395)

At this point he begins to address Sancho as *vos*, a linguistic marker of his emotional distress and displeasure because it reasserts the hierarchical distance that separates the two. Having demeaned him in this way, Don Quixote then turns Sancho's initial rhetorical ploy against him by insinuating his henpecked dependence on his wife and pretending to assume that the final decision rests with her.

Finally, Don Quixote declares the entire relationship up for grabs. Either Sancho will resign himself to the old order or Don Quixote will find a new squire. "'And finally, what I mean, and what I hereby say, is that if you don't want to come with me, and trust to what may come your way, and take your chances with Fate, as I do, may God be with you and keep you, because I won't have any problem finding squires who are more obedient, more attentive, and nowhere near so clumsy—or so talkative'" (II, 7, 395).

Sancho is crushed; he had been counting on the personal relationship he had established with Don Quixote in their previous sally to outweigh his request to replace it with a new relationship mediated by money. In effect, Sancho has been bluffing, and Don Quixote has called his bluff. And just at this point who should arrive but Sansón Carrasco, who offers himself as Don Quixote's new squire. Now Don Quixote is on the defensive; he either has to make good on his own bluff and choose another squire, or find a way not to exclude Sancho. His tactic is to continue bluffing and raise the stakes. Let Sansón stay at home and honor his family, he says, "'for I shall be satisfied with whatever squire I find, now that Sancho won't condescend to journey with me'" (II, 7, 396).

It works. Sancho returns to the fold in a welter of allusions to the feudoaristocratic order: "'my lord, . . . I wasn't born into some ungrateful family, and the whole world knows . . . what the Panzas, from whom I'm descended, have always been like, . . . I can see you want to make it worth my while.'" He also includes a lengthy assertion of his masculine independence from his shrewish wife: "'so if I've made a big fuss about this business of my salary, it's only been to humor my wife, because, once she makes up her mind about anything, there isn't a mallet in the world that can bang the hoops on a barrel the way she can keep going after what she wants. But in the end, a man's got to be a man, and a woman's got to be a woman, and since I'm a hundred per cent man, because how could I deny it, I'm going to be a man in my own house, no matter what anybody says'" (II, 7, 396).

Sancho places himself explicitly in the old order, in the company of the squires Don Quixote had thrown up to him as examples only a moment before: "'So I hereby offer all over again to serve your grace faithfully and loyally, just as well or better than all those squires who've ever served and are still serving however many knights errant there were or ever will be'" (II, 7, 396). The crisis is averted, "Don Quixote and Sancho embraced and remained friends," and the third sally begins, with the disastrous expedition to El Toboso that culminates in Sancho's enchantment of Dulcinea.

The second confrontation occurs in part II, chapter 28, after the braying adventure, in which Sancho has received a drubbing along the entire length of his back. He begins by renouncing any ambition to increased material well-being, suggesting he would be better off to return to his family and support them "'with whatever God chooses to give me, instead of dragging along after your grace'" (II, 28, 510). He then complains of the unpleasant physical conditions he is forced to endure, and finally moves on to criticize the institution of knight-errantry itself. After Don Quixote hears "those oldtime knights errant" stigmatized as "the idiots they must have been," his ire is engaged and he again threatens to end the relationship. Here it is Don Quixote who invokes the salary. If Sancho really wants to return home, that's fine, and Don Quixote volunteers to pay him for the time he has put in: "'you have my money: count up how long we've been away . . . , think about what you ought to be earning every month, and pay yourself off'" (II, 28, 511). What follows is a labor-wage negotiation between an employer and an employee.

Sancho recapitulates his employment history with Tomé Carrasco, the twenty-two reales per month we have already noted. He then attempts to assign a monetary value to the increased physical privation he has experienced as squire to a knight errant. Don Quixote agrees with the principle that the salary should reflect the conditions of labor. Sancho calculates a surprisingly low two reales per month, an insignificant increase of .067 real per day over what Tomé Carrasco was paying. But as we have seen, Sancho is unwilling to renounce the ínsula, and here he considers it a formal obligation to be discharged. Since no actual ínsula has been forthcoming, Don Quixote owes him equivalent compensation in the form of money. Sancho calculates an additional six reales, apparently also per month, for a total of thirty reales: twenty-two the equivalent of his old salary, plus two for service as escudero, plus six more for the ínsula. Don Quixote accepts the entire package, and agrees to pay Sancho for the twenty-five days he calculates they have been on the road. Here the negotiation breaks down, and Sancho's real strategy becomes apparent. His numbers are so small, his demands apparently so modest, because he has calculated the time on the road as slightly over twenty years. Sancho thinks in volume, like a *mercader grueso*.

Don Quixote professes to be shocked, but agrees to be bankrupted by Sancho's demands, "'I'll be delighted to be poor and penniless to get rid of the worst squire in the world'" (II, 28, 512). Nevertheless, it is at this point that he begins to fight back. Abandoning the new order labor negotiation, he counterattacks from within his encyclopedic knowledge of the old, calling Sancho a "'corruptor of the squirely laws of knight-errantry.'" Can he find a single precedent for a salary in all of chivalric literature? Of course not. Then Don Quixote invokes the essential feature of the old order, the interplay of reciprocal obligations unmediated by money, in which he had participated in good faith but which Sancho has perverted: "'Oh, the bread ungratefully broken! Oh, the promises misplaced!'" (II, 28, 512). Finally, he holds out anew the promise of the ínsula and calls Sancho an ass for turning it down.

The old order triumphs by this combination of recrimination and vituperation. Sancho is brought back into line, "and he felt such intense sorrow that the tears came to his eyes, and at last, his voice low and sad, he said: 'My lord, it's true: all I need to be a complete ass is a tail.'" Don Quixote agrees to pardon him "'as long as you mend your ways, and as long as, from now on, you're not always looking out for your own interest'" (II, 28, 512).

There is no rational economic explanation for this outcome; it is produced by each man's underlying need for the relationship to continue. It is troubled on the surface by Sancho's desire to change its economic base and Don Quixote's insistence on maintaining that base. Twice now Sancho has been made to realize that changing the economics of the relationship would undo its fundamental human dimension, and twice he has decided that being with Don Quixote is more important than his economic self-interest.

Something new happens in part II, chapter 60. The issue of Dulcinea's disenchantment, by means of Sancho's self-inflicted lashes, has now become paramount. There comes a moment when Don Quixote can no longer sit idly by while Sancho invents one excuse after another to avoid beating himself. Finally he attempts to lower Sancho's pants while the squire is asleep and administer at least two thousand lashes himself. Sancho wakes up and reminds Don Quixote of the conditions he had negotiated: "'These have to be lashes I volunteer for, not lashes anyone forces on me, and right this minute I'm not a bit interested in being whipped. You'll have to be satisfied, your grace, with my promise to thrash and flog myself when I happen to feel like it.'" Don Quixote insists, and again inserts the discussion into the context of feudal social relationships: "'I can't wait for you to be chivalrous, Sancho, because you're not only a hard-hearted, rude peasant [*villano*], you're a soft-skinned one, to boot'" (II, 60, 676).

He attempts again to untie Sancho's belt, whereupon the squire "stood up and threw himself at his master, first grabbing him with his bare hands, then knocking his legs out from under him and throwing Don Quixote flat on his back, after which he set his right knee on his master's chest and pinned both Don Quixote's hands to the ground, holding him so he could neither roll over nor breathe." This is a shocking infraction of the hierarchical relationship, an open physical rebellion against the authority of the master. Don Quixote reacts from within his class, and again invokes the unmediated personal relationships of feudalism: "'What, you traitor? You show yourself thus disrespectful of your master and natural lord? You dare do this to the hand that feeds you?'" (II, 60, 677).

It is clear that feudalism has been rendered inoperative. Respect for his obligations to his master is not sufficient to compel Sancho to administer the beatings. Don Quixote's attempt to impose his authority by force has resulted in insurrection, and the master now finds himself physically subordinated to his servant.

Instead of seizing institutional power, Sancho uses his physical domination of Don Quixote to impose a social contract in place of the automatic assumptions of feudalism. "'I'm not knocking a king off his throne, or putting anybody up on one. I'm just helping myself, because I'm my own lord. Promise me you'll keep your hands to yourself, and you won't try to whip me, and I'll set you free as the breeze. Otherwise, "Traitor, Doña Sancha's foe, / here is where you die"'" (II, 60, 667). It is surely significant that Sancho frames his ultimatum in the language of feudalism as it is encoded in a traditional proverb and in fragments of traditional medieval ballads. Don Quixote gives Sancho his promise; the preexisting feudal relationship is reestablished, but in a modified form: the "master and natural lord," as Don Quixote had described himself a moment before, has become a lord who enjoys his prerogatives at his vassal's pleasure.

Don Quixote attempts without success to revive the traditional relationship in part II, chapter 68. He notes ruefully that Sancho has failed to beat himself, and he throws up to him the play of reciprocal obligations that defines the feudal social relationship: "'When you sleep, I lie awake; when I weep, you're singing; when I'm faint from fasting, you're lazy and breathless from too much food. But good servants should share their masters' suffering, and feel what they feel. . . . Get up . . . , and give yourself three or four hundred lashes toward the total necessary to disenchant Dulcinea, and I simply beg this of you, because I have no desire to be clutched in your grip, like the last time, because your arms are mighty ones'" (II, 68, 717).

When Sancho refuses, Don Quixote invokes his own part in the feudal bargain in an attempt to shame him into action: "'Oh merciless, merciless squire! Ah the wasted bread I've given you, and the ill-considered favors I've granted you, and still plan to grant you! Because of me you've been a governor, and because of me you can see yourself close to becoming . . . a count'" (II, 68, 717). All to no avail. Sancho makes an eloquent and elegant speech in praise of sleep, and suits action to the word. Feudalism, whether by imposition or supplication, has become impossible.

Following their return engagement at the ducal palace Don Quixote and Sancho resume their journey home. In part II, chapter 71, Sancho changes the course of the entire question by comparing himself, with his gift for disenchanting, to a physician with his ability to heal. He breaks the salary-mercedes impasse by proposing a third possibility: a fee for services. Don Quixote agrees with the principle. He expresses some reservations in the case of Dulcinea, on the grounds that the introduction of payment might cancel the magical efficacy of the treatment, but then decides it's worth a try. "At this offer, Sancho opened both his eyes and his ears a full foot or more, and assured himself that, on these terms, he'd be delighted to whip himself" (II, 71, 730).

The question now becomes agreeing on a figure per stroke. Sancho asks how much Don Quixote is willing to pay. In a parody of the theologians' debates concerning the "just price," Don Quixote first allows that "'in consideration of what the magnitude and immensity of what this remedy truly deserves, all the treasure of Venice, plus that in the mines of Potosí, would not be sufficient,'" then tells Sancho to set his own fee (II, 71, 730). This Sancho does, in a paragraph that fixes the value of each stroke and converts the unit price into a total stated in reales. Not only that, Sancho calculates twice, dividing the thirty-three hundred lashes at one *cuartillo* each into three thousand, and working that out to 750 reales, then taking the remaining three hundred lashes at one cuartillo each and working that out to seventy-five reales, then adding the two together. This is the second time that the illiterate Sancho has performed an arithmetical calculation in his head. He uses a shortcut that reduces the calculation to round numbers but necessitates retaining a partial total in memory while the second calculation is being performed. It is true that Sancho could simply have divided the total number of azotes by four, but by narrating the calculation in such detail the text calls attention to precise amounts, to the materiality of this exchange, and allows us to see the wheels turning in Sancho's brain.

This is an important event in the history of the economic relation between Sancho and Don Quixote. Because the fee-for-services principle does not involve replacing the concept of mercedes with that of a salary, it does not violate the demands of the chivalric code, which in turn allows the interpersonal relationship to continue. Don Quixote is so pleased with this new arrangement that he offers Sancho a bonus of one hundred reales for prompt completion. But this is only the beginning, for as the "powerful, flexible whip" begins to crack on Sancho's flesh he begins to think he has underpriced his services. "Once Sancho had given himself six or eight good strokes, the game stopped being funny, and the price began to seem far too low, so he stopped for a moment and told his master he'd been cheated, because lashes like these deserved to be paid at half a real, not a cuartillo" (II, 71, 732).

Sancho is clearly taking into account the value of his labor in the production of the commodity (stroke) he offers for sale to Don Quixote. We take this approach for granted nowadays, but a labor theory of value such as this had traditionally been subordinated to a utility theory based on the triad of the *raritas, virtuositas,* and *complacabilitas* of the commodity: its scarcity, its ability to satisfy a human need, and its particular appeal to an individual buyer. In scholastic thought, to consider the question of how much it cost the supplier to bring the commodity to market was to encourage merchants to plead high costs as an excuse for charging exorbitant prices. There are a couple of exceptions to this general rule. The first is Juan de Medina, who proposed in 1550 that if a new kind of merchandise is brought into a place, and there is no law to determine its price, then we should consider the factors proceeding from the vendor (including costs, labor, care, industry, and risk), from the purchaser (the need felt, the number of prospective purchasers, and individual taste), and the commodity itself (its scarcity or abundance, the advantages it offers).[42] The second is Pedro de Valencia, whose treatise on witchcraft Cervantes must have known and whose economic writings were probably familiar to him as well. In his "Discurso sobre el precio del trigo" (1605), he defends the *tasa* (controlled price) and argues that it should be assessed in terms of labor rather than money.[43] Sancho situates himself among a small minority of avant-garde economic theorists.

Don Quixote readily agrees to double the price, and Sancho promises to lay on with a will. It is at this point that Sancho quits whipping himself and begins whipping the trees instead, which is what everyone remembers about this episode. And it is here that the real turning point in the relationship between the two men occurs. An interpersonal crisis has been created precisely by the resolution of the economic relation. Until now Don Quixote has been concerned for Sancho's welfare only insofar as Sancho will or will not be able to beat himself the required thirty-three hundred times. If he should die before completion, Dulcinea will remain forever enchanted. Consequently, Don Quixote admonishes him not to "'whip yourself so hard that, before you reach the desired number, you leave this life behind'" (II, 71, 731). Now, as he hears the sound of the "pitiful voice, and the fierce, biting thud of the whip," he is forced back to a kind of mirror image of Sancho's choice earlier in the game, between self-interest and the interpersonal relationship. He chooses the relationship with Sancho, not to the exclusion of Dulcinea, for he wants to be able to "'conclude this business to everyone's satisfaction,'" but clearly subordinating her to Sancho. In addition, he recognizes Sancho's economic function in the support of his family, and he locates Dulcinea within a presently disadvantageous economic conjuncture. That is, Don Quixote's final choice takes place in an environment defined by economics, in the narrow sense of *oikos* as well as the broader one including himself, Sancho, the fee-for-services arrangement, and Dulcinea. "'Sancho my friend, may Fate forbid you give up your life, just to please me, for you are your wife's and your children's support. Dulcinea can wait for a better opportunity, and I will keep myself within the bounds of hope soon to be satisfied, and wait until you have recuperated and recovered your strength, and then we can finish this business to everyone's satisfaction'" (II, 71, 732). It has taken almost the entire second part of the novel to work out this interplay between the two protagonists, the crisis in their economic relationship crystalized in the question of salary and mercedes, and the relationship of both to Dulcinea.

Marxism is presumed to offer a dialectical vision of history but has always seemed to me more like a master narrative divided into chapters. Chapter 1 establishes the dominance of the feudal system. In chapter 2 feudalism is succeeded by capitalism, which in turn will give way to socialism in chapter 3. Seen in retrospect, the ingredients of the master narrative change in value according to where we are in the story. Capitalism is clearly better than feudalism at the beginning, because it opens up a world of new possibilities, the creation of unlimited wealth, and the promise of dramatically enhanced material well-being for everyone. But later in the story, a nostalgically evoked feudalism takes on a more positive value because the triumph of capitalism has torn human relationships asunder. Cervantes's text catches the question at the point in early modern European history when these choices were still choices, before the definitive triumph of capitalism and the division of humanity into exploiters and exploited. Don Quixote and Sancho dramatize that moment in the master narrative when the dialectic of individual self-interest and interpersonal solidarity was still a real dialogue.

# 2

## Guilds and Entrepreneurs in Sevilla

In *Rinconete y Cortadillo,* two boys meet on the road, team up, and make their way to the great commercial metropolis of Sevilla. Their plan is to go into business for themselves as thieves and burglars. Instead they discover that all illegal activity in Sevilla is tightly controlled, and they find themselves inducted into a crime syndicate presided by the wonderfully named Monipodio. Various of the criminal activities, as well as the organization and membership of the syndicate, are described in detail. A venerable scholarly tradition considers this *novela ejemplar* in terms of Cervantes's relations with the picaresque genre. This line of inquiry yields formal questions relating to narrative point of view (first or third person, protagonist, witness, or something aproaching an omniscient narrator), and ethical questions such as the relative evil of the two youthful protagonists in comparison with such picaresque stalwarts as Guzmán de Alfarache. Julio Rodríguez Luis, for example, writes: "This *novela* is generally considered to be picaresque, with allowance made for the differences between the picaresque and Cervantes's characteristic style, which are so great that many critics have doubted that the presentation of Rinconete and Cortadillo, and Monipodio's brotherhood can be called picaresque at all."[1] Similarly, Juan Bautista Avalle-Arce devotes most of the introduction to his edition of the *Novelas ejemplares* to the contrast between Cervantes and Alemán, dealing with both the formal and the ideological questions. Care has also been taken to distinguish between *Rinconete* as a product of the cultural moment called Baroque and nineteenth-century naturalism in its depiction of criminals and lowlifes.[2] My colleagues and I have all read many student papers that grapple with the generic identity of Cervantes's text with greater or lesser theoretical sophistication and rhetorical precision. The sequences at Monipodio's patio have also been related to the theater, specifically to the *entremés* and Cervantes's acknowledged mastery of that genre, by Domingo Ynduráin and José Pascual Buxó.[3]

This brings us to a less strictly literary line of inquiry in which the critical tradition centers on Monipodio's patio and what it reveals about Cervantes's knowledge of the Sevillian underworld at the end of the sixteenth century. Here there is room for everything from lyrical evocations of the colorful world of pimps, whores, cutpurses, and hit men for hire, to more sober considerations in light of documentary evidence such as that offered by Pedro Herrera Puga and Mary Elizabeth Perry.[4]

I want to follow this last avenue, not to assess Cervantes's knowledge of organized crime but to inquire into his representation of the structures of society and especially of commerce in the commercial capital of the Spanish empire. As in the preceding chapter, the ultimate goal of this inquiry is to shed some light on the organization and structure of the text as a verisimilar fiction. Once again there is a dialectic of two competing socioeconomic systems, an old one and a new one. Once again what is at stake is the quality and potential of the interpersonal and economic relationships determined by the two systems. But this time the setting is urban Sevilla instead of rural La Mancha, and the conflict arises not between individuals but between groups, between free enterprise and monopolistic control. In the reading I want to offer here, the protagonists and the phenomenon of crime are both considered as signifiers, but the categories they point to are specific and historical rather than timeless and archetypal.

I find that my habitual approach to literary characters in terms of the categories proposed by psychoanalysis, as though they were real people whose overt behavior can be seen to conceal unconscious motivation, fails to yield any insights when applied to the two protagonists of this story. These two youths are the opposite of what we find in Don Quixote and Sancho, for example. Those old friends are most emphatically two separate subjects whose oppositions and interactions form an evolving and problematical human relationship, which we have just surveyed in its specifically economic dimension. Rinconete and Cortadillo, on the other hand, are virtually interchangeable. They are the same age. Although the text refers to "el grande" and "el menor," the fact is that they are "two kids about fourteen or fifteen years old; neither of them was more than seventeen."[5] They look and dress alike: "Capes, they didn't have; their pants were of canvas, and their stockings of skin. They were both sunburned, their fingernails chewed ragged, and their hands not very clean" (191–93). They talk alike, with their exaggerated *señor gentilhombre* and *señor caballero*. They have similar family histories to tell. Both are estranged from their place of origin and from their fathers: "'my homeland isn't mine, because all I've got there is a father who doesn't recognize me as his son and a step-mother who treats me like a stepson,'" says one (193). The other has stolen his father's earnings, for which he has been "'exiled from Madrid for four years'" (195). Both have left in a hurry: "'in such haste that I didn't have time to find an animal to ride,'" says one (195); "'in such haste that I didn't have time to arrange for an animal to ride,'" says the other (197).

As soon as they discover how much they have in common, they decide to form a team. Together they bilk a passing *arriero* (mule driver.) Together they travel to Sevilla. Together they steal the shirts from the Frenchman and the purse of coins from the sacristan. Together they observe the people and events at Monipodio's patio. Together they are inducted into the crime syndicate. Nowhere do their wills cross. In fact, after the initial dialogue, they never again speak to each other. Even their names become entangled. It should be observed in passing that both *Cortado* (the name of a profession) and *del Rincón* (a toponymic) are typical of the kind of names taken by New Christians upon conversion and baptism, suggesting a common membership in a marginalized segment of society, somewhat estranged from the ruling orthodoxies. When they first meet, Cortado puns on the other's name: "'my bad luck has me cornered [*arrinconado*]'" (194). Cortado is dubbed "Cortadillo el Bueno" by Monipodio (218), but later the text refers to "Rinconete el Bueno" (237). Finally, on the last page of the text, these two characters become one. Cortado suddenly disappears. The text does not report his absence, and consequently has nothing to say about when he left or where he has gone. The concluding summary of events and value judgments is focussed entirely through Rinconete. If we come to this text with ideas of character, of individuals engaged in dialogic relationships whose respective consciousnesses impinge upon each other and whose lives are mutually affected in consequence—that is, if we expect Rinconete and Cortadillo to be anything like Don Quixote and Sancho, or Campuzano and Peralta, or Cipión and Berganza, or even the pastoral Elicio and Erastro—we are disappointed and disoriented. For a reader with my particular interest in individual personality, this text is especially disquieting. I have no choice but to abandon my usual reading strategies and consider Rinconete and Cortadillo not as personalities but as the representation of something abstract.

I am similarly disoriented if I attempt to interpret Monipodio's crime syndicate in light of my training in the Castro/Gilman school of hispanism, as an alternate society that, although composed of criminals and outsiders, offers a more positive vision of the possibility of community than the official social order. I find it equally difficult, however, to accept the generally held view of Monipodio's outfit as a "grotesque deformation," or a perverse mirror image of the official society, in Julio Rodríguez Luis's phrase.[6] Francisco López Estrada considers it a "reverse utopia," an "inverted reality" that derives ultimately from the Renaissance topos of the world upside down.[7] José Pascual Buxó insists on the inversion of normal social values and the corresponding radical estrangement of Monipodio's subgroup from society's norms: "In the secret brotherhood all the normative and dogmatic impositions of civil and religious life are unconsciously inverted." Pascual Buxó passes in review every aspect of the straight society and notes its deformed mirror image in Monipodio's operation. Thus the objects in Monipodio's patio and the adjoining rooms, the people who congregate there, Monipodio himself ("paternal icon of an inferior, monstrous humanity"), the "christening" of Rinconete and Cortadillo and their reception as new members, the linguistic barbarisms, the self-serving use of proverbs, the discordant music, the references to chivalry, to business, to religious confraternity, all demonstrate the social and moral inferiority of Monipodio's crew, perversely and/or ineptly aping their betters.[8]

There is no question that Monipodio's patio is an image of the larger society; the question is what kind. Suppose the patio is indeed a distorted reflection. If that is the case, the normal society presumed to lie outside its confines would embody positive social and moral values, and the text would be a celebration of society's virtues by presenting their contrary. I personally find it offensive to Cervantes's genius and his ideological posture, or more precisely to my idea of them, that the meaning of this text should come down to praise for the status quo and finger wagging at society's criminal substructure. Let us suppose instead that, rather than a distortion, Monipodio's patio is more like a microcosm, a synecdochic representation of the larger society and the official values.

Here is where we can start to observe the dialectic of the old and the new orders within the historical and cultural context of fin de siècle Spain with specific reference to Sevilla. Everything that happens within Monipodio's patio represents some aspect of the old order. Let us begin with reference to the ruling political and religious orthodoxy.

Manuel Criado de Val, Julio Rodríguez Luis, and José Pascual Buxó, for example, have all noted the presence of chivalry, that social and artistic codification of the ruling orthodoxy of feudalism, in Monipodio's patio. With the exception of Criado de Val, who remarks that it becomes harder and harder to define the border separating knights and hidalgos from pícaros,[9] these critics consider the incongruous chivalresque language and behavior another manifestation of the social and moral inferiority of Monipodio's crew.[10] I am inclined to agree with Criado de Val; all I see is the pervasiveness of the chivalresque ideals and the technical language of chivalry. It is the narrator, after all, and not any of the lowlifes, who observes that the *hidalguía* of the two new-comers is affirmed by the group (218). In the Porras manuscript Rinconete is literally dubbed knight by a whack from one of the *bravos*. When he reacts, Monipodio intervenes: "'Hold, Rinconete my son, for with that blow you have been dubbed a knight, and you have been spared six months' novitiate.'"[11] This passage was eliminated in 1613. Rodríguez Luis conjectures that perhaps Cervantes considered the explicit comparison with induction into the chivalric order too crude.[12] In the definitive text Cortadillo is dubbed "el Bueno" in accord with chivalric practice but without the commentary.

The *rufianes* and *valentones* Chiquiznaque, Maniferro, and Repolido are the paladins of Monipodio's court. The missions they are charged to perform are seventeenth-century versions of what the romances of chivalry and Don Quixote would call *enderezar tuertos* (righting wrongs). These acts of vengeance are the violent underside of at least one aspect of the dialectic of competing socioeconomic systems. They are not random, but rather appear in the text as the instruments of class conflict. A character identified only by his class and age, a nameless *caballero mozo* (young aristocrat), appears in the Monipodic court with a complaint. It seems he had ordered and paid an installment on a fourteen-stitch slash on the face of an equally nameless *mercader de la encrucijada* (merchant down by the crossroads) (233), which Chiquiznaque had inflicted instead on the merchant's servant. The lengthy dialogue between the dissatisfied aristocrat and the ministers of his orders centers on the legitimacy of the substitution. Chiquiznaque invokes the authority of the proverb "who loves Beltrán loves Beltrán's dog," and the whole encounter is played for laughs on the surface. The underlying dynamic, however, is anything but humorous. The aristocratic caballero is twice called *"galán,"* or *"señor galán,"* suggesting that he and the bourgeois mercader are rivals in love (234). The amorous competition is an obvious displacement of the real class conflict, where aristocratic economic interests are threatened, onto a conventional literary substitute. Monopodio's cutthroat paladins are the guardians of the values and interests of the aristocracy. This little vignette depicts the technology of the new—the professionalization and commercialization of physical violence—in the service of the preservation of the old. The young aristocrat makes ostentatious display of wealth in the form of cash and a gold chain. "'The thirty ducados I left as good-faith money won't make a dent in my wallet,'" he remarks as he prepares to forfeit his deposit; and later, when a new contract is agreed to, "he took a finely wrought chain from around his neck and gave it to Monipodio, and it was clear from the color and the weight that it was real gold" (235). This display suggests the economic power that the entrenched old order can mobilize in the defense of its interests.

The most visible occurrence of chivalry, however, is Monipodio's assumption of the role of the father-king who in the chivalric tradition defends the rights of the weak and redresses wrongs done them. Here the damsel in distress is Cariharta, who bursts tearfully into the Monipodic court and demands "God's justice and the King's" in a language loaded with the technicisms of the chivalric code. Monipodio reassures her: "'Calm yourself, Cariharta. I am here, and I shall do justice. Tell us your grievance, and you will be longer in the telling than I am in rectifying it'" (224). At one point Cariharta complains: "'I'm supposed to eat bread on cloths, and lie together with him?'" (224). She comes close to casting herself in the role of Jimena demanding vengeance on the Cid, as the old ballad says: "A king who does not do justice should not reign, nor ride a horse, nor frolic with the queen, nor eat bread on cloths, much less bear arms." It need hardly be noted that the king's function as supreme dispenser of justice was still a feature of the political orthodoxy of 1600 and was embodied as such in Lope's theater. That is to say, Monipodio's operation reflects the official feudomonarchical organization of society, with Monipodio in the role of king, and simultaneously the contemporary idealization of that social order in reactionary literary genres such as the *comedia,* the *libros de caballerías,* and the *romancero.* This might be the moment to invoke the picaresque, and to suggest that within the context of literature Rinconete and Cortadillo are representatives of a different genre, which instead of glorifying the present by identifying it with an idealized past depicts the contemporary reality of nascent urban capitalism and the social tensions resulting from attempts to create new patterns of distribution of wealth. Monipodio and his group represent the feudomonarchical social order enshrined in the majoritarian literary genres noted above; Rinconete and Cortadillo seem instead to have something to do with bourgeois capitalism and the picaresque.

Before turning to the economic questions at the heart of this inquiry I want to consider the religious practices current at Monipodio's and their relation to contemporary religiosity in general. My thesis is simply that instead of a deformation of the Roman Catholic orthodoxy promulgated at Trent and imposed as the law of the land, concretely as "Ley 13, título 1, libro 1 de la Novísima recopilación," the practices chez Monipodio are the salient features of that orthodoxy carried to their logical extreme. It is customary to list as particular preoccupations of the resurgent Catholic orthodoxy the following, most of which are reactions to Protestant heresy: in general a renewed emphasis on the public forms of religious behavior, in opposition to the subjective interiority associated with Protestantism; the importance of works, as opposed to the Protestant variations of faith and predestination; transubstantiation in the Mass; the veneration of saints and the efficacy of their intervention; the veneration of images; the efficacy of ceremonies; the dignity of the clergy and sanctity of the monastic state. Many of these concerns are present in Cervantes's text.

The members always give a part of what they steal for "'oil for the lamp at a very devout image in this city, and in truth we have seen great things come of this good work'" (208). La Pipota needs to "'go and complete my devotions and light my candles at the image of Our Lady of the Waters and at the Holy Crucifix of Saint Augustine'" (219). She later asks the group for money to pay for the candles. La Ganancia provides it, and requests that Pipota buy a candle on her behalf as well, "'and light it at the altar of Señor Saint Michael; and if you can afford two, place the other one at Señor Saint Blas, for they are my advocates. I'd like to light another one for Señora Saint Lucy, to whom I am devoted because of my eyes, but I don't have the change. But someday I'll do my duty by all of them.'" Pipota responds: "'You'll be doing very well, my daughter, and don't be cheap, for it is of great importance to place the candles yourself before you die, and not leave it to your heirs or your executors.'" Escalanta speaks up "and ordered two more candles for whichever saints she deemed most profitable and grateful" (222).

It need hardly be noted that Monipodio's operation is organized like a religious order with its particular rule, which includes a year of novitiate. The lad who leads Rinconete and Cortadillo to Monipodio is in "the year of the novitiate" (207). The protagonists themselves are subsequently relieved of the same "año del noviciado" (216).[13]

The practices chez Monipodio are not opposed to Roman Catholic orthodoxy; they are an exaggeration of it. They are opposed to Protestantism and, more pertinent for Cervantes in his Catholic context, to Erasmian spirituality and the Erasmian ideal of the Christian life. These values are associated instead with Rinconete and Cortadillo, who inquire about restitution (208), and whose point of view structures the explicit contrasts offered at the end of the text.

> He was especially tickled when she wanted the labor she had invested to earn the twenty-four reales to be applied against her sins, . . . and he was amazed by the certainty and confidence they all displayed of going to heaven as long as they performed their devotions, even though they reeked of thefts, murders, and offenses against God. And he laughed at the other old lady, Pipota, who took the stolen basket of laundry home and went to light candles at the images and with that believed she was on her way straight to heaven without stopping to change her clothes. (240)

It need hardly be observed that ironic distance and mocking laughter such as we find here are the hallmarks of the Erasmian attitude toward the kind of religiosity exemplified by Monipodio's crew. What is noteworthy is the identification of Monipodian religiosity with the official orthodoxy promulgated at Trent, incorporated into the civil code by Felipe II's government, and put into practice by all the law-abiding members of society.

Monipodio's patio, in short, incorporates the official political and religious values of Cervantes's society: feudomonarchism and Roman Catholic orthodoxy. It presents not a grotesque deformation, which would valorize the official institutions positively by contrast, but a caricaturesque exaggeration that throws the salient features of those institutions into prominence and invites our critical meditation on them. We can turn our attention now to other aspects of the old social order. First among these is the organization of commerce. Antonio Domínguez Ortiz offers this description of the model: "The characteristics of production, as it subsisted into the eighteenth century, are: organization by guilds, tight controls, exclusion of competition, hierarchy of workers (apprentice, journeyman, master)."[14] Monipodio's operation is organized in this way, as a guild in the medieval tradition, with closed membership, rules for apprenticeship, and a monopoly on the activities within its purview. Julio Rodríguez Luis observes that if it weren't for the reference to vengeance, we might think Monipodio is the head of the guild of tailors.[15]

This association prompts consideration of the name Monipodio and its relation to this particular form of organization. The word is a corruption of *monopolio.* In the sixteenth century it had three interrelated meanings. *Monipodio* is first a crime syndicate. *Autoridades* defines it as a "convenium or contract among certain individuals who unite for some evil purpose. It is a corruption of 'monopoly.'" Rodríguez Luis reports that in Luis de Zapata's *Miscelánea* (1566) there is a reference to the existence of a brotherhood of thieves in Sevilla, similar to Monipodio's, which required all its members to be Old Christians. He also calls attention to similar confraternities in other texts—in Naples, in Martí's *Guzmán de Alfarache;* in Rome, in Alemán's *Guzmán*—and concludes that such organizations were a familiar part of the landscape of urban Europe since the middle ages.[16]

*Monipodio* is also a commercial monopoly on a particular commodity in order to control prices. Covarrubias, s.v. *monipolio:* "*Monipolios* are purchases in quantity by one person, or two or three, for resale to the surrounding merchants. They are prohibited by ancient laws, but still practiced, to the detriment of the society." Pierre Chaunu reports the existence of such a practice at the time and place that interest us:

> The trade in grain constituted a kind of state within the state, with its powerful and tyrannical agents, jealous of their prerogatives, the "señores monipodios." Their presence was felt more than seen, in the contracts that provided for the provision-

ing of the fleets. A place was reserved for them along the length of the Street of the Alhóndiga, in the Sancta Catharina district. This is where they had their fortress-like houses, with their interior patios, their great vaulted storerooms upstairs and down, where they stored quantities of wheat, flour and barley.[17]

These "señores monipodios," their enclosed patios, and Chaunu's graphic characterization of them as a "state within the state" are particularly relevant for Cervantes's Monipodio and his operation.

In addition, Francisco Márquez Villanueva called to my attention that *monipodio* is also a monopoly on local government offices. There is finally the pervasive use of the term *monopolio* by contemporary historians to denote the government control of commerce with America (through Sevilla) in the sixteenth century. Thus Domínguez Ortiz, for example, evokes "the economic doctrines in effect then, which we might classify as premercantilist, one of whose premises was rigid state intervention in foreign trade and commercial monopoly with the colonies."[18] It should be noted that, although this last meaning of the term is not documented in sixteenth-century texts, the analogy between control of crime, control of prices, control of offices, and control of trade with America would not be beyond the reach of an observer of average human intelligence, let alone a particularly gifted one such as Cervantes. The name Monipodio, in other words, suggests not only the crime syndicate explicitly present in the discourse, with the monopoly on crime standing for the monopoly on commodities practiced by the "señores monipodios," but also the commercial monopoly exercised by Sevilla over commerce with the American colonies. This monopoly is the logical extension of the medieval guild mentality to the new transatlantic economy.

The Sevilla monopoly was exercised through the Casa de Contratación. Michèle Moret observes: "The famous *Casa* was founded in 1503 for the purpose of assuring state control over commerce with America. . . . The *Casa* assured both economic and fiscal control, with a view to collecting entry and exit duties at Sevilla and in America."[19] We recall that in the Porras manuscript the description of Monipodio's lair is set apart from the preceding narrative by the heading "Casa de Monipodio, padre de ladrones de Sevilla." It is not too far-fetched to posit an analogy between these two *casas*.

The combination of legal requirements to be completed at the city gates ("the Customs Gate, because of the *registro* and the *almojarifazgo* that are paid" [199]) and again at Monipodio's (206) evoked in Cervantes's text surely recalls the customs formalities to be executed by merchants bringing goods into the city up the river from Sanlúcar. Pierre Chaunu characterizes the registro as an instrument of total control:

From the beginnings of commerce with America and its founding in 1503, the *Casa de Contratación* was to keep lists of all merchandise going to or coming from America. These lists of merchandise were the first form of the *registro*. The control exercised over everything shipped to or from the New World was from the first a fiscal and an economic control, with a view to collecting entry and exit duties at Sevilla and in America. These duties were essentially *ad valorem* taxes, the *almojarifazgo* . . . and the *avería*. The Spanish state was not only interested in establishing fiscal and commercial control over the traffic with America, but also had political, juridical, and even theological ends in mind. The state attempted, in effect, to preserve the innocence of the New World. This purpose is expressed through the control of subversive merchandise such as books, and also through the control of people. State control, exercised through its intermediary the *Casa de Contratación,* went far beyond the domain of merchandise; it extended to everything that went to America: objects, animals, black Africans, passengers.[20]

As for the *almojarifazgo,* Henri Lapeyre reports: "It was part of the Muslim legacy, consisting of revenue from diverse sources, but which came principally from customs duties. . . . Import duties were generally 5% *ad valorem.* . . . The *almojarifazgo de Indias,* which was not established until 1543, affected only traffic with America."[21] Surely this coincidence between the apparatus of control at Monipodio's and that put in place by the state is too great to be insignificant. Harry Sieber refers, somewhat obliquely, to this in his introduction to our text, where he remarks that it is not a coincidence that our heroes enter the city by the Customs Gate, nor that Monipodio has a monopoly on all merchandise stolen there (26).

As it happens, the administration of the Sevilla monopoly was under the personal control of one of Cervantes's "favorite" aristocrats, the Duque de Medina Sidonia, immortalized in the sonnet "Vimos en julio" and present beneath the surface of *La española inglesa.* Michèle Moret reports that from May 1602 until his death on 12 July 1615, Medina Sidonia was

the head administrator whose jurisdiction went beyond his own district of Sanlúcar. He was also the Captain-General of the Andalusian coast. Let us recall that his family, possessors of one of the greatest fortunes in Spain at the time, had a terrible reputation. . . . Let us admire his talent for creating the impression of a loyal vassal ready to place his own fortune at the king's disposal. An Inspector-General once remarked his ability to turn his authority to his own advantage, and recognized his sense of organization. . . . He oversaw "maritime matters" such as the security of the coast and the provisioning of ships, but he also oversaw grain shipments for the entire province. He took an interest in the foreigners who came to do business, keeping an eye on them and making sure they paid the required duty and respected local conventions. He was charged with making sure that royal orders concerning the conditions of commerce were obeyed. All this put him in contact with mercantile society and he, like most administrators, did not deprive himself of the opportunity to put his own capital to profitable use.[22]

In fact the Duque was always alert to the possibility of profit. In 1611, for example, he sold his office of *alcalde mayor* to Don Pedro Girón de Nivera. Don Pedro let the office appreciate for about a week and then resold it to Don Luis de Carranza. Speculation in lucrative municipal offices was apparently a popular and remunerative exercise among the highest-ranking Sevillian aristocrats. It was the city, that is, the people, who ultimately paid.[23] Modesto Ulloa further observes that in addition to the receipts from the almojarifazgo at Sanlúcar, which was always under his personal control, in 1581–1582 Medina Sidonia received over a million maravedís from the Sevilla almojarifazgo when it was controlled by the merchant guild of the city.[24]

In a very real sense, Medina Sidonia *was* the monopoly. It is even possible that the *modelo vivo* for Monipodio was Cervantes's old "friend" the Duque himself. Furthermore, Medina Sidonia is present, by name, in the text. When Cortadillo returns the sacristan's purse Monipodio recognizes his act by dubbing him "el Bueno." The text observes that "Cortado was confirmed with the name of *Bueno*, as though he were Don Alonso Pérez de Guzmán, who threw his knife off the walls of Tarifa to slay his only son" (218). The first Pérez de Guzmán to be known as "el Bueno" was the present Duque's (1550–1615) ancestor, the siege of Tarifa having occurred in 1294. But their names are the same, including the epithet "el Bueno," as Peter Pierson makes clear in his biography of the Duque, which suggests that the present Duque might be lurking ironically inside the reference to his heroic ancestor.[25] At the very least, there is an identification of Monipodio's order with the proud heritage of feudalism and with its most powerful Sevillian avatar.

It is not difficult to discern several parallels between the historical monopoly on commerce administered by Medina Sidonia and the fictional monopoly administered by Monipodio. Both are the inevitable product of the prevailing mentality, the central concern of which can be expressed in the word "control" and which was responsible for the proliferation of exclusive corporations ranging from craft guilds and religious confraternities to *colegios mayores* to cathedral chapters and aristocratic military orders with their statutes of purity of blood. This pervasive apparatus of control was mobilized to keep everyone in his place, to inhibit social mobility, and to assure that power remained in the hands of those who had traditionally wielded it. Maravall mentions in passing that there seems to have existed in Sevilla a commercial confraternity whose members were all aristocrats.[26] Monipodio's organization is simultaneously a representation of all the exclusivist corporations of that society. It unites religious orders as well as lay confraternities, feudalism and chivalric orders, commercial monopoly and control of the judicial system. Aurora Egido has observed that the announcement that "Monipodio was to give a lecture of the type required at competetive examinations" (239) suggests the presence of the academic hierarchy as well.[27] Monipodio's organization, in short, constitutes a synechdocical representation of the organization of all society into a vast series of guilds and hence of the dominant mentality and ruling orthodoxy.

But Monipodio's syndicate does not stand alone in Cervantes's text. It is opposed to and by the vision of Rinconete and Cortadillo, who attempt to practice a form of entrepreneurial capitalism, concretely a partnership. When they reach Sevilla their first act is to raise capital from the sale of the objects stolen from the Frenchman. "The next day they sold the shirts in the flea market outside the Arenal Gate, and cleared twenty reales" (199). This sum is capital to be invested in the equipment required for their new business: "They bought everything out of the profits from the Frenchman's shirts" (201). The appeal of this particular business is precisely that it is free of control. "You didn't pay an *alcabala*, . . . you didn't have to find a master, . . . you could eat whenever you liked, . . . you didn't have to take an examination" (200). Additionally, this is a business that operates in the modern manner, on "credit, which was the most important aspect of that business" (202). Finally, the trade of *esportillero* is not an end in itself, but is itself an investment in the more lucrative business of thievery. "It was perfect for practicing their trade without fear of discovery, because it allowed entrance into every house" (200). The firm's first enterprise, their theft of the "holy and blessed money" derived from "rentas" in the sacristan's purse, is a victory of a new form of enterprise based on individual initiative and wit over the old order, based on stable tributary relationships. It is no wonder that the protagonists are dismayed to find that the free enterprise they envisage is impossible in monopolistic Sevilla. When Cortadillo returns the sacristan's purse on Monipodio's command he is not being generous; he is capitulating. He simply has no choice but to incorporate himself into the prevailing order. And when Monopodio dubs him "el Bueno" and identifies him with the Duque de Medina Sidonia he is symbolically celebrating the defeat of free enterprise and Cortadillo's apparently voluntary embrace of the monopolistic order.

And what is the practical result of all this monopoly? We know that the Duque de Medina Sidonia attempted to exercise total control over all commercial operations under his sweeping jurisdiction. An example of this rigorous control was the general embargo of 1601, which had disastrous effects on commerce, as Michèle Moret reports: "One has the impression that the embargos, especially the one in 1601, paralyzed commercial activity and unleashed a general discontent in Andalucía." She cites a letter from a Flemish businessman, who observes that "'the grief resulting from this embargo is impossible to believe.'" Bankers and businessmen were going broke all over the place. "Sevilla witnessed numerous bankruptcies, including the banker J. Mortedo and Juan Castellanos de Espinosa, the receiver of *bienes de difuntos* and treasurer of sales tax revenues. Few businessmen were able to resist the unfavorable current; more bankruptcies were expected as a result of creditor insolvency. The Juan Castellanos affair put everyone at risk."[28]

Moret cites a letter from the Marqués de Montesclaros to the Duque de Medina Sidonia: "'It is my duty to commmunicate to you the great affliction this city has felt as a result of such generalized losses, especially the businessmen . . . ; among the reasons given for this bankruptcy, and by no means the least significant, are the recent embargos, which always seemed very dangerous to me. . . . The few businessmen left are being severely squeezed."[29]

It is worth pointing out that fewer businessmen, or 'hombres de negocios,' meant a greater share of the profits for the Duque. In the language of Cervantes's fiction, the *caballero mozo* (young aristocrat) cuts out the *mercader de la encrucijada* (merchant from down by the crossroads).

I am not the first critic to call attention to the conflict in Cervantes's text between free-agentry and monopolistic control; Francisco López Estrada sees this clearly. "The experience of Rincón and Cortado in Sevilla is to see how their possibilities for action are constricted, and how they finally enter the crime syndicate, which is the opposite of what they expected. . . . In search of liberty, they find the organized tyranny of Monipodio."[30] Harry Sieber also calls attention to the total control exercised by Monipodio, contrary to the boys' expectations. The evocation of space in the text enacts this progression from free-agentry to control, as the scene moves from an inn on the open road to the institutionalized space of the city of Sevilla with its walls and gates to the still further restricted enclosure of Monipodio's patio. Henri Pirenne observed some time ago that capitalism did not develop in the urban bourgeois milieu, with its closed corporate organization that placed so many limitations on economic expansion, but rather grew in various other centers, frequently rural, where the absence of heavy-handed guild restrictions permitted new and more appropriate forms of industrial relations.[31] What I want to emphasize, however, is not the abstract polarity of freedom versus control but the concrete historical reality of the clash between the old and the new mentality acted out on the terrain of commerce in the commercial capital of the Spanish empire. I cannot resist noting, however, that in a larger context the boys' integration into the order presided by Monipodio is a reintegration, as sons, into a patriarchal order that they both had abandoned before the narrative begins. Monipodio as "padre de ladrones de Sevilla" is nothing if not, in Lacan's phrase, the locus of the Law. And it is certainly not for nothing that he demotes Rincón and Cortado back to childhood by renaming them with diminutives.

Rinconete and Cortadillo are the representatives of the new order, destined not to flourish but to be crushed by the old. What makes them difficult to accept as the locus of positive value is their status as thieves. But in this text everyone is a crook. The operative structural opposition, therefore, is not between being a thief and being honest, but between thieving in the old, safe but limited, premercantilist way and thieving as a modern entrepreneur. Being a thief becomes a metaphor for being a businessman. Monipodio and company stand for the way commerce was in fact organized, as a rigidly controlled monopoly tied to the medieval guild mentality and safely in the hands of the most powerful aristocrats, while Rinconete and Cortadillo stand for an incipient bourgeois free enterprise, which turns out to be both *arrinconado* (cornered) and *cortado* (curtailed). It is they who are outside the offical order presided by Monipodio, but the rhetoric of the text turns the tables and makes it appear otherwise. The text converts Monipodio's operation into the Other by presenting it as the object of scrutiny from without. The text estranges the reader from Monipodio by causing us to identify with Rinconete and Cortadillo. This identification is effected by the pervasive disparity between the linguistic practices of Monipodio's community and those common to Rinconete and Cortadillo and to ourselves. We share membership with the protagonists in the common linguistic community of cultured speakers and especially as readers of standard Spanish. This "linguistic perspectivism" allows us to feel superior to Monipodio and company. It is in this way that Cervantes encodes a revolutionary ideological statement, a kind of lament for the bourgeois capitalism that was not to be, in the superficially humorous anatomy of a picturesque crime syndicate with which no reader is tempted to identify, even though in fact it incorporates all the official values and stands for the prevailing social order.

# 3

## Ricote the *Morisco* and Capital Formation

The episodes concerning the morisco Ricote and his family, his clandestine return to Spain from exile in Germany (*Don Quixote* II, 54), and the love and Mediterranean adventures of his daughter Ana Félix and the Old Christian Don Gregorio (II, 63 and 65), are to the second part of the *Quixote* as the story of Ruy Pérez de Viedma and Zoraida are to the first: two stories of Christians and Moors, part of a venerable thematic tradition in Spanish letters. There are, nevertheless, fundamental differences between the two episodes. The first difference is structural. Everyone recalls that contemporary reaction to *Don Quixote*, part I, had criticized Cervantes for having "availed himself" of various interpolated stories, especially the one about the *curioso impertinente* (I, 33–35) and the one about the captive captain Ruy Pérez (I, 39–41). In part II, chapter 44, Cervantes responds to this criticism, and declares that "in this second volume, he had decided not to introduce any separate, artful tales, but only such narratives as, to his mind, emerged out of the strictly historical facts" (II, 44, 586). The episodes concerning Ricote and his family are part of this new narrative strategy; they have indeed "emerged out of the strictly historical facts." In contrast to Ruy Pérez's more genre-piece story of Christians and Moors, whose literary filiations have been admirably elucidated by Francisco Márquez Villanueva,[1] Ricote's is anchored in the painful, life-wrenching experience of thousands of Spaniards between 1609 and 1614 known as the expulsion of the moriscos.

The sense of verisimilitude and historical urgency in Ricote's story is heightened, paradoxically, by the presence of the fictional Sancho Panza and their equally fictional relationship as friends and neighbors. Their common identity as Spaniards is heightened by their joint juxtaposition to the band of Germans with whom Ricote is travelling. Leo Spitzer and Helena Percas de Ponseti have called attention to this common Spanish identity as manifested in their natives' command of the Castilian language in contrast to the international argot favored by the Germans.[2] Américo Castro elucidated the semiosis of the ham bones and the wineskins the pilgrims carry with them as a kind of passport or safe-conduct through a Spain defined by purity of blood and an obligatory state religion. Ostentatiously eating ham (or sucking on the dry bones) and drinking wine in public freed one from both Muslim and Jewish "taint."[3] The pork products conferred a double seal of approval, as the bishop of Segorbe (Valencia) noted in an antimorisco tract of 1587: "They all abstain from wine and pork, and they do so doubtless because it is Mohammed's precept and they are his disciples; and with respect to the pork, Mohammed himself got this ceremony from the Jews."[4]

It goes without saying that Ricote, who is in the country illegally and subject to the death penalty if his real ethnicity should become known, takes cover under these outward and visible signs of pure Old Christian blood, but the wine has a second semiotic function as well. Differing drinking styles distinguish Ricote and Sancho from their companions. The Germans drink until all the wine has been consumed and they pass out. The two Spaniards drink less, and instead of falling asleep they fall to conversing in Spanish. They are identified as Spaniards by their attitude toward alcohol as well as by their language. "Finally, the wine used up, they fell asleep, sprawling out on the same grass they'd been eating on, only Ricote and Sancho still awake and alert, because they'd eaten more and drunk less, so they walked away a bit and seated themselves under a beech tree, leaving the pilgrims buried in sweet sleep, and Ricote, never once slipping into his own Moorish speech, spoke what follows in the purest Spanish" (II, 54, 646).

The narrator's introduction to Ricote's speech, the subject of which will be his Spanish identity and his love for his country, brings together all the markers of Spanishness we have seen: his Castilian language, his relative sobriety, and his friendship with Sancho. In addition, their location "al pie de una haya" recalls Garcilaso's shepherds "al pie de una alta haya," and Virgil's "recubans sub tegmine fagi." Not only does their relative sobriety set them apart from the Germans in early modern Europe, their conversation under the beech tree locates them within a continuity of Mediterranean civilization that reaches back through Garcilaso and comes to rest in the undisputed cultural authority of Virgil.

The foregoing is nothing new. It is customary to observe that Ricote is just as Spanish as Sancho, and that his clandestine return to Spain is motivated in part at least by his love for the homeland he can no longer live in. It is less well known that Cervantes's fictional presentation is at odds with the vision that has emerged of the history of the moriscos and their relations with the dominant Old Christian majority. Thanks largely to French historical scholarship, the image we now have is that of a "total cultural confrontation," in Braudel's phrase.[5] In particular, the work of Louis Cardillac, Jeanne Vidal, and Bernard Vincent, as well as Antonio Domínguez Ortiz and Julio Caro Baroja, reveals the existence of a strong, cohesive morisco community that clung to its identity and the markers of that identity: the Arabic language at home, clandestine Arabic names in addition to the official Christian "nombre de pila" imposed at baptism, circumcision of boys, forms of dress, marriage and funeral customs, and the practically universal clandestine practice of Islam.

The Old Christian establishment used every means at its disposal, including providing tax incentives for mixed marriages, to wean the moriscos from their cultural identity and cause them to assimilate to the majority beliefs and practices. More stringent measures were also proposed. One of these "final solutions" involved the deportation of the moriscos to Newfoundland, where they would perish in the harsh climate, "especially castrating the male adults and children, and the women as well," as Don Martín de Salvatierra, bishop of Segorbe, noted forcefully but redundantly.[6] In 1588 a certain Don Alonso Gutiérrez proposed that, if expulsion should prove impossible because the moriscos were, after all, baptized Christians, all those above a certain quota could be castrated.[7] This solution was rejected by Pedro de Valencia in 1606 and again in 1609 by Manuel Ponce de León, who wrote: "cutting off their organs of generation is inhuman, barbaric, and alien to Catholic zeal."[8] The morisco community proved amazingly resistant and resilient. The story that has emerged of the hundred years from the conversions of 1501 through the revolt in the Alpujarra and consequent expulsion of moriscos from Granada in 1570, to the final expulsion of all the moriscos from Spain in 1609–1614, is the story of a struggle between oppression and resistance. The expulsion may be read as a confession of defeat on the part of the authorities.[9]

The most useful study of the fictionalized reflection in Ricote of the religious and especially the human dimensions of the expulsion is Francisco Márquez Villanueva's essay, "El morisco Ricote o la hispana razón de estado." Much of what follows is indebted to Márquez's exemplary humanism and humanitarianism. The expulsion is clearly bound up with religion, a theme that offers two subdivisions. There is first the general question of the legitimacy (or the logic) of a Christian monarch expelling Christian subjects from a Christian realm on religious grounds. For this to work it was necessary to argue convincingly that the moriscos, although made Christian by the sacrament of baptism, were really all hypocritical in their religion, all practicing Islam in secret, and all traitors in their loyalty to the state. Carried to its theological extreme, this tactic raises the knotty and ultimately unaskable question of the efficacy of the sacrament, as well as challenging the Pauline doctrine of the mystical body of Christ. But Ricote and Sancho are already members of a society where some Christians are more equal than others, where the entire founding notion of *limpieza de sangre* and the institutions that depended on it routinely ignored St. Paul's message, and we have seen that the clandestine practice of Islam was in fact widespread among the moriscos.

Ricote's sojourn in Germany, where "the Germans . . . let everyone live as they choose, and most of that country enjoyed religious freedom" (II, 54, 647), raises the question of religious orthodoxy as imposed in Spain against the freedom of conscience that obtained in Germany. Critics seem to have felt compelled to take sides in the surviving form of a debate that divided Europe and set off wars that exhausted its land and people for most of the sixteenth and seventeenth centuries. It is therefore not surprising to find Leo Spitzer affirming that Ricote has come to know religious tolerance as he saw it practiced in Augsburg, in the very heart of Protestantism, and concluding that in Counter-Reformation Spain it was impossible to write more boldly than this about religious liberty.[10] And it is certainly no shock to read Joaquín Casalduero's rejoinder, that those who believe that having Ricote live in Germany meant that Cervantes was praising religious freedom are laboring under a misapprehension.[11] It is clear that for the Spaniards of 1615 Germany did indeed represent freedom of conscience, and that the ruling orthodoxy in Spain considered that freedom an abomination. Fray Felipe de Meneses, for example, rhetorically contrasts Germany, sundered by heresy, with Spain, where the Inquisition assured uniformity of belief and behavior. He accuses Luther of having seduced the German people with the promise of "freedom and exemption from many of God's laws and all of the Church's, because that is his cry: freedom! Thank God there is no freedom like this in Spain."[12]

Within the German religious panorama the city of Augsburg, where Ricote had established himself, is particularly intimately associated with the question of liberty of conscience and the birth of Protestantism. Pedro Aznar Cardona, a violent apologist for the expulsion, laments the end of religious unity in Carlos V's German domains unleashed at the Diet of Augsburg, where liberty of conscience was officially determined as imperial policy. Aznar Cardona calls it "the German pestilence, where, even having considered the difficulties that attend a plurality of religious opinions, they obtained a decree at the Augsburg Diet of 1555, according to which any imperial Prince may choose whichever religion he prefers."[13] In addition, the basic theological document that defined Lutheran belief was hammered out by Luther and Melancthon in the same city of Augsburg, and is still known to Lutherans as the Augsburg Confession. Of all the German cities where Cervantes might have located Ricote in exile, only Augsburg has this specific relation to this specific religious and political issue.

The bibliography on the religious aspects of the expulsion of the moriscos is extensive; certainly the socioreligious questions raised were fundamental. But if we return to Cervantes's text we search in vain for anything more than superficial references to religion and theology. Ricote allows that his wife and daughter are "'good Catholic Christians,'" and that he is still praying to God "'to open the eyes of my mind and show me how I can serve Him'" (II, 54, 648). The religious question is not absent, but neither is it the principal focus of the novelistic episode. The text instead foregrounds first the painful human situation of those like Ricote and his family who have been forced from their homes and their country, and second, money. The text is loaded with references to money, which invites us to make money the focus of our critical inquiry as well.

It is a commonplace of historical scholarship to observe that military and religious considerations prevailed over the economic interests of the great landowners of Aragón and Valencia in determining the expulsion of 1609–1614. The prosperity of their estates and of the entire region depended on the skilled agricultural labor force composed of moriscos. An earlier expulsion, which had been approved by the Consejo de Estado in 1582, was in fact aborted because Felipe II had been persuaded during a visit to Valencia that the loss of the morisco labor force would wreak havoc on the economy. Historians generally agree that the principal economic effect of the expulsion was precisely the dramatic loss of most of the agricultural labor force, which indeed ruined the economy in Aragón and Valencia, just as cooler heads had predicted in 1582.

But economic ruin was not limited to the loss of the agricultural labor force. Fray Antonio Sobrino, a supporter of the expulsion, describes a memorial addressed to the king in 1609 proposing various alternatives, because expulsion would mean the ruination of all aspects of the economy. Sobrino himself rejects this thesis:

> "Yesterday afternoon the Conde de Castellar showed me a Memorial he was about to send to His Majesty, whose thesis is that the exclusion of the moriscos would be the universal ruin and desolation of this kingdom. This grounds the food and shelter of all elements of society in the service and usefulness of the moriscos, absent which, the incomes of the great aristocrats, the burghers, the ecclesiastics and religious orders, the alms of all the poor, the hospitals and churches, the wages of the mechanical trades, all would disappear, and in consequence, the entire kingdom would perish."[14]

Sobrino, as well as the royal authorities, should have paid more attention to this document, because it predicted exactly what recent historical scholarship has discovered to be true. In their indispensable *Historia de los moriscos: Vida y tragedia de una minoría* (1978), Antonio Domínguez Ortiz and Bernard Vincent identify the first economic consequence of the expulsion as simply a significant loss of population. This is divided into agricultural workers, who formed the majority, followed by merchants and traders. The consequences of this loss spread like the concentric ripples of a stone in water. The Cortes of 1625 complain of "'the great decrease in trade and commerce which has resulted from the expulsion of the moriscos, because many of them were in business, and they were all useful because they tilled the land and worked at other trades, which brought in significant tax revenue, which has now ceased.'"[15] The text singles out the loss of agricultural workers and traders, and points to another kind of economic consequence of their expulsion, namely the loss of tax revenue. The secular and ecclesiastical dues that moriscos paid just like everyone else disappeared along with the expelled moriscos themselves. In places where moriscos had been the majority of the population, this meant a crippling loss of revenue. Ironically, members of the ecclesiastical hierarchy were particularly vulnerable to its effects. In Almería, for example, the annual income of the bishop was reduced to twenty-five hundred ducados, and the chapter revenues fell from 1,728,069 maravedís in 1568 to 949,418 after the expulsion of 1570. This resulted in a forced downsizing of the cathedral personnel; the twenty canons, twenty racioneros, and twelve chaplains originally provided by the Reyes Católicos shrank to six of each, or a loss of thirty-four of fifty-two ecclesiastical positions.

There is ample testimony from the sixteenth century linking the morisco population with capital and capital formation. This association is in part a function of the officially feudoagrarian organization of society and its official aversion to commerce, capital formation, and capitalism in general, by banishing those practices to its margins. It was widely believed, for example, that the moriscos as a class were wealthy and that their pernicious habits of hard work and thrift allowed them to sponge up all the wealth of the country.

In 1587 the aforementioned bishop of Segorbe, Don Martín de Salvatierra, complained that the moriscos had monopolized the production and distribution of comestibles, all the jobs related to "'the provision of foodstuffs, such as vegetable gardeners, water sellers, tavern keepers and the like, where most of the money in this country is spent, and these moriscos are grabbing up everything and depriving Old Christians of their means of sustenance.'" The moriscos have become wealthy "'because they take in everything and spend nothing, not on food or drink or clothing or shoes.'" Some of the emigrés from

Granada have become wealthy enough to become tax farmers (which in turn leads to even greater capital accumulation) who can post their bonds in cash: "'And in Guadalajara, Pastrana, Salamanca and other places there are moriscos worth more than 100,000 ducados.'"[16]

A year later the aforementioned Don Alonso Gutiérrez affirms: "'These moriscos are very wealthy, and the *real* that comes into their hands never leaves. In Sevilla and Andalucía they buy and sell foodstuffs, and they bake and sell the greater part of the bread that is consumed; both are very lucrative businesses. They are porters for hire, cord makers and other similarly high-paying jobs, and this wealth in them is suspicious and hateful.'"[17]

The venerable patriarch Juan de Ribera, archbishop of Valencia, repeats the same accusations: "'They made themselves masters of money because they had taken over all the trading and contracting, especially of foodstuffs—which is where the real money is—and the better to do so they had become storekeepers, stewards, bakers, butchers, tavern keepers and water sellers, pie makers and vegetable gardeners.'"[18]

Finally, here is the testimony of the apologist Fray Marcos de Guadalajara: "'Item, because they are in general covetous and greedy, and most attentive to putting money away and keeping it without spending any, . . . they have chosen the highest-paying trades and businesses, such as storekeepers, notion sellers, pie makers, vegetable gardeners and the like, so that they come to be the sponge of all the wealth of Spain, and this is doubtless why they have such immense quantities of gold and silver in their possession.'"[19]

It was widely believed, or professed to be believed, that the humble petit bourgeois occupations enumerated throughout these polemical writings were first of all deliberately chosen by the moriscos (as though real alternatives existed), and second that these same modest trades were the key to runaway financial success, more lucrative than the great landholdings of the aristocracy, than the mines of America, and so on. It was also widely believed that the moriscos got even richer by retiring their wealth from circulation, by refusing to spend anything, not a single real, on consumer goods. This testimony is all "interested," in the economic sense of being enlisted in the service of justifying the expulsion, but the general trend of morisco professions and the accumulation of wealth is documented in more objective sources as well.

Domínguez Ortiz and Vincent quote the Cortes of 1593, which complained that the moriscos had become "'storekeepers, stewards, bakers, butchers, tavern keepers and water sellers, which allowed them to take in and save a great deal of money.'"[20] On other occasions, municipal authorities addressed themselves directly to the central government, as Guadalajara did in 1598, requesting that the moriscos be put to work in animal husbandry because they have become "'storekeepers, traders, messengers and other occupations related to business,'" in which they enjoy "'great profit and little work.'" A report from Sevilla in 1608 identifies the majority of the moriscos as "'businessmen, silkworm raisers, tavern keepers and mule drivers.'" Fray Alfonso Fernández, whose *Historia y anales de la ciudad de Plasencia* appeared in 1627, observed that many moriscos had "'grocery stores in the best locations in the cities and towns, and most of them lived off their own labor.'" The Cortes of 1598 requested that no morisco be allowed to be a "'storekeeper, steward, baker or maker of fritters, trader or dealer in any kind of foodstuffs either wholesale or retail, with grave penalties for infraction, but that all should till the land and be allowed to sell the products of their farming and grazing.'"[21]

Going characteristically against the grain, Pedro de Valencia considered that restricting the moriscos to the petit bourgeois occupations was in fact the most effective means of controlling them and simultaneously generating increased tax revenues:

"As long as the moriscos who are scattered throughout the kingdom refuse to mix with the natives and to show signs of being true friends and Christians, and since we cannot be sure of their intentions, we should try to diminish their physical vigor. We should not allow them to be farmers or have other jobs that might keep them fit and in shape for war. Instead, let them be only storekeepers and traders in the cities and towns. If they get rich there is no problem, since they would then be able to pay higher taxes, and they would become effeminate and cowardly, a well known side effect of wealth."[22]

Domínguez Ortiz and Vincent conclude that given the presence of so many moriscos in the petit bourgeois occupations and their virtual exclusion from the more remunerative kinds of activities, their general standard of living must have been modest and only a few of them acceded to a genuine bourgeois status. A few more facts will help us put Ricote's situation into perspective. Seven hundred morisco families expelled from Granada in 1570 settled in Córdoba. A census of property taken in 1592 reveals that about half of them owned no property at all, and that the total assets of the remainder amounted to something like one hundred ducados per family. But Fernando Aceite and his son-in-law, who traded in spices, had twenty-eight hundred ducados, and the brothers Miguel and Jerónimo López, silk merchants, had eighteen hundred.[23] Ricote's fortune of more than two thousand ducados compares very favorably with these figures.

We are in a position to conclude that the fictional Ricote is a verisimilar representation of a typical morisco economic profile as it emerges from the documentation: a *tendero* (storekeeper) in that nameless "lugar de la Mancha" who has sneaked back into the country to recover his accumulated wealth. In particular, we can tentatively identify him with the moriscos expelled from Granada in 1570 following the Alpujarra revolt and resettled in other areas. In a study of love and marriage among the moriscos, Bernard Vincent observes that many of those expelled from Granada were in fact concentrated in the large villages of La Mancha.[24] Vincent and Domínguez Ortiz remark that small business and transport were typical morisco occupations, practiced especially by those expelled from Granada in 1570. They aver that the moriscos that Cervantes knew must have been mainly those expelled from Granada and scattered over Castile, many of them small storekeepers.[25] Julio Caro Baroja remarks that following their expulsion from Granada and resettlement with Old Christians in integrated communities, the moriscos became accustomed to speaking Castilian, as Ricote does so fluently.[26] This might be the place to note the presence of moriscos named Ricote in Esquivias, the home town of Cervantes's wife and the place he knew best in La Mancha.

The accumulation of money, in its two modes of monopolizing the most lucrative businesses and hoarding every real, is presented in the antimorisco polemics as a fault: a selfish, divisive, unpatriotic act. The validity of the accusation depends on the meaning and value of the acts of saving and spending. The official attitude toward wealth and its uses would hold that wealth is to be spent, preferably on either of two things: individually on ostentation as a validation of social status, especially on luxury consumer products imported from abroad, and collectively on the propagation and defense of the faith. The paradigmatic case of the latter are the wars against the heretics in the Low Countries. In a funeral sermon in honor of Felipe II, Fray Agustín Salucio explicitly contrasts the ethos of spending money to defend the faith with that of accumulating it for secular purposes. "'Who does not understand,'" he asks rhetorically, "'that we could have saved some 60,000,000 ducados if we had only let the Low Countries live in liberty of conscience, as they call having no conscience of God in the world? A worthless saving, for we Catholics know that gold is not made to be worshipped, but to be spent in the service of the Faith.'"[27]

Fernand Braudel has shown how in the Low Countries religious orthodoxy was subordinated to the possibilities of the new economic order. "Amsterdam became a great city by welcoming foreigners and turning itself into a melting pot, taking advantage of everyone's skills and allowing everyone free practice of religion. Amsterdam transformed the throng of Flemings, Walloons, Germans, Portuguese Jews and French Huguenots into 'Dutchmen.' In 1650 one-third of the population was of foreign birth or extraction. Toleration meant accepting people as they were, since whether workers, merchants or fugitives, they all contributed to the wealth of the Republic." Braudel cites a 1701 guide-book: "'All the peoples of the world can serve God here according to their hearts and following the movement of their conscience and although the dominant religion is the Reformed Church, everyone is free to live in the faith he confesses and there are as many as 25 Roman Catholic churches where one may go to worship as publicly as in Rome itself.'"[28]

The result of this policy was a massive influx of capital, making possible the takeoff of the Dutch economy.

> Among the stream of refugees—French Protestants, Antwerpers, Jews from Spain and Portugal—were many merchants, often with substantial capital. The Sephardic Jews in particular contributed to Holland's fortune. . . . They were also good advisors, and were instrumental in setting up commercial links between Holland and the New World and the Mediterranean. But the Jews were not the only contributors to Amsterdam's success. Every trading city in Europe sent a contingent. Antwerp merchants were especially important. When Antwerp fell to Alessandro Farnese in August 1585 its citizens obtained generous conditions, notably that merchants were permitted to leave the city and take their property with them. So those who chose exile in Holland brought capital, competence and commercial contacts, and this was unquestionably one of the reasons for Amsterdam's rapid take-off. Half of the first deposits in the newly created Bank of Amsterdam (1609) came from the southern Netherlands.[29]

In Spain it was the other way around: the material possibilities that capitalism might have offered were sacrificed on the altar of racial and religious purity. The progressive aristocrat Don Sancho de Cardona, admiral of Aragón, attempted to imitate the Dutch (and Ottoman, and Papal) practice of religious toleration by allowing his morisco vassals to return to Islam and practice their religion upon payment of certain fees, keeping his agricultural labor force intact and content. Don Sancho even allowed the reconstruction of some mosques on his estates, and planned to denounce the forced conversions of the moriscos to the pope and the sultan in an effort to have them nullified. For his efforts Don Sancho was tried and convicted by the Inquisition in 1569, putting an end to his attempt to harmonize religious freedom and economic well-being. The opinion expressed by the implacable Fray Jaime Bleda prevailed: the moriscos had always wanted freedom of conscience, "'as Christians and Jews enjoy in the Ottoman empire, and Jews enjoy in papal lands, and all the heretics enjoy in most places in Europe,'" but, according to the logic of fanaticism that organized Fray Jaime's thought, this freedom is "'forbidden by Divine Law.'"[30]

According to the official thinking, money not spent has a negative value, and the moriscos' thrifty habits were stigmatized as antipatriotic. This mentality helped mobilize the violent denunciations we have seen. Viewed from another perspective, however, the moriscos' propensity for saving might appear as an exercise of that "primitive accumulation of capital" Marx defined as the essential precondition for the takeoff of a capitalistic economy. In this sense, the humble moriscos who work and save represent the most advanced and potentially the most productive sector of the Spanish economy. Their expulsion signifies not only the loss of the agricultural labor force that everyone has noted but also the stillbirth of a native petit bourgeois capitalism grounded in values and ideals that triumphed in northern Europe, and that might have at least contributed to preventing or attenuating the seventeenth-century decline in Spain. The expulsion of the moriscos, seen from this perspective, is a double economic disaster, affecting both labor and capital formation. The fictional character's name, Ricote, subsumes both these dimensions. With respect to labor, it is well known that in Murcia the Valley of Ricote was home to a morisco agricultural community that was exceptional for its docility and productivity, but was finally sent into exile along with everyone else. The allusion to this labor force in the character's name could not be more transparent. In addition, the embedded adjective *rico* and its augmentative *ricote* clearly point to the dimension of accumulated wealth.

This sobering view of what the expulsion meant for labor and capital in the Spanish economy is available in Cervantes's text for anyone willing to read it there in Ricote the morisco storekeeper. But Cervantes has by no means exhausted the subject. Ricote has returned to Spain to recover the capital he left hidden when he went into exile. He is travelling with a group of German pilgrims whose first word when they spy Sancho coming along is "Guelte," a Castilianized form of the German *Geld*. Money is on everyone's mind in this story. Even these foreigners who have come ostensibly to tour the holy places of Spain, as Ricote explains, are really there in pursuit of cash. "'Many of them make regular annual trips to Spain, visiting its shrines and holy places, which they regard as their golden Indies, and a source of absolutely certain, tried-and-true profit'" (II, 54, 647). Ricote is referring to what has become known as the colonialization of the Spanish economy. Spain is to Europe as America is to Spain: the source of wealth that exists to be extracted and transported to the metropolis. As early as 1558 this relationship had been made explicit by the prescient Luis de Ortiz: "the foreigners make fun of our nation, . . . they treat us worse than barbarians, . . . much worse than Indians, because at least we give the Indians a few trinkets in return for the gold and silver, while they not only get rich and make up for what they lack at home by taking our commodities, but they take our money as well with their sneaky thievery, not even bothering to dig it out of the earth, as we do."[31] It is further ironic that it is the holy places of Spain, the most representative of the official ideology of money spent in the propagation of the faith, that the probably Protestant Germans regard as the prime source of extractable wealth.

The illegal export of capital in which Ricote participates was another real consequence of the expulsion. Many moriscos were able to smuggle relatively large sums of accumulated capital out of the country. Domínguez Ortiz and Vincent report that some moriscos hid the wealth they could not export, possibly in order to deny it to the Old Christian authorities and possibly in the secret hope of being able to return for it some day. This practice was denounced in a royal decree of 24 February 1571, which claims all hidden treasure for the Crown: "'And because we are told that the said moriscos have left money, gold, silver and jewels buried, covered over, hidden or otherwise concealed in diverse parts and places of this kingdom, [we declare that] all of this too is ours and belongs to us.'"[32]

Julio Caro Baroja offers a series of examples given in the violently Old Christian *Expulsión justificada de los moriscos españoles* (1612), by Pedro Aznar Cardona, of moriscos from little places in Aragón who at least purportedly smuggled what we can only describe as serious money across the border: Francisco Pariente, from Brea, took more than forty thousand ducados in gold and silver across the frontier of Navarra, and his companions had with them a total of 250,000 ducados in coins. Manuel Granada, from Epila, and his grandson Compañero took twenty thousand. A certain Fierro, from Lérida, "'took out great quantities of gold and silver on various occasions, and transported it all to Turkey mixed in with dried fruits he pretended to be selling.'" This tactic recalls the modus operandi of Ricote's companions, who hide the coins "in the hollow parts of their staffs, or sewn into the patches on their cloaks, or by using other tricks they know about, they manage to smuggle back into their own country, in spite of the customs guards and the official control points" (II, 54, 648). The Oveje brothers from Almonacir de la Sierra smuggled out more than twenty thousand ducados, while Lope and Baltasar Alexandre, from Barbastro, took fifteen thousand. If we compare these figures to Sancho's annual wage of twenty-two ducados we can grasp the magnitude of these operations.[33]

The practice seems to have been widespread, even allowing for Aznar Cardona's obvious animus toward the moriscos. Caro Baroja offers the fictional episode of Ricote, among other literary texts, as evidence that many moriscos did indeed return from exile to recover the money they had left behind. The expulsion of the moriscos of the Valley of Ricote was motivated in part, he says, by their having given shelter to some of the clandestine returnees.[34] Aznar Cardona fulminates against the moriscos who sneaked back into Spain to reclaim their treasure and against those who protected them. Possibly as a result of his influence, the government decreed on 26 October 1613 that aiding or hiding a repatriated morisco was punishable by confiscation of all property. This was the penalty that awaited Sancho had he agreed to help Ricote. In fact, the fictional episode of their chance meeting, precisely in Aznar Cardona's Aragón, in 1614, Ricote's mission to recover his treasure, and Sancho's reluctance to get involved shares so many features with Aznar Cardona's treatise that one wonders whether Cervantes was responding more or less explicitly to the intransigent Aragonese author's diatribe and evoking the human consequences of those policies that turned Spaniards into foreigners and neighbors into enemies.

At this point we can identify Ricote as a paradigmatic figure who enacts, or in whom is enacted the whole gamut of personal and economic consequences attendant upon the expulsion of the moriscos. His name recalls the productive capacity of the agricultural labor force. His trade as village storekeeper was his personal contribution to the distribution of merchandise and the circulation of money in the local economy. His hidden treasure is a primitive accumulation of capital that in other circumstances might have produced a petit bourgeois capitalism. Finally, his exile and his new association with the dubiously pious German pilgrims makes him an agent of the clandestine export of Spanish capital to Europe. Through him is enacted, in miniature and at the personal level, the classic trajectory of Spanish capital in the sixteenth century: from the mines of America, through Spain, to the waiting coffers of foreign bankers. Pierre Vilar has defined the American treasure as the accumulation that made capitalism possible in northern Europe but which passed unproductively through Spain. "Enterprise dies while parasitism thrives. If the money coming from America into private hands served only to pay for luxury imported goods, the king's money was already pledged to the bankers in Augsburg and later in Genoa. This policy also diverted from Spain the flow of money that would make possible the nascent capitalist production elsewhere in Europe."[35]

Let us return for a moment to Augsburg, which Vilar mentions along with Genoa as the final resting place of the American silver that passed through Spain contributing nothing but rampant inflation to the Spanish economy. Besides its special significance in the religious conflicts of the sixteenth century, the city of Augsburg had another automatic association in the Spanish mind, as the home base of the Fugger banking dynasty, which controlled the Spanish economy until the Genoese took over in 1557. Of all the cities in Europe and around the Mediterranean basin where Cervantes might have sent his fictional Ricote into exile, Augsburg is the only one that brings together the religious and economic themes bound up in the expulsion of the moriscos.

There is an apparent but significant anachronism in Cervantes' text, set in 1614, long after the Fuggers had been replaced by the Genoese as the royal bankers and not long before the Genoese themselves would be replaced by a consortium of Jewish and converso financiers from Portugal and Amsterdam. It is true that the Fuggers remained on the scene and influential in Spain. They owned the rights to enormous revenues from such operations as the mercury mines of Almadén that so incensed Mateo Alemán, and in 1615 a certain Don Jorge Fúcar was made a Knight of Calatrava. But the reference in the *Quixote* is to pre-1557 Augsburg. Cervantes takes liberties with chronology, I think, to bind the personal tragedy of Ricote and his family to the great national questions raised by the expulsion of the moriscos, and to offer a miniature version of the catastrophic results of a policy so inadequate to its historical moment and to the social conditions it attempted to address.

I want to conclude by coming back to Ricote's accumulated capital and its function in the fiction. Francisco Márquez Villanueva observes somewhat facetiously but without making a value judgment that any storekeeper who had amassed more than two thousand ducados in Don Quixote's and Sancho's little village was not only "rico," but indeed "ricote."[36] Michel Moner, however, considers that the positive valence of the allusion to the hardworking New Christians of the Valley of Ricote is undone by the seme *rico* and the word *ricote*, with its vulgar augmentative suffix. This semantic orientation, argues Moner, which the text amplifies with its discussion of alms, hidden treasure, and coins secreted in the pilgrims' clothing, associates Ricote the character with the accusations hurled by the antimorisco polemicizers of ill-gotten wealth concealed behind a façade of poverty. Moner observes that neither Sancho nor Don Gregorio accepts Ricote's offer of money (II, 54 and 63). He concludes from this that morisco capital, if it is good for anything, is to be used to ransom captives from Algiers, but not to make gifts or loans to Old Christians. And finally, in a curious echo of the sixteenth-century apologist Don Alonso Gutiérrez, Moner stigmatizes Ricote's wealth as "of suspicious origin."[37]

Moner also argues that the hidden treasure is superfluous as a motivation for Ricote's return to Spain. It is more than sufficient that he wanted to reunite his dispersed family: "In addition, it should be noted that the treasure, so frequently mentioned by Ricote and his daughter, turns out to have a minimal narrative payoff[!] when we consider the role it plays in the plot. In fact, it was not at all necessary to invent a buried treasure to justify Ricote's return to Spain."[38]

Moner concludes that "literary imperatives," by which he means things like parallelism and other kinds of formal patterning, may be interfering with the text's value as testimony. It is true that Ricote's presence in Spain can be readily explained without recourse to his hidden treasure, although Ricote himself announces he has returned "'to find my daughter and dig up the great treasure I had hidden'" (II, 63, 701). And if the treasure is narratively superfluous, what is it doing in this narrative? I would argue that the presence of the redundant treasure might also be explained by positing that money—its ownership and uses—is an important theme in this story, and the fact that it is not necessary for the plot simply underscores its thematic importance.

Ricote's fortune is first mentioned in a general way by Ricote himself. He offers Sancho two hundred escudos, or close to ten years' wages, if Sancho will help him recover it. Without specifying any amount or the form in which his wealth is held, he tells Sancho that "'there's so much of it you can really call it treasure,'" and he adds that he can give Sancho enough to live on (II, 54, 648). Ricote's wealth is established at first by contrast with Sancho's poverty. Later, his daughter Ana Félix specifies the form in which the wealth is held: "'He left, secretly buried and in a place that I alone know, a great horde of pearls and immensely valuable gems, along with gold coins of all sorts'" (II, 63, 699). A specific amount is finally mentioned, in connection with the rescue of Don Gaspar Gregorio from Algerian captivity: "'And then they immediately set themselves to thinking how best to rescue Don Gregorio from the peril in which he'd been left; to save the young man, Ricote offered more than two thousand ducados in pearls and other gems'" (II, 63, 702). This amount, more than two thousand ducados, does not include the coins Ana Félix had mentioned earlier, so the total fortune must be even greater. In any case, Ricote's offer is turned down; the *renegado* and the Christian oarsmen will instead free Don Gregorio and spirit him away, commando-style. Ricote does pay these individuals handsomely after the rescue has been effected (II, 65, 708). Finally, Ricote offers Don Gregorio one thousand ducados, but the offer is turned down. Don Gregorio prefers instead to borrow a modest five ducados from Don Antonio Moreno, promising to repay him in Madrid (II, 65, 709). Michel Moner has argued that the refusal of Ricote's largesse, either as a gift to Don Gregorio or to ransom him, identifies the morisco's wealth as tainted; I am not so sure. There is a suggestion, certainly, that the Old Christian aristocrat Don Gregorio makes a distinction between Ricote's daughter and his money, finding the former desirable and worthy but the latter not. This may simply be a manifestation of the official aristocratic disdain for wealth in any form except land, it may suggest that Don Gregorio is an extreme exemplar of this economic backwardness, and it may bode ill for his marriage to Ana Félix should it occur. On the other hand, perhaps the offer of one thousand ducados to Don Gregorio was by way of a dowry, Don Gregorio understood it as such and declined, preferring to let his future father-in-law retain his capital.

However, Moner continues, the money might be functional in the sense of establishing a "homology" between Ana Félix's story and Zoraida's, suggesting a new aspect of the relationship between the two stories we observed at the beginning. In both cases there is a treasure (lost/kept) in the relation of father and daughter (separated/reunited).[39] Although the structural symmetry had already been observed by Luis Murillo in a note to his edition,[40] it is worth repeating. The discovery of this relation invites us to consider the other half of Ricote's story, the intercaste (and international) love of his daughter Ana Félix and the aristocratic Old Christian Don Gaspar Gregorio that offers so many analogies with the story of Zoraida and Ruy Pérez de Viedma. Various scholars have suggested the idealized fictionality, the deliberate rewriting of history inherent in the Zoraida–Ruy Pérez story. The most recent and most eloquent of these is E. Michael Gerli, whose contributions we shall consider in detail later. For the present suffice it to say that the reconciliation of ethnicities and religions effected by Zoraida and Ruy Pérez, and desired by Ana Félix and Don Gregorio, is just not verisimilar.

As early as 1526 the government had attempted to foment a policy of integration (read: assimilation) of the morisco New Christian population. Mixed marriages were encouraged, with generous tax exemptions. A royal decree of 8 December 1526 stated:

> "We make a gift to all Old Christian men who marry New Christian women, and to the Old Christian women who marry New Christian men, and to the Old Christians who go and live among the New Christians. They shall be exempt from the requirement of housing members of the royal court and soldiers. Neither shall they be required to make payment in clothing nor in animals nor birds nor in anything else by way of lodging. And beyond this, in order to do a greater favor to those who accomplish the foregoing, we promise to give land from royal and municipal holdings to themselves and their posterity."[41]

It is interesting to note in passing that all the inducements are directed toward Old Christians. It is they who are presumed to be making a sacrifice by marrying out of their ethnicity or by moving into the other neighborhood. It is only they, ultimately, who are real in the eyes of the authorities. Perhaps this tendency to address the morisco 'problem' without addressing the moriscos themselves is in part responsible for the failure of the entire project. Vincent concludes dryly that there were very few mixed marriages; the difference between the two communities was such that neither Old Christians nor moriscos looked favorably on these unions. He remarks elsewhere that mixed marriages were particularly rare among the moriscos expelled from Granada in 1570 who settled in the large villages of La Mancha.[42] Ricote and Sancho would agree. When he discovers that Don Gaspar Gregorio is pursuing his daughter, Ricote remarks: "'very few Moorish women, or even none at all, ever fall in love with Old Christians, and I think . . . this rich young man wouldn't have been able to woo . . . my daughter'"; to which Sancho replies: "'May it be God's will, because it wouldn't have done either of them any good'" (II, 54, 649).

The analogy between Ana Félix and Zoraida is still worth pursuing, especially now that we know how unrealistic the intercaste love stories are. Besides the mixed marriage theme, these two stories have in common their casts of characters. As Moner has reminded us, they are both stories of daughters and fathers separated or reunited and of family wealth lost or recovered. These similarities suggest another, to my mind more fecund analogy, between another father and daughter in another Cervantine text. When he makes his presence known among the crowd in the harbor at Barcelona, Ricote links his material treasure to his daughter and her beauty: "'I came back to find my daughter and dig up the great treasure I had hidden. I did not find my daughter; I did find the treasure, which I have with me. . . . And now I've found the treasure that most enriches me, which is my dear daughter. Anna Félix is her name, her surname being Ricote, and she herself as well-known for her beauty as for her father's wealth'" (II, 63, 701). This simultaneous recuperation of material wealth and lost daughter is experienced also by Isabela's father, the converso merchant whose return to material prosperity is the story of *La española inglesa*. This relationship, one of analogy rather than homology, serves to suggest the identification of Ricote's recouped treasure as capital and of Ricote himself as at least a potential merchant.

In both texts there is an inverisimilar scene of public recognition, reconciliation, and restoration, possible only in fiction. In *La española inglesa* it occurs when Isabela is just about to enter a convent and Ricaredo appears and claims her. The assembled company, which includes the representatives of church and state as well as the international banking community, celebrates the couple's union and the incorporation of the English Catholic into the Sevillian converso haute bourgeoisie. In the *Quixote*, the description of the lovers' reunion, with the father's implicit blessing and the approbation of the assembled company, which once again includes the representatives of public authority, is replete with the clichés of sixteenth-century romantic fiction: "Ricote and his daughter came out to welcome him, the father weeping, the daughter shy and bashful. The two young people did not embrace, for when love is deep and real, modesty usually prevails. But their beauty, side by side, was noted and admired by all who saw them. It was silence that spoke for these two lovers, and the chaste and happy thoughts their eyes revealed" (II, 65, 707–8).

In *La española inglesa* there is a happy ending dramatized in the text. In Zoraida's and Ana Félix's stories, however, the conclusion is left in doubt. In the first story we are led to believe that Ruy Pérez and Zoraida will indeed wed, following her baptism. What is left uncertain, as Márquez Villanueva and others have pointed out, is the affective quality of their December-May marriage and Zoraida's second-class social and religious status, which we shall discuss in more detail in the following chapter. If the ending of the Zoraida–Ruy Pérez story in part I offers at least the illusion of happiness, in part II there are fewer (if any) reasons to rejoice. Nothing has been resolved, everything is up in the air, and the prognosis is not good. Don Antonio Moreno, a prototypical Catalan businessman in spite of his Castilian name, has offered to bribe the authorities "allá dalt" in Madrid so that Ricote and his family may remain in the country. Ricote expresses his scepticism in a wonderfully sarcastic speech about how upright and uncorruptible is Don Bernardino de Velasco. Don Antonio arranges an inverisimilarly harmonious disposition of the characters, in which the viceroy of Catalonia shelters the criminal Ricote in his home "'while we wait to see what I can do in this business'" (II, 65, 708).

"Don Antonio's departure date arrived . . . . Don Gregorio's parting from Anna Félix was accompanied by tears, moans, sobs, and fits of fainting" (II, 65, 709). The last scene is a tearful parting. The text refers to Don Antonio's departure (while concealing the purpose of his trip) and to the lovers' tearful parting. This separation has been occasioned by Don Antonio's somewhat illogical insistence that Don Gregorio accompany him to Madrid to visit his parents, who are presumably in La Mancha. This chain of events causes the lovers' separation to be a subordinate function of Don Antonio's mission to Madrid. The dénouement of the love story hinges on Don Antonio's success or failure, his ability, as he says, to "'see what I can do in this business'" in Madrid. The real question left unanswered, therefore, is whether business, in the form of Don Antonio's *negocio,* will triumph over ideology. The ultimate conflict dramatized in this story is not between ideology and young love but between ideology and business. At the risk of falling out of favor with the practitioners of British cultural materialism, to say nothing of the guardians of the Reagan-Bush-Clinton new world order, I feel compelled to conclude by observing that the dependence of the love story upon material wheelings and dealings reproduces and in that sense validates the currently discredited relationship between base and superstructure so central to classical Marxist analysis.

Part 2

# Gender, Class, Modes of Production

# ~~ 4
# Women and Men, Christians and Muslims

In the captive captain's story (*Don Quixote* I, 39–41), we return to the theme of "moros y cristianos" that we saw in the story of Ricote the morisco in *Don Quixote,* part II. This time, instead of a confrontation between the majoritarian values and an unassimilated ethnic minority in Spain, we witness an international religious conflict between Christianity and Islam, in which the deliverance of Ruy Pérez and Zoraida into Christian Spain is traditionally taken as a triumph of the true faith. The most interesting recent variation on this theme expands the focus to include the religious dimension within Cervantes's racist and exclusivist society, in which religion and ethnicity are fused. In E. Michael Gerli's reading the captive's narrative becomes "a deconstruction and rewriting of Spain's foundational fiction of Reconquest."[1] In an argument poignantly reminiscent of the later work of Ruth El Saffar, Gerli detects the possibility of an idealized "Spain presided over by peace and justice," the result of a replacement of a central patriarchal myth by a "symbolic recovery through maternal love, fellowship and domesticity."[2] Gerli's is the most recent in a long series of fundamentally idealistic accounts of the text. This idealism takes two forms: there are studies that simply focus on poetic-universal abstractions such as harmony and goodwill, and those that, although they consider real social questions such as ethnic tensions and an immobile social order, discover an upbeat message of redemption or reconciliation encoded in the text. I want to call attention to another confrontation, quite explicit but generally ignored by critics, which is the confrontation between two different socioeconomic systems: an old one that contains the Pérez de Viedma family in the mountains of León and a new one that operates in Algiers. An investigation of this particular confrontation yields a more pessimistic vision of Cervantes's perception of the possibility of reform in his society.

The old order, as it is represented in the text by the Pérez de Viedma family, may be succinctly described as a feudoagrarian patriarchy. Wealth is synonymous with the ownership of land. Lineage is counted, and property is inherited, "por línea recta de varón," according to the Spanish legal cliché that Don Quixote recalls in relation to Gutierre de Quijada, "from whom I trace my own descent, in the direct male line" (I, 49, 337). *Patri-mony* is the family property to be passed on to the next generation. It is designated by its name as the *father's* property. Covarrubias defines it as: "what the son inherits from the father." In this traditional economic order the preservation of the patrimony, to be passed on intact from generation to generation, is the first order of family business. In fact, it *is* the "family business." Its implementation is aided first by the pervasive institution of primogeniture, in aristocratic families normally formalized in the creation of a *mayorazgo* (entailment) for the firstborn son, and secondly by specific strategies of marriage to avoid or at least minimize the disintegration of the patrimony. Similarly, "increase" is defined in this system as augmentation of the patrimony, and is accomplished through advantageous matrimonial alliances.

One such strategy documented in the period that interests us was to keep as many daughters as possible off the marriage market, thus eliminating the need to provide a dowry, which would have to come out of the patrimony. Angel Rodríguez Sánchez observes, with reference to powerful propertied families in Extremadura: "Examination of genealogical trees reveals a significant dedication to the religious life on the part of the female descendants. Explaining why so many feminine progeny are 'destined' for the cloister sends us back to the possibilities for entailment, the savings in dowries should entailment occur, and above all, to the family interest in limiting access to entitlement."[3]

More pertinent for the all-male Pérez de Viedma family is the institution of primogeniture. Javier Salazar Rincón observes that the survival of the family patrimony "was assured by the laws of the mayorazgo, an efficient instrument for avoiding the dispersion of aristocratic property and the weakening of aristocratic power. These laws established the right of the firstborn son to all the property left by the holder, on condition that it be preserved and transmitted intact to his successor."[4] Mayorazgo automatically has the effect of keeping the patrimony together, as it is passed on in its entirety to the eldest son.

But *mayorazgo* and *primogenitura* are not synonyms. Promogeniture was the custom, introduced as part of the feudal system, of the eldest son inheriting all the property. The evidence suggests that by the fourteenth century primogeniture was taken for granted as the norm, whereas a mayorazgo had to be founded by a written legal document. Its purposes were to keep the patrimony together and to preserve the memory of the founder and his family name.

The mayorazgo rests on the tradition of primogeniture, but from the legal point of view it subordinates it to the precedence of the property itself. As Marx observed wryly in the *1844 Manuscripts:* "The lord of an entailed estate, the firstborn son, belongs to the land. It inherits him."[5] The mayorazgo also has the practical effect of codifying the custom into law in those cases where a mayorazgo had been founded. The foundation of a mayorazgo was only reasonable in aristocratic families who owned considerable property in the form of land. Bartolomé Clavero makes this point explicit in his monumental study of feudal property in Castile from 1369 to 1836: "The doctrine and the law of mayorazgos clearly reflect the historical relation in Castile between entailment of the estate and control of the land, as manorial or feudal property in the broad sense, including estates and vassals. The mayorazgo embraces the totality of rents, taxes and rights of a given place."[6]

Since it is clear from the foregoing that the Pérez de Viedma family does not qualify for a mayorazgo proper, I want to focus principally on its essential underlying assumption, the rule of primogeniture, relying principally on Clavero's work.

Prior to the *Siete Partidas,* the practice of the firstborn son inheriting the father's arms and horse, that is, the outward signs of hidalgo status as well as the tools of the warrior's profession, is codified in the Fuero de Usagre, the Seudo-ordenamiento de Nájera, and the Seudo-ordenamiento de León, among others.[7]

Ernst Mayer considers that the institution of the mayorazgo depends on that of hidalguía and the inheritance by the firstborn of the *casa solariega* and the arms and horse (which by the way identifies Don Quixote as a primogénito, with his "great-grandfather's suit of armor"). Mayer derives this ultimately from Germanic law. This tradition is in turn simply assumed by the 1505 Leyes de Toro.[8]

Rudolf Leonhard claims that the tradition of straight-line succession and the preference for males are of Germanic provenance, while the right of primogeniture and the indivisibility of the inheritance are the contributions of feudalism. In the same vein, continues Clavero, Joseph Calmette writes that "'the privilege of the firstborn is, in any case, a trait *sui generis* of feudal society,'" adding that "'the point of origin was neither Roman nor Germanic.'"[9]

In the *Partidas,* succession by primogeniture is already assumed to be the rule. The question of the mayorazgo is developed in Partida 2, título 15, ley 2, which is concerned specifically with royal succession. Again, the rule of primogeniture is assumed: "'The title to the kingdom shall be held only by the firstborn son upon his father's death. If the eldest son dies before inheriting, if he has left a legitimate son or daughter, then that child inherits. If all these should die, then the kingdom should be inherited by the closest male relative.'"[10]

So pervasive was the mentality of primogeniture that the obligation to provide something (*alimentos* or *dote*) for the issue left out of the mayorazgo by the law of primogeniture was by no means clear or certain. At least one theorist recognized a general moral obligation: "If my father founds a mayorazgo for me which includes all the property and income, so that nothing is left for my sister, the founder's daughter, then I have the obligation to provide her dowry out of the property included in the mayorazgo."[11] Clavero concludes that in spite of this, "the integrity of the mayorazgo prevails over the right of the excluded issue to maintenance and dowry."[12]

Luis de Molina's *De hispanorum primogeniorum origine ac natura libri IV* (1573), the principal legal-scholarly authority on questions of primogeniture and mayorazgos in the period that interests us, formulates the basic premise unequivocally: "'Hispanorum primogenia ex propia natura indivisibilia sunt.'"[13]

We might consider these the principal economic characteristics of the old order of which the Pérez de Viedma family, hidalgos from the mountains of León, was part. The basis of wealth is land, with whatever tributary rights go with it. The land belongs to a family; indeed, the family derives its identity and social status from its relationship to the land. The object of the system is to allow the transfer of this land, intact, undivided, and undiminished, from one generation to the next. The immemorial custom of primogeniture ensured that the land would remain undivided. The legal institution of mayorazgo, where it was in effect, imposed further restraints on the dispersion of the patrimony through the prohibition of alienation and confiscation. The emphasis is on conservation as opposed to expansion, and on orderly succession from father to firstborn son, who immediately becomes the new patriarch upon his father's death, and whose mission in life now becomes that of conserving his patrimony and passing it on intact to his own firstborn son. This occurs at the expense of the other children, who because they are disinherited are in effect rendered nonexistent. It might be argued that these disinherited *segundones* constituted the only potentially dynamic sector of the society. This is true, but their economic dynamism occurs in spite of, not because of the system, and their activity, however productive it may have been, is not officially valued. There is no official place in the system for individual initiative (except that connected with military enterprises) and the notion of economic growth, let alone social mobility, is officially unrecognized. This is an order that privileges stasis over dynamism.

Let us turn now to the new order, an incipient capitalism based on notions of commodification and commerce. Fernand Braudel has already traced the spread of capitalism in Europe from Venice to Amsterdam by way of Portugal and Antwerp. What we are interested in here is nascent capitalism in its extra-European, specifically Muslim-Mediterranean context.

Subhi Y. Labib begins an article on capitalism in medieval Islam by observing that "Islam approved of trading," and that "the Islamic merchant was born into an active trading community." He further notes the existence of the *funduqs* which he characterizes as "virtual stock exchanges and commodity futures trading in dates and tuberous vegetables." The *letra de cambio*, that staple of early modern European financial capitalism, has its exact equivalent in the *suftajah*. Labib observes in passing that "interest and usury were legally prohibited; however they were customary. Usury and excessive profit played an important role in Islamic capitalism. Neither Muslims nor Christians nor Jews shunned usurious business dealings."[14]

Within the particular Ottoman context, Halil Inalcik in an article on Ottoman socioeconomic structures distinguishes three subcategories of what in Spain would be *pecheros* (commoner-taxpayers) in Ottoman society: peasants, craftsmen, and merchants. Peasants and craftsmen were subject to strict government regulation, but merchants were not. They were free to increase their capital by any means, and "in all classes of Ottoman society there was apparent a great desire to put cash into making profit; and the most profitable field for investment of cash wealth was commerce." "Partnerships on credit (*shirkat al-wujuh*) and *commenda* (*mudaraba*) were important means of bringing together capital and specialist skill." In a *shirkat al-wujuh* the partners borrowed money to trade on and at the end of a stipulated time returned the capital to its owner. A *mudaraba* is a relationship in which one party puts up the capital and the other party does the trading (the labor), and both share in the profit. If the capital was used for manufacture instead of trade it was a *shirkat al-sana'i wa 'l-takabbul*, where one party might put up the capital and the other the labor and expertise, or they might both borrow capital from a third party and engage jointly in manufacturing the product. The point is that doing business on credit was normal. Inalcik remarks that "there is much truth in the suggestion that Islamic law and the Islamic ideal of society shaped themselves from the very first in accordance with the ideas and aims of a rising merchant class," but goes on to clarify that the commercial mentality antedates Islam and was in fact "the traditional concept of state and society that had prevailed in the Near East in pre-Islamic times."[15]

Merchants were prized and accorded privileged treatment by the imperial Ottoman government. There was, however, a popular opposition to the capitalist mentality, the same thing we find in Spain directed by Old Christian peasants toward Jews, and a serious antagonism between the manufacturing sector, controlled by craft guilds with the guild mentality (closed corporation, control), and the merchant-banker-traders (buy cheap, sell dear, loan money at interest, make as much as the traffic will bear in an unregulated free-market situation). The government finally supported the guilds in that there never developed a system of state-financed manufacture or mercantilism proper. "As regards industrial production, the state . . . sought to solve the new problems within the old guild framework; it never considered moving in the direction of a system of mercantilist economy as Europe did."[16] The same conflict was occurring in Spain, and the response of the Spanish government was identical to that of the Ottoman state. As we have seen, Cervantes dramatizes it in *Rinconete y Cortadillo,* where Monipodio and Company represent the official mentality, still tied to monopolies and closed corporations.

There was no ethnic association with trading as there was in Spain, where trading was associated with Jewishness. Ronald Jennings observes in the case of Cyprus that "until the Ottoman conquest, credit and moneylending seems to have been very much under the control of a small group of Jews. As the only source of credit, they were eagerly welcomed by businessmen and other people needing cash. Under the Ottomans, that system changed drastically, for under the Sharia, lending money at a fair interest rate was in no way reprehensible. Suddenly one finds people of all faiths involved in lending money for interest."[17] Jews were certainly active in trading, however. Inalcik calls special attention to the Nasi family: Doña Gracia Mendes and her nephew João Miguez-Juan Micas-Don Joseph Nasi-Duke of Naxos, who acquired the monopoly of the wine trade and later of beeswax and became fabulously wealthy. He had a part also in the financial relations between France and the Ottoman Empire. In 1555, Henri II, pressed for money, floated a loan in France at an extra-high rate of interest. Many Turks found it profitable to invest in this loan. Apparently Joseph Nasi covered some 150,000 *scudi,* and King Henri welched, whereupon the sultan confiscated French merchant ships calling at Ottoman ports until the debt to Nasi was satisfied.[18]

In sharp contrast to Spain, commerce, including the very profitable activity of tax farming, was practiced by all. "There is no question that since the fifteenth century Jews had had a large share in the farming of taxes at Bursa and Istanbul, but Greek and Turkish capitalists do not seem to have been less active. Thus in 1476, when a five-man consortium of Greeks bid 11 million *akches* (ca. 245,000 Venetian ducats) for the farm of the Istanbul customs for three years, a four-man consortium of Muslims outbid them by 2 million and won the contract. Next year a Muslim Turk of Edirne and a Jew jointly put in a higher bid, but were outbid by a consortium of Greeks. From the middle of the sixteenth century, with the coming of the Marranos, Jewish influence and control of the money market seem to have increased. But there is no clear evidence that they introduced a new mercantilist tendency into the Ottoman economy; it seems that they brought rather their own activities into conformity with the already existing pattern."[19]

At the other end of the Mediterranean, Diego de Haedo describes a dynamic trading economy in the hands of a diversified merchant community in Algiers. As elsewhere in the Ottoman empire, there are no ethnic restrictions on trading, nor is trading incompatible with soldiering. "Merchants are also numerous. Many are native Muslims, others are renegade converts and their sons. Some are native Jews who converted to Islam voluntarily, as we see happening every day. Many of these merchants were janissaries and common soldiers first, and when they discovered the trading life was more comfortable and less dangerous, they gave themselves over to it."[20]

The Algerian merchants traded in a broad range of commodities, generally agricultural products and raw materials from Algiers in exchange for manufactured products from Muslim and Christian lands. The commonly exported commodities included wheat, barley, rice, cattle, oxen, camels, sheep, wool, olive oil, lard, honey, raisins, figs, dates, and silk. Export of hides was controlled through special contracts with the king, along the lines of the Spanish *asientos*. The Algerian merchants bought merchandise from as far east as India for resale to European merchants. They also bought merchandise from the Christian ships that traded there under safe conduct for resale to an expanded local market that included all of western North Africa, and for export to the Muslim east, "because no Barbary port has more commerce with European merchants and their ships than Algiers." Quality textiles came from Genoa, Naples, and Sicily; ironware, glass, and soap came from Venice; iron, lead, tin, copper, pewter, gunpowder, and textiles came from England; pearls, fragrances, perfumed water, herbed olive oil, scarlet cloth, salt, wine, "and lots of golden *escudos* and *reales,* which is the principal and most profitable merchandise," came from Spain. From Marseilles and elsewhere in France came candle wicking, iron, steel, nails, saltpeter, gunpowder, alum, sulpher, vitriol, cutlery, needles, pins, oats, chestnuts, salt, wine, "and many of these commodities, which are prohibited and contraband in Spain, are actually loaded there onto French ships saying they are bound for France, but when they are out at sea they change course for Algiers." It would appear that the Spanish merchants suffered under a heavy burden of regulation and prohibition, which their French colleagues managed to circumvent, so that Spanish-manufactured products could be sold in the "enemy" market, much as weapons technology is now exported to unfriendly countries through intermediaries. Finally, the Algerian merchants also resold European merchandise seized by corsairs back to the Europeans, "but principally, they ransom many captives."[21]

The Barbary economy was dominated by corsair activity, which included trade in seized merchandise and the commodification and sale of human captives. Haedo describes a highly organized and disciplined operation, where control resided ultimately with the sultan. The *galima* (spoils), including captives, merchandise, money, and jewelry, were the property of the *arráez* (captain of the ship) and of the partners who shared the cost of outfitting it. Seized clothing became the property of the *leventes* (common soldiers), who shared equally. One-seventh of all booty was reserved for the king of the port from which the expedition had sailed: Algiers, Tunis, or Tripoli. The corsairs in each port were subject to a field commander appointed directly by the sultan. This commander led all expeditions, and had the authority to compel participation under his command by all corsairs. He received one-fifteenth of all booty taken.[22]

The economic concept is primitive; wealth is generated by taking it away from somebody else. Investment of the profits seems to be unknown, but each corsair vessel was an investment vehicle for the *arráez* and his partners, called *armadors,* who in Ciro Manca's summary limit themselves to the investment of a certain capital, becoming *pro quota* owners of a ship and participating in the same proportion in the profits of the corsair expeditions.[23] Salvatore Bono considers that these capitalists might be large-scale players such as wealthy businessmen, powerful state functionaries, or high-ranking military officers, who owned shares in several ships, or more modest businessmen, artisans, or small savers who had committed their own capital to a single corsair ship.[24] Manca, however, considers the concentration of the corsair enterprise and the resulting profits in the hands of a restricted group of privileged capitalists "simply irrefutable."[25] What is clear is that this aspect of the corsair economy was organized along capitalist lines.

Within this system Manca delineates the internal divisions of socioeconomic class familiar from Marxist analysis: capital and labor; directors and directed; exploiters and exploited; free and slave. The extremes are peopled respectively by arraeces and armadors, who own the means of production and take the lion's share of the profits, and at the other end by slaves, who contribute only labor and do not share in the profits. A "dynamic middle class" was composed of off-duty janissaries, *moros,* and renegades who had no capital to invest, but who contributed their labor and shared in the profits. This means they could aspire to a primitive accumulation of investment capital and ultimately to become arraeces or armadors themselves.[26]

The corsairs and their partners preferred to consume the profits immediately, stimulating the local economy without producing any long-term gain. Haedo reports that when the ships return to port,

> the arraeces and common soldiers begin immediately to throw money around on lavish parties they call *sosfias,* and on wine and *arrequín* or spirits, and on every type of gluttony and lechery they spend everything they have stolen on their voyage. Then all Algiers is content, because the merchants buy many slaves and other merchandise the corsairs bring, and the storekeepers sell everything they have in stock to those who come from the sea, because many get themselves up in complete new outfits, and everything is eating and drinking and feeling good.[27]

The corsair economy was built on slavery as the chief source of labor and as the chief commodity. The capitalization required for the exchange of captives, on which the entire economy rested, had consequences that went far beyond the immediate goal of redeeming souls (and bodies) for Christianity. The economies of Algiers and western Europe were in fact mutually interdependent. Since raising the cash required for large-scale ransom operations was difficult, the practice of ransoming captives on credit became pervasive. The ransoming agency (a Christian religious order) could borrow money from the Algerians at 10 percent per month, or they could do business with European merchant-bankers established in Algiers, whose rates were slightly less onerous. The friars who ransomed Cervantes, for example, borrowed 220 escudos from various merchants in Algiers to add to the 280 they had already received in *adjutorios* for him.[28] The entire corsair economy, based on the sale of captives, in fact depended on these Christian intermediaries, who, because they were integrated into the North African economic system, kept it open to the outside world and assured the insertion of the corsair economy into the international economic concert.[29] Not only did the European merchant-bankers provide the funds necessary for the redemption of Christian captives, they also put the indispensable Spanish *escudos de oro en oro* into circulation in the Algerian economy. "In the hands of these Christian merchant-bankers," continues Manca, "the ransom of captives, trade in merchandise and the affairs of finance became closely intertwined. And all of them, for one reason or another, introduced significant quantities of European currency into Barbary, independently of the exchange involved in the redemption of captives and the trade in merchandise, simply as financial speculation."[30]

These merchant-bankers controlled a financial market extending from Europe through North Africa, buying local money for escudos de oro, selling it to European Christians who needed it for purposes of ransom or trade in merchandise, in exchange for escudos de oro worth more on a different market, in bills of exchange (*letras de cambio*) payable at a European *plaza*, usually Lyon. The merchant buys five Algerian *doblas* for the Algerian price of one escudo. He then sells the five doblas to, say, the Trinitarians, at the European price of 1.66 escudos, payable at Lyon. Finally, a good part of the foreign exchange flowing into Algiers in exchange for captives was reexported to Europe to satisfy the demand for durable and nondurable goods, especially products required for the corsair operation. Each galley put into service in Algiers required an expenditure on the European market of some three thousand escudos de oro en oro, for masts, rigging, sails, oars, anchors, cannon, and other items of equipment in excess of the amounts generated by direct corsair activity.

Ellen Friedman offers a small caveat with regard to the ransoming agencies. "The apparent financial probity of the friars who carried out the expeditions does not necessarily lead to the conclusion that the orders or their hierarchies did not profit from redemptionism. Only a thorough examination of the financial records of the orders themselves would reveal how much of what was collected actually went toward the ransom of captives and how much was diverted to other uses."[31]

Friedman offers further evidence of the commodification of captives on the Spanish side.

> Upon their return to Spain . . . the rescued captives were expected to participate in a series of religious processions in various cities. . . . The emotional impact of a returning redemption was very powerful, and an important factor in generating contributions for future ransoming expeditions. The instructions that the generals of the orders issued to the friars make it clear that this was the purpose of the ceremonies. . . .
>
> For the massive campaigns to raise funds for the ransom of captives, the printed and widely circulated accounts of their sufferings and of the difficulties encountered by the redemptionist fathers in North Africa, the processions held when the ransomed captives returned, the visibility of former captives begging alms, the chains and shackles hung in churches and public buildings throughout Spain, all served to confirm for many Spaniards that the long struggle with the Muslim world was not over.[32]

We may now turn to a discussion of the respective economic orders as they are represented in Ruy Pérez de Viedma's story. The Pérez de Viedma family belongs to and indeed embodies what we have been calling the old order. Wealth is based on the ownership of land, which in turn is tied to hidalgo status. The wealth is the father's, the patri-monio, to be passed on in patrilineal succession. The patrimonio is finite and not expected to grow.

Within this general paradigm the Pérez de Viedma family presents some peculiarities. First, this is an all-male family, consisting of the father, his brother, and his three sons. There are no mothers, wives, or daughters. Second, in this family an equal division of the patrimony, derived from folkloric and biblical sources, takes precedence over the rule of primogeniture, which as we have seen prevailed in fact. This is of crucial importance, yet it is all too easy for it to pass unperceived. Our collective familiarity as professional readers of literature with traditional texts and stories—folktales and the Bible—tends to make history invisible to us, with unfortunate consequences for our comprehension of and indeed our entire relation to texts such as this one. Because we recognize a pattern inherited from older formulaic modes of storytelling, in this case the traditional division of the property among the sons and their subsequent going forth to make their fortunes, we tend to read the text in terms of the conventions of folk narrative, in opposition to those of verisimilar fiction, which is in fact what we are reading and where we would have been led had we been attentive to the presence of real social practice. This presence, paradoxically, is revealed by its absence from the text, but only if we are alert enough to be looking for it. Within the fiction, the father's radical departure from the norm has profound psychic consequences for Ruy Pérez, which we shall explore later. For now I want to focus on the economic consequences, which cannot be overemphasized.

The entire point of the traditional economic order, as we have seen, is the preservation of the family patrimony intact, with primogeniture working in tandem with specific matrimonial strategies. This father's decision to ignore the rule of primogeniture effectively converts all his sons into segundones, with the attendant economic obligation to make their own way in the world. There is thus a general sense in which all three brothers participate in the new order. Ruy the soldier and Juan the judge form part of what Maravall has called the two great pillars of the modern nation-state: the professional army and the professional bureaucracy.[33] But soldiering is clearly a vestige of the old order, and soldiering was still held to be incompatible with commerce. Similarly, lawyering is merely the modern manifestation of the medieval cleric's function. In addition, Juan Pérez de Viedma's membership in the old order is signalled by his interest in marriage strategies as the means of social mobility and economic increase. He has already benefitted from such a marriage, by keeping his wife's dowry for himself after she died in childbirth (I, 42, 293). His daughter and only heir Doña Clara is the object of the affections of a certain Don Luis, the son and only heir of a "'gentleman from Aragón, lord of two villages'" (I, 43, 298), "'so noble and rich I'm not fit to be his son's servant, much less his wife'" (I, 43, 299), and "who wanted to secure a title for his son."[34] Juan Pérez, who knew about the father's plans for his son, and who "as a sensible man was well aware what an advantageous match this would be for his daughter" (I, 44, 308), could not be keener on the advantageous alliance that now offers itself.

The only true capitalist, or true representative of the new economic order, is the nameless third brother. He is physically absent from Spain and the Mediterranean (in the *new* world, in fact), and he is absent from the discourse except as a second-hand reference, which only emphasizes his absence. The nameless third brother is also the invisible support, through the money he regularly sends, of the visible lifestyles of his father and his brother Juan, who both belong to the old order. As Juan Pérez de Viedma explains: "'My youngest brother is in Peru, and so rich that, with what he's sent my father, and me as well, he's easily fulfilled his share of the bargain, indeed, putting so much into my father's hands that he's been able to satisfy his natural generosity, while I've been able to apply myself, comfortably and with authority, to my studies, and to reach the point at which you behold me'" (I, 42, 294). The father is free to engage in the aristocratic exercise of *liberalidad,* one of the visible signs of his hidalguía, and the son can pursue his studies in greater material comfort and visible social prestige, a marker of his own hidalgo status, thanks to the profits generated from an unnamed business conducted by an unnamed son in a far-off place. This family dynamic enacts perfectly the relation between invisible economic base and visible cultural superstructure familiar from classical Marxist theory.

The father, brother Juan, and the unnamed entrepreneur brother all belong to a system in which the exercise of the new economic order supports the visible manifestations of the old. Only Ruy Pérez de Viedma is left out, as he soldiers on in the king's service. A couple of significant throwaway references to Genoese commercial enterprises suggest that Ruy Pérez might have preferred to go into business himself. He does not take up arms and enter the king's service immediately, in Spain, but travels to Italy instead. And instead of taking the most direct route, from the mountains of León to Barcelona or Tortosa and thence by sea to Italy, he goes by way of Alicante, "where it was said there was a Genoese vessel taking on a cargo of wool bound for its home port" (I, 39, 266). The economic historian Felipe Ruiz Martín identifies Alicante as the principal port of embarcation for Spanish merchandise bound for Italy from 1577 to 1585, noting in particular the tendency after 1569 of sheepowners to send their wool to Genoa and Livorno by way of Alicante.[35] That is, Ruy Pérez postpones the assumption of his military career, and he seeks the society of Genoese merchants instead of Spanish soldiers. His brief narration of these events also points to the colonialization of the Spanish economy in the form of export of raw materials to be reimported later as manufactured products. Later in his narrative Ruy Pérez locates a military objective by its proximity to Genoese commercial activity: "Tabarca, a little port or freight station run by Genoese in the coral-fishing business" (I, 39, 269). If these fleeting references mean anything, they suggest that Ruy Pérez is the victim of a double whipsaw effect brought on by his father's decision: he is deprived of his birthright and stuck in an unprofitable career not of his choosing. And he is out of the loop, behind the door, invisible, in what Francisco Márquez Villanueva calls his "recia honradez castellana" (tough Castilian honor), with respect to any share of the profits his nameless brother generates in Perú.[36]

In contrast, the new economic order is pervasive in Algiers. As we have seen, the Algerian economy is based on trade in merchandise, which includes the commodification of humans. Wealth is not preexistent and finite, but is continuously generated (by that primitive form of entrepreneurship known as stealing), and in theory presents the possiblity of infinite growth. Commodification divides captives into two classes that correspond to the two aspects of a commodity delineated by economic theory: the *cautivo de rescate,* such as Ruy Pérez himself, has a cash or exchange-value; the *cautivo de almacén* has a use-value. This division also leaves the role of the capitalistic entrepreneur to the Algerians, who own the means of production and who extract profit from both captive classes in their respective ways.

The family composed of Hajji Murad and Zoraida resembles the Pérez de Viedma family in that there is no mother. They are similar also in that the father's wealth is a patrimony to be inherited by his daughter. The text names Zoraida specifically as heir: "Hadji Murad, rich as could be, who had just one daughter, heiress to his entire estate" (I, 40, 276). But here the resemblance begins to break down. Hajji Murad is an *alcaide.* His wealth is derived from tribute levied on rural *moros* and *alarbes* subject to the king of Algiers, and from stealing, corsair fashion, from others. Here is Haedo on alcaides in general and Hajji Murad in particular: "The alcaides extract lots of money from these people, becoming vey rich in a very short time. Among the richest of these alcaides living in Algiers in 1581 were: first, Hajji Murad, a Slavonian renegade, the father-in-law of Muley Maluch, King of Fez."[37]

But Cervantes's Hajji Murad is not characterized in this rapacious, Algerian, new-economic-order way, except indirectly. The alcaidía is present as part of Hajji Murad's unnarrated prehistory, but assimilated to the Spanish old-order notion of "quality." The informed reader has to supply the Algerian context, both with reference to the real meaning of having been an alcaide and with respect to Hajji Murad's status as a European convert to Islam. He is introduced in Cervantes's text as "a principal and rich Moor named Hadji Murad, a man who'd been in charge of the fort at La Pata, which among the Moors is a post of great quality" (I, 40, 273).

Cervantes's text mutes Hajji Murad's participation in the Algerian economy in order, I think, to allow the chain of protocapitalistic economic practice to begin with Zoraida. Her wealth is clearly designated as the result of theft; it is generated by stealing from Hajji Murad. It is then invested in various ways: to exchange for Ruy Pérez, to finance the escape, and to take to Spain as a form of dowry. Therefore, Zoraida's thievery might be defined as a primitive accumulation of investment capital. The escape operation is indeed a textbook example of capitalist enterprise as it was practiced in the Algerian corsair economy and described by Bono and Manca, and known generally in the Ottoman world as *mudaraba*.[38] Zoraida puts up the capital, and Ruy Pérez supplies the labor. In this way she becomes a full participant in the Algerian economic system.

The Algerian economy is also based on (forced) trust, that is, on credit. Of necessity, deals are made through intermediaries such as the renegade and the merchant. "'I finally made up my mind to confide in a renegade from Murcia, who'd said he was a true friend and made promises that would require him to keep any secret I entrusted to him'" (I, 40, 273). That is, Ruy Pérez didn't really trust him, otherwise the promises wouldn't have been necessary. This is followed by a description of various practices common among renegades. If they return to Spain they carry signed statements from Christian captives stating they were always kind to Christians and always wanted to escape from Algiers. Some are legitimate; others use the statements to get themselves released after they have committed robberies, or to get reconciled with the Inquisition. The renegade finally wins over Ruy Pérez and his comrades by a performance: "'He said all this with so many tears, and such signs of repentance, that we were all of the same mind and agreed to tell him the entire truth, which we proceeded to do, holding back not a single detail'" (I, 40, 275). In the end the renegade assumes control of the entire escape operation, overruling Zoraida's plan. He is also responsible for taking Hajji Murad prisoner, and for brutally telling him the truth about his daughter and the Christians.

The eight hundred escudos for Ruy Pérez's ransom are given "on the pledge of a merchant from Valencia, who happened to be in Algiers at the time, giving him the money and arranging that he'd pay it after the next boat arrived from Valencia, for if the money were handed over at once the king might suspect" (I, 40, 277). That is, the merchant did not give the king money. Instead, he gave him his word, and the ransom is effected on credit. Ruy Pérez also arranges for the ransom of his three comrades, because although they are good guys, he cannot be sure that they wouldn't be so envious of his freedom that they might do something "that would injure Zoraida." Their ransom is arranged, on credit, through the same merchant, whom they never take entirely into their confidence. "'I had them ransomed the same way I'd arranged it for myself, giving the merchant the whole sum, so he could assume our bond with perfect safety and certainty. All the while I told him nothing of what we were really up to, because that might have been dangerous'" (I, 40, 278).

In capitalism's master trope, the new economic order is figured as fecundity, especially the male phallic function, leading to increase. The Greek word *tokos* signifies both interest and offspring. Even such a staunch supporter of the feudoagrarian system as Quevedo knew that capitalism and fecundity are related. In *La hora de todos* he figures commerce as a stud horse: "commerce is the stud horse of money, who impregnates the doubloon and makes it give birth every month."[39] It is the old aristocratic order that is represented by sterility, in the sense of the absence of growth and increase. Wealth is finite, to be lived off of and held on to. An ethic of investment and growth opposes an ethic of preservation (or its alternative, a desperate dialectic of preservation and consumption).

Ruy Pérez's nameless father is not really sterile; he does engender three sons, but this act is not mentioned in the text. The text is concerned with preserving and passing on a finite patrimony defined as preexisting. Ruy Pérez's father practices the aristocratic virtue of *liberalidad*, but he is generous to the point of profligacy, an activity analogous and assimilable to the biblical spilling of seed on the ground. He divides his property finally in order to allow his sons to inherit something before he fritters it all away. Instead of increase, the elder Pérez de Viedma actually gives us decrease.

Zoraida's father presents a marked contrast. First, he has a name, an attribute his aristocratic Leonese counterpart lacks. Second, Hajji Murad has a garden, which because it is mentioned as the site of gathering salad greens and other fresh produce from a presumably ever-renewable supply is at once a symbol and a literal representation of fecundity, growth, and other protocapitalist practices. That is to say, Hajji Murad fecundates. His engendering of Zoraida is symbolized in his garden, which in turn symbolizes her inviolability. Françoise Zmantar has written: "Cervantes's garden is the open garden of Hajji Murad, a space of freedom and generous abundance. It is also the garden-cloister of the chaste and pure Zoraida."[40] The biosexual act of engendering Zoraida is specifically, although negatively, evoked in the text when he curses "'the hour when I begot you'" (I, 41, 287).

Zoraida also fecundates. She steals from her father and invests the proceeds in Ruy Pérez, ultimately for her own profit. The narrative makes clear that Zoraida owns all the means of production, literally as the money necessary for the ransom and escape operation, and figuratively as ownership of the discourse and of the biosexual means of reproduction. Her assimilation to "Lela Marién" places her simultaneously at the origin and the end of a matrilineal succession in which men are simply superfluous. In this she is like Preciosa and the gypsy women of *La Gitanilla*, who as we shall see also form part of the same matrilineal chain, which again stretches from the humblest elements of society to the Holy Family and the Virgin Birth.

Zoraida owns the phallic *caña* (cane pole) that symbolically impregnates or at least inseminates Ruy Pérez with infusions of money and text. But this caña is ambiguous (or androgynous), and worth considering in some detail. First, Zoraida's window is described as a vaginal opening complete with pubic hair: "not only were these more like holes in the wall than what we call windows, but they were covered over with heavy, tightly-coiled iron grillwork" (I, 40, 272). From this opening protrudes the caña, "its tied-on handkerchief sagging so heavily that we expected a singularly joyous birth" (I, 40, 276). When he takes the money the first time, Ruy Pérez breaks the caña, which is not described in the same detail nor with the same associative power as the vagina/*ventana*. We have to infer its phallic function because of the female genital associations of the window and the references to pregnancy and birth. In fact, the caña is normally a harmless substitute for the phallic *lanza,* attested in a wealth of real practice in aristocratic tourneys and in the cliché phrase "las cañas se vuelven lanzas" (the cañas become lances), to indicate that something is no longer a game. And yet this caña is potent. Hanging beneath it is the bag filled with *cianiís* (golden coins). The generative organs figuratively evoked are both male and female—vulva, phallus, scrotum—all melded together in a self-sufficient autonomous system. They all belong to the woman, and the male figure is reduced to the role of passive receptor. Is this why Ruy Pérez breaks the caña after the first insemination? Is it a futile gesture of assertion of masculine primacy? The text doesn't offer any clues, or does it? " 'I took that lovely money, broke the stick, and then went back to the square where we'd been standing, looked up toward the window, and saw a singularly white hand' " (I, 40, 273). Breaking the caña is part of a series of events narrated in rapid succession that moves from taking the money to contemplating the white hand now visible in the window. If we place it in the context of the genital imagery that pervades the passage we are led to identify the hand as a representation of the clitoris, the only organ, male or female, that has no function other than sexual pleasure and that assures female autonomy in that area. In consequence, we might conclude that the textual representation of the tiny semi-internal organ figured in the white hand suggests a real, physical, material, and anatomical power of woman behind and beyond the appropriated and easily broken artificial phallus. It is not necessary for every reader to accompany me to the end of this line of thought; the primacy and power of woman over man is demonstrated by the caña, by the bag, by the coins, and subsequently by the "document written in Arabic" that adds ownership of the discourse (another instance of generative power, as every reader of Chomsky knows) to the biosexual figurations.

In an eloquent aside immediately preceding the second insemination, Ruy Pérez wonders "'if there'd be any more gold coins raining down'" (I, 40, 273), suggesting a precise analogy with the story of Jupiter's insemination of Danae in the form of a shower of gold, but again with the gender roles reversed.

It is customary to note Zoraida's assimilation to the role of the Virgin Mary, noting such attributes as her virginity, her beauty of spirit, her marriage to Ruy Pérez as a version of Mary's marriage to Joseph, their arrival together at the inn, and so on. E. Michael Gerli has discovered in the positive references to Mary the negation of the Spanish national myth of La Cava Rumía.[41] But Mary's most salient attribute is surely the joining of virginity and motherhood in the miracle of the Virgin Birth. Assimilation to Mary is therefore also assimilation to the ultimate representation of women's empowerment and independence from men. Ruy's brother Juan Pérez de Viedma's offhand reference to "the miracle of the caña" (I, 42, 294) suggests again, from an unexpected quarter, the idea of the Virgin Birth and Mary's nondependence on masculine insemination.

The invocation of Mary and the Virgin Birth raises the question of mothers in general. As we have noted, there are no literal mothers in either the Christian or the Muslim family, but there are two surrogate/symbolic mothers in Islamic Algiers: Zoraida's Christian nanny and the Virgin Mary or Lela Marién. "'When I was a little girl, my father had a woman slave who taught me, in my own language, how to say Christian prayers, and told me a great deal about Lela Marien. But the woman died, though I know she did not burn in eternal flames, but went with Allah, because since then I've twice seen her, and she's told me to go to the Christian world to see Lela Marien, who loved me dearly'" (I, 40, 274).

The Christian captive/surrogate mother is the representative of the real mother, who is Lela Marién herself. María Caterina Ruta notes that Lela Marien appears as a loving mother toward whom Zoraida feels an undefined sentiment founded in the memory of pleasant suggestions received in childhood and nurtured by the absence of her real mother.[42]

If we consider these relationships in a religious context as the text presents them, then the female Christian captive is to Lela Marién as Mohammed is to Allah, and Lela Marién opposes Allah at the respective apices of two parallel but opposing divine hierarchies. We are witnessing the germ of a matriarchal religion, which here at least opposes patriarchal Islam. This hypothetical matriarchal religion also opposes orthodox Christianity, but in the Algerian segment of our text, where the character of Zoraida predominates, the Church is resolutely feminized. The renegade who translates Zoraida's letter wants nothing more than to "bring himself back into communion with the Holy church, his Mother" (I, 40, 275).

If we consider the relationship of Zoraida to Mary in a social context, the phrase "Lela Marien will find someone who'll marry me" assumes great importance, as it transfers the traditional prerogative to choose the daughter's husband from the father to the mother, and we are witnessing the germ of a matriarchal social order as well as a matriarchal religion.

When the party reaches Spain the feminization of Christianity through Zoraida is abruptly and without commentary replaced by the triumphant patricentricity of true Christian orthodoxy: "'with tears of sheer joy, we thanked God, our Lord, for the incomparable grace He had shown us'" (I, 41, 289).

In addition, upon reaching Christian Spain Zoraida is rendered mute, suddenly deprived of her ownership of the discourse and converted into an object. Indeed, her silence is the subject of everyone else's speech at Palomeque's inn: "The veiled woman made no reply; her only response to everything said to her was silence. 'My dear ladies, this young woman scarcely understands my language, and knows indeed none but her native tongue.' 'Tell me, sir,' said Dorotea, 'is this lady a Christian or a Moor? Because by her clothing and her silence we are led to believe . . .'" (I, 37, 258).

And to top it off, Ruy Pérez, who in Algiers was dependent upon the services of the renegade for access to Zoraida's Arabic, now assumes the role of bilingual interpreter, speaking to Zoraida in her own language and reversing their earlier relationship of linguistic dominance and subordination.

In this context it is not difficult to interpret the renegade's jettisoning the chest containing Zoraida's treasures at sea (I, 41, 288) as the loss of what was left of the accumulated capital she would have brought to her new life in Spain. In one brutal blow after another Zoraida is deprived of the instruments and attributes of personal autonomy.

The discourse of orthodox Christianity offers a suitably patricentric counterversion of Zoraida's abandonment of her Muslim father in the story of the convert Martín Forniel recounted by Cervantes's friend, Dr. Antonio Sosa. Forniel disowns his Muslim mother while coldly proclaiming his adopted Christian faith:

> His mother embraced him, shed torrents of tears, beat her breasts, pulled her hair and scratched her face as Moorish women do. And showing him the breasts that had suckled him, she begged and pleaded with him to show compassion for her worn

and solitary old age, and to return with her to her house and to the religion of his fathers and forefathers. The constancy this brave Martín Forniel displayed in the face of all these importunings is worthy of eternal fame. Like a strong, hard rock the sea crashes against in vain with its waves and furious impetus, he was immovable, constant, invincible. And his only response to his mother was to say that he did not recognize Moors as mother or relatives, that he was a Christian and he would live and die as such.[43]

The coincidence of Sosa's riparian imagery and the location of Zoraida's final abandonment of her father on the beach is remarkable.

Alison Weber once observed that Zoraida's conduct is not explained by either religion or love.[44] María Caterina Ruta suggests a "possible unconscious conflict" involving her father at the heart of Zoraida's search for autonomy.[45] Francisco Márquez Villanueva has characterized Zoraida's devotion to Mary as excessive, beyond the limits of Christian orthodoxy, to the point where he is moved to suggest a mental imbalance as the cause of her cruelty to Hajji Murad.[46] All these critics have seen clearly that what is at stake here is not religion, but Zoraida's attitude toward her father.

I think Zoraida's behavior is explicable in terms of a confluence of master tropes and narratives from capitalism and psychoanalysis, and I would suggest that the Marian rhetoric provides her a doctrinally acceptable outlet for a preexisting hostility toward Hajji Murad. Given the absence of her mother, a probable inference is that she blames him for the mother's death (perhaps in childbirth), and that she seeks a substitute, a better mother who doesn't need a man, and whom no man can cause to disappear.

Or again, her hostility toward her father could be a reaction-formation thrown up as a shield against her own unacceptable incestuous impulses, which would be stronger than usual in her situation as the woman in her father's life, and which she displaces onto the socially acceptable father-figure of Ruy Pérez. Luis Murillo wonders, without attempting to analyze "the full implications of her choice," why she chooses "a lover and husband who was twice her age."[47] This age difference points to the identification of Ruy Pérez with Hajji Murad. This association would suggest another meaning for her theft of her father's "jewels," and it likens her precipitous flight from home to Don Quixote's. Alban Forcione has observed that "the protagonist and the heroine are, through allusion, associated with Joseph and Mary" as they arrive at the inn.[48] Françoise Zmantar also remarks their similarity to "le modèle biblique offert par Marie et Joseph."[49] Choosing Ruy Pérez and simultaneously casting herself in the role of the Virgin is another means of defending against her own unacceptable desire. Ruy Pérez stands in simultaneously for Hajji Murad (the object of unspeakable desire) and for Mary's husband Joseph (the guarantor of the absence of desire). He is at once the desire and the defense against it.

My reading of these actions and their possible motivation from Zoraida's perspective complements Alison Weber's, made from the point of view of Hajji Murad. Weber considers that Hajji Murad casts Zoraida in the role of her own absent mother, who is also his wife. He simultaneously identifies her with sexual pleasure when he curses the moment he conceived her.[50] He also accuses her openly of converting to Christianity only because she believes "'how much easier it is to practice indecency, in your lands, than it is in ours'" (I, 41, 287). There is an implicit suggestion that he harbors the same incestuous impulse toward her as she does toward him. This reciprocal incestuous attraction recalls and strengthens the hypothesis I proposed concerning an analogous reciprocal attraction of Marcela and her uncle in *Don Quixote,* part I, chapter 13.[51] It is also interesting to observe that Ruy Pérez identifies Zoraida as Hajji Murad's only heir, and remarks that "'many of the viceroys who'd visited that house had sought her as their wife, but she refused to be married'" (I, 40, 276). This denies the experience of the historical Zoraida, who in fact married the king of Fez, in order to recall another aspect of the relationship between the fictional Marcela and her uncle.

As the narrative begins its return to Spain I would like to come back to the relation between Ruy Pérez and his father, and consider for a moment the psychic consequences for the firstborn son of the father's decision to ignore the rule of primogeniture. In addition to, or prior to its legal force, the institution of the firstborn son carries a powerful affective charge that is specifically recognized and celebrated in the *Partidas:* "Majority means to be born first; it is a very great sign of God's love toward children, those to whom He gives it among the others who are born afterward. For it is clear that with this honor He bestows He moves the firstborn forward and places him above the others, because they must obey him and regard him as lord and father."[52]

Primogeniture defines a special relationship between Ruy Pérez and his father. Ruy will (or should) inherit what he himself identifies as *nombre y ser* (name and being), which includes property as well as lineage. But the father squanders his wealth and then divides his property equally among his three sons instead of reserving it all for the firstborn. The father denies Ruy Pérez his birthright, symbolically his *ser* (being). In fact, Ruy makes this point explicit (I, 39, 265). Ruy should feel angry with his father, but instead he turns his anger into generosity and filial devotion through reaction-formation. He returns two-thirds of his share of the inheritance to the father, and he dutifully (or more or less dutifully) enters military service according to his father's wishes.

Throughout his military career Ruy Pérez seeks a surrogate father with whom to do the entire relationship over again and get it right this time. In his narration he converts virtually every man to whom he is subordinated into some kind of a father. This includes a series of Christian leaders culminating in the pope and a series of Muslim leaders culminating in the sultan, who is evoked specifically in the father-son relationship and who combines the roles of both father and son: "There are only four family names denoting lineage among them, which all descend from the Ottoman house . . . the Grand Turk, who is also son and heir of all those who die, and shares in the inheritance with the other sons left by the deceased" (I, 40, 271).

On the Christian side we can count first "a famous captain from Guadalajara, Diego de Urbina," to whom he is subaltern. Ruy Pérez gives up a promotion to captain himself in order to follow Don Juan de Austria, "the natural brother of our good king Don Felipe," as he had given up enlisting in Italy in order to follow the Duque de Alba. The first of the Muslim father-surrogates is Ruy Pérez's first master, Alí Pasha or Ochalí, whose moral qualities he praises. He is inherited by Ochalí's surrogate son, Hasán Pasha or Hasán Veneciano. The father-son relationship between the two pashas is explicit in the text, and its homosexual component is played down in favor of affect. Hasán is evoked first as a boy, a *grumete,* of whom Ochalí "was so fond that he became one of the man's most pampered favorites" (I, 40, 271).

While he is rowing in the Turkish galleys Ruy Pérez witnesses and perhaps even participates in a particularly horrible father-son interaction. The unnamed captain of a galley called *La Presa* is identified as "a son of that famous corsair Barbarroja" (I, 39, 267). He was so cruel to his slaves that when it became apparent that *La Presa* was going to be captured by a Christian galley, commanded incidentally by "the soldiers' father" Don Alvaro de Bazán, the slaves/sons seized the captain, "and passing him from bench to bench, from the stern to the prow, they bit into him so savagely that before he'd gotten much further than the mast his soul was down in Hell" (I, 39, 267). The sons ingest the father's still-living flesh in a particularly gruesome version of the totemic meal. This is also a reverse reenactment of the story of Cronus and his children, suggesting that fathers and sons can be interchangeable, or rather, the identity as father and son is simultaneous. The "father" eaten by his "sons" on the galley is also identified as the son of Barbarroja. And it is worth remembering that although Cronus is best known for eating his children, he is also a son who castrated his father, Uranus. Clearly, there are powerful psychic forces, of both individual and universal scope, behind the folkloric division of the father's property among the conventional three sons.

During this time Ruy Pérez decides to refrain from writing to his father and

telling him "the news of my disaster" (I, 39 268). Is he just a man who stoical-
ly accepts whatever fate dishes out? Is he ashamed? Does he fear he would dishonor his father? Or might he unconsciously want to be punished for some
imagined breach of filial devotion? He might reasonably be angry with his
father, and even hold him ultimately responsible for his situation of captivity,
on the grounds that he wouldn't have been a soldier at all except for the father's exercise of authority, but he is not. It might well be that his refusal to
trouble the old man now is a continuation of that reaction-formation that
resulted in his turning back two-thirds of his inheritance in the first place.
Everybody (practically) can be a father, except Ruy Pérez. He engenders nothing: not wealth and not offspring. His narrative repeatedly refers to fathers who
are also sons, and sons who are also fathers. But he is only a son.

The story comes full circle, ending in Christian Spain where, as Paul Julian
Smith observes, "the phallic order seems complete once more."[53] Both protagonists are incorporated into the feudoagrarian patriarchy presided by the
unnamed Pérez de Viedma *padre*. Ruy Pérez returns too, and Zoraida is defini-
tively incorporated into the same order. Her empowerment, which we have
seen figured in Algiers as the ownership of the discourse, as the accumulation
and investment of capital, as the ownership of all the symbolic genitalia, and
the identification with Mary and the Virgin Birth, ceased when she boarded
the little boat bound for the promised land. Zoraida's empowerment, her
emergence as a person, an entrepreneur, and as an agent of history, was possible only in the protocapitalistic Algerian economy. It is difficult to decide whom
to feel sorrier for: Ruy Pérez, who returns to what he had left, older and with
the melancholy resignation noted by Márquez Villanueva, or the silent Zoraida,
for whom the reality of life in Spain, as a morisca or second-class Christian,
will bear no resemblance to her Algerian fantasies.

The ending of the captive's tale anticipates what we are going to find in *La
Gitanilla*. Like Preciosa, Zoraida is assertive and empowered only as long as
she remains outside the parameters of official society, in a socioeconomic order defined as Other, whether among the gypsies in Spain or the Muslims in
Algiers. As soon as the presumably happy ending is reached and she is incorporated into the "normal," "official" order, she is silenced and stripped of her
power. A feudoagrarian economic order replaces any kind of nascent capitalism, preservation and stasis replace growth and change, sterility replaces fecundity, and woman is reduced to chattel. In a word, the old triumphs over
the new. Social order and conformity are purchased at the price of personhood.
This is why I cannot accompany the idealistic readers of these texts; I think
the price is too high.

# ~ 5
# Women and Men, Aristocrats and Gypsies

The first sentence of *La Gitanilla* identifies and stigmatizes the gypsies as a deviant and dangerous minority in late-sixteenth-century Spanish society: "It seems that the gypsies are born into this world to be thieves: their parents are thieves, they are raised among thieves, they are instructed in thievery, and finally, they come out true died-in-the-wool thieves, and their desire to steal is finally conquered only by death."[1]

This value-laden sentence continues to resonate even in the late twentieth century. In 1973 the gypsy Juan de Dios Heredia reported that the Dirección Nacional del Apostolado Gitano protested its inclusion in a text for schoolchildren in Enseñanza General Básica as an example of the Spanish language in its classical period. This violently antigypsy diatribe, which brings together all the racial and ethnic stereotypes held in sixteenth-century Spain, was duly withdrawn from the elementary school reader and replaced with a less offensive example of Golden Age prose. But Heredia goes on to observe, "'I have before me several articles, the products of twisted minds that, in seeking to defend Cervantes, stridently reaffirm that we gypsies are a race of criminals.'"[2] The anecdote reveals that the mindless clichés have lost none of their vitality in the last four hundred years. Gypsies were automatically marginalized and stigmatized in the Franco era as they were in the time of the Reyes Católicos and the Hapsburgs.

Another anecdote specifically relates the Franquista mentality to the ruling orthodoxies of Cervantes's society. On 23 October 1939, as part of the celebration of Franco's victory in the Spanish Civil War, a performance was staged at the Teatro Español in Madrid that featured among other acts a poem by the gypsy poet Ramón Charlo. The next day the performance was reviewed by Araujo Costa, who commented: "'The Spanish empire always had a clear concept of hierarchy: hierarchy in society, in social mores, in literature, in the theater. As we revive the noble traditions of the Spanish empire in the present moment we must continue to respect the notion of hierarchy in all areas of our national life. In particular we must never allow gypsies to invade the genteel and courtly stage of our most prestigious theatrical venue.'"[3]

As early as 1499 the gypsies in Spain had been identified as a disruptive element in the newly forming state and had came under governmental scrutiny. On 4 March 1499 the Reyes Católicos gave the gypsies a choice: either settle down in one place like everyone else and start doing some useful work, or be denied permission to travel within the country.[4] It didn't work; the gypsies simply disregarded the law.

Gypsies, vagabonds, and thieves came to be synonymous. In 1544, in addition to the usual penalty of public flogging, convicted thieves were marked by having their ears notched so they could be more easily identified the next time they were caught. In 1548 the notched ears were replaced by a brand on the cheek. In 1559 the brand gave way to a tattoo on the arm, with the name of the place where the thief was first caught.

In 1594 a law was proposed that would have provided a "final solution" to what we might call the "gypsy question." Very simply, gypsy males and gypsy females were to be forcibly segregated so that procreation would become impossible and the race would disappear.[5]

Not only were gypsies marginalized and stigmatized, those operations were performed from within the official value system and the official discourse of a racist, conformist society in which individual worth, or indeed individual character, was seen as a function of genealogy. Cervantes's narrator characterizes the gypsies as a subgroup of society defined by heredity, or in the language of the time, by *linaje* or *sangre,* set apart by that genetic determinism from the rest of society and raised in a kind of isolation so that the genetic characteristics might be intensified and brought to fruition. Gypsies, according to Cervantes's narrator, are born into the world with a genetically defined mission, and raised so that the mission can be fulfilled. "They are born into this world to be thieves: their parents are thieves, they are raised among thieves, they are instructed in thievery, and finally, they come out true died-in-the-wool thieves" (61).

The late-twentieth-century reader's reaction to this opening sentence is a function of what he or she thinks about Cervantes. The reader for whom Cervantes is a spokesman for the offical values will identify the source of this opinion about gypsies as Cervantes himself. Consequently this reader breathes a sigh of relief to learn, on the next page, that the heroine of this story isn't really a gypsy at all. As this reader reads along he or she formulates a series of questions having to do with when, how, and under what circumstances Preciosa's true identity will be revealed. And it doesn't really matter what her identity turns out to be; the essential thing is that she is "born of better than gypsy stock" (62). So to accept the narrator's characterization of the gypsies implies certain attitudes toward both Cervantes and gypsies.

The most authoritative reading of *La Gitanilla* is still Alban Forcione's "Cervantes's *La Gitanilla* as Erasmian Romance," the lead study in his book, *Cervantes and the Humanist Vision* (1982). Forcione identifies *La Gitanilla* as a fictionalized version of Erasmus's ideas on Christian marriage, in which the union of Preciosa/Costanza and Andrés/Don Juan acts out on earth and in the present the ideals of marriage embodied in the royal union of Felipe III and Queen Margarita and in the two biblical marriages of Joachim and Anne, and Joseph and Mary. The spiritual marriage of Christ and His Church, although not evoked specifically in Forcione's text, is undoubtedly present beneath the surface. This series of ideal marriages, according to Forcione, is opposed by the fractious union of the *teniente de asistente* and his wife Doña Clara, to which Forcione applies the adjective "demonic." Forcione considers Cervantes's text to be a celebration of the existing social order and the official vision of society. It is relatively easy to coax out Forcione's academic and ideological preferences, and to discover how his reading of the text is a function of those preferences. Academically, Forcione is guided by the vision of the Christian-European Américo Castro of the *Pensamiento de Cervantes* (1925), with its insistence on the influence of Erasmus, humanism, reason, and what was for Castro a vision of the truest form of Christianity. Forcione goes far beyond Castro in his documentation of Erasmus's presence, with a wealth of references to particular Erasmian dialogues, in Cervantes's texts. Ideologically Forcione seems to be guided by a hierarchical vision of the world and the cosmos, a universe divided spatially into high and low, with social class, authority, and moral values distributed accordingly. In this scheme, gypsy society has to be the demonic reflection of the ideal/proper/divine social order, the highest earthly embodiment of which is the aristocratic society into which Preciosa/Costanza and Andrés/Don Juan are finally and truly integrated.

If the reader's Cervantes is out of tune with the official values, he or she cannot read this opening sentence without some discomfort. Georges Güntert, for example, decides that Cervantes's narrator only pretends to adopt the official attitude toward the gypsies.[6] Even though chances are good that no late-twentieth-century American reader has actually met a gypsy in the flesh, many are opposed to ethnic stereotyping in general and unwilling to believe that Cervantes could be indulging in it. Accordingly, these readers fall back on some good ideas about literary analysis internalized from Henry James and Wayne

Booth, and distance the narrator who makes this outlandish accusation about gypsies from the ideal Cervantes, who must have some surprise egalitarian message up his sleeve. Such a reader might also, in a reverse but powerful intertextual association, bring to bear a reading of Lorca's *Romancero gitano* and its casting of gypsies in the role of free spirits, or simply as freedom or the life force, opposed to the deadening official conformism personified by the Guardia Civil. This reader will also formulate a series of questions to ask the text, all concerned with what the "true" or "hidden" message will turn out to be and by what signs he or she shall know it. This reader reads against the grain, subjecting every narrative assertion to intense scrutiny, and standing the narrator's expressed opinions on their head. With respect to the question of gypsies and aristocrats, such a reader is inclined to invert the official relationship and to seek a kind of moral superiority in the gypsies, with their healthful outdoor lifestyle attuned to the rhythms of Nature and their refusal to join the rat race of honor and social prestige. All this might indeed signify moral superiority, but the notion is seriously weakened if not totally undone by the fundamental fact that the gypsies in the narrative are all thieves.

I want to go back for a third time to the first sentence, this time to relocate it within its own temporal dimension. I made a point of genetic determinism, of a subgroup born into society with a mission that sets them apart, a system of child rearing that segregates them and concentrates on preparing them to achieve their genetically determined destiny. What would happen to the logic of this sentence if instead of *gitanos* it said *nobles* or *hidalgos,* and instead of *ladrones* it said *dirigentes* or *gobernantes*? Absolutely nothing; the logic would remain intact. We would still be talking about a genetically defined subgroup, born into society with a genetically determined mission, raised apart from the rest of society in order to prepare them to achieve their genetically determined destiny. The substitutions I have suggested reveal within Cervantes's text a connection between gypsies and aristocrats that Bernard Leblon made on other grounds and in a more general way some time ago.[7]

Leblon documents a series of real historical relations between gypsies and aristocrats. He remarks that from the time of their arrival in the Peninsula in the fifteenth century, the gypsies had sought to establish bonds of fictional kinship with the most powerful families in the regions they passed through. They systematically sought out aristocrats as the godparents of their children at baptism, and they adopted the godparents' family names. This accounts for the abundance of illustrious *apellidos*—Castro, Maldonado, Mendoza, Salazar—among gypsies. Leblon remarks that these "godfathers" could be very useful when the gypsies ran afoul of the law.[8] In addition, he postulates a "secret sympathy" between the two groups based on the value both attach to living free, that is, unbound by convention and the rules that apply to most people; by their common love of singing, dancing, and women, that is, of pastimes and amusements; and finally by their mutual interest and expertise in horses: "Women, horses, music and dancing are the visible aspects of a centuries-old communication between two societal extremes that everything would seem to separate. But, just at that time the feudal world is disappearing, it seems reasonable to posit an ensemble of secret affinities between them—their conception of freedom, their vision of the world and the art of living—which the advent of the new bourgeois order would soon relegate to oblivion."[9]

Leblon considers gypsies and aristocrats a kind of last bastion of the feudal mentality and lifestyle that was going to be swept away forever by a new "bourgeois" social order, which we still live under today. The observation of the secret sympathy is very suggestive. For one thing it is easy to document in the first sentence of our text, and doing so immediately redefines the terms of the ideological debate surrounding it.

Leblon's notion of a secret sympathy between gypsies and nobles plays hob with the hierarchical worldview enunciated by Forcione, especially when one considers that relationship in the context of Cervantes's own family experience. This is old knowledge, but it is not generally taken into consideration in a critical context where author-functions and authorial discourses tend to replace real writers, so I beg my reader's indulgence for a moment of anachronism and apparent theoretical naïveté. The story is that the very aristocratic Don Diego Hurtado de Mendoza fathered an illegitimate son by a gypsy woman named María Cabrera. The son, known as Don Martín "el Gitano," was easily placed by his father's influence in a high position in the ecclesiastical hierarchy, as Archdeacon of Guadalajara. Apparently he went on to become a cardinal. When Cervantes's grandfather, Juan de Cervantes, was residing in Guadalajara in the service of Don Diego de Mendoza as a kind of accountant, the Archdeacon Don Martín dishonored his daughter María. The fruit of this illicit union of the Archdeacon Don Martín "el Gitano" and María de Cervantes was Miguel's cousin Martina. This is recounted with copious documentation by Bernard Leblon in *Les Gitans dans la littérature espagnole*. So if one is inclined to take this kind of biographical data seriously it is not hard to conclude that Cervantes could have formed some fairly unflattering opinions of aristocrats and their abuses of power, on the basis of the effects of those abuses on his own family. This anecdote contributes to undermine Forcione's hierarchy, which situates aristocrats at the top and gypsies at the bottom. It also suggests an important sense in which Forcione's thesis is not about society, even though he passes in review every social class from gypsies on up through minor officials to aristocracy and royalty. Forcione is ultimately concerned not with society in history but with some kind of platonic universals, moral absolutes of good and evil that happen to be embodied in human social classes, what Aristotle (and the Castro of 1925) would call "the universal poetic." Leblon's vision, in contrast, is very much anchored in "the historical particular."

A recent echo of Forcione's hierarchy of high and low, aristocrats and gypsies, and good and evil is formed by a little group of studies that make the contrast in terms of something Forcione leaves out: money and economic systems. The inspiration for the general orientation of these studies is probably Harry Sieber's excellent introduction to *La Gitanilla* in his edition of the *Novelas ejemplares*. I want to concentrate on this group's evocation of what they see in opposition to the affinities discovered by Leblon, as two radically different economic systems that characterize gypsies and aristocrats respectively. Once again, the aristocratic values are seen as normative.

Robert ter Horst observes that the gypsy economy is based on theft, which in turn arises from "a feeling of want and emptiness. The emblem of this kind of appetite is the clutching, grasping talon." A very nice observation, especially the figuring of economic theory and practice in the grasping talon, which indeed appears several times in the text. Opposed to this "tight-fisted acquisitiveness" is the aristocratic model, arising from material abundance and characterized by the bestowal of largesse emblematized in the "open, aristocratic hand of Andrés, which is abundant, liberal, prodigal in contrast to the predatory sterility, or lack, of the gypsies."[10]

The problem with this part of his analysis is its anachronism. In 1600, what he describes and recoils from as "greed" was in fact the emergence of a bourgeois mentality, the wave of the future elsewhere in Europe. Ter Horst later opposes the plebeian (an economic class that subsumes the gypsies) to the aristocratic in a slightly different way: "Madrid is . . . a mixed marketplace featuring both the aristocratic idea of merit and the plebeian pursuit of profit. The plebeian principally values gain while the aristocrat prizes merit. Yet essential worth is not at its best unadorned and unaccompanied by material wealth."[11] This begins to make more sense. "Merit" seems to mean "essential worth," an attribute presumably characteristic of aristocrats but lacking in gypsies and other plebeians. The name for this "essential worth" in the sixteenth century was *sangre* or *linaje*. This is what distinguishes the aristocrat from his fellow citizens, and the aristocrat's sangre is what is "not at its best" unless accompanied by material opulence. Material opulence therefore becomes the outward and visible sign of an inner grace called "noble blood." Now we have an accurate description of the system. Ter Horst's sleight of hand consists in hiding the aristocratic *sangre* (a concept probably repugnant to most Americans) behind *merit,* with its impeccable associations to the Protestant work ethic, to meritocracy, and so on, all much more congenial to our inculcated habits of thought and official national rhetoric. Ter Horst's move is a version of Alexander Hamilton's earlier conflation of "the rich, the well born, and the able."

Finally, ter Horst relates the sterility of the Teniente's household to the insitution of the *residencia,* which he apparently believes to be an Ottoman administrative practice, with its corollary that "everything is for sale" and that consequently the road to success is through bribery. As we shall see when we consider *El amante liberal,* this turns out to be exactly backwards; the residencia was in fact a Spanish practice. He then contrasts the Teniente's sterility with the prodigality displayed by Andrés's father, the noble Don Francisco de Cárcamo, and reasons that if prodigality is aristocratic, and if sterility is gypsy, and if gypsies and Turks see the world as a giant marketplace where everything is for sale, then the Turks must be coming from sterility too, and the gypsy economy is like the Turkish: "The gypsies are the Turks of the tale."[12]

Ter Horst's study, along with William Clamurro's and Joan Ramon Resina's, has the merit of placing the question of economics at the center of critical inquiry, and of identifying two different economic systems at play in *La Gitanilla.*[13] If aristocratic values are to be seen as normative then the aristocratic economic system must be found to be better, at least in some moral sense, than the gypsy system.

I want to suggest a different framework in which to consider the issue of the two economies. The readings that identify with the aristocratic (i.e. the official) values oppose sterility, by which is meant scarcity and a corresponding niggardliness, to liberality, by which is meant generosity born of abundance. Suppose instead that we oppose sterility to fecundity, or its economic analogue, productivity. In both sets sterility is the negative term. If we oppose sterility to liberality it goes with the gypsies, but if we oppose sterility to productivity, then sterility becomes a feature of the aristocracy.

The aristocratic economic order might be characterized as backward and unproductive, not to mention frivolous and wasteful. The aristocrats are never depicted in the process of creating wealth; wealth is assumed to be always already there. They are shown in the act of dispensing it, gambling it away, throwing it around in an exercise that simultaneously identifies them and assures their authority.

The aristocratic economic order is visible in the Madrid gambling house, which is populated exclusively by aristocrats. They are engaged in consumption of both money and time: "many caballeros who passed the time strolling around or playing at various games" (72). These unproductive activities identify them as noblemen by exhibiting the aristocratic attribute of *otium cum dignitate.* They are also identified by the semiotics of clothing, as one swears "'on my honor as a caballero'" by "'the insignia I wear on my breast'" not to molest Preciosa and her girlfriends sexually (72). The threat of sexual rapacity is added to the identifying features of the aristocracy, along with their dress and their unproductive economic activities, which in addition to gambling include giving away money to the kibbitzers around the gaming tables, an exercise of largesse appropriate to their condition.

When young Don Juan accosts Preciosa and declares himself to her he presents himself as an aristocrat, as aristocrats have just been defined at the gambling house. "'I am a caballero, as my habit proclaims (and opening the clasp of his cape he showed on his breast one of the most prestigious insignias of nobility in Spain). I am the son of Fulano, I am under his care and guardianship. I am his only son, and I expect a reasonable mayorazgo. My father is in Madrid seeking a government appointment, which he is almost certain to obtain'" (84). He shows her his *hábito;* he locates himself within an aristocratic patrilineal succession, where he remarks his father's legal and financial authority over him; and he locates that lineage within the feudoaristocratic economy of tributary relationships and *mercedes.* He also offers Preciosa money: "'I have here one hundred escudos in gold to give you as a pledge and a sign of what I plan to give you'" (84). Finally, he locates himself within an aristocratic and idealized system of relations between the sexes, the visible and respectable surface of which the rapacity of the gambling house is the seamy obverse. "'I am not courting her because I'm trying to seduce her,'" he declares; he wants only to "'to serve her in the way she finds most appropriate'" (84). This veritable paradigm of courtly love is superficially opposed to the threat of rapacious sexual exploitation we have just seen among the noble gamblers, but in fact the two are necessary complements.

Don Juan's home, that is to say his father's house, also offers a view of the aristocratic economic order. The noble Cárcamo père is described in terms of the "red-colored-cross of knighthood on his breast" and his exercise of *liberalidad,* which we now recognize as markers of aristocracy. His first words to the gypsy girls are: "'Come on up, my children, for here you will be given a handout'" (92). Later he offers a coin, a "doblón de oro de a dos caras," for a performance. He insists on the pattern of patrilineal descent as he demotes his son back to childhood by calling him "'don Juanico mu hijo,'" the significance of which is not lost on Preciosa, who in turn diminutizes her future husband five times in quick succession.

The aristocratic economic order provides a context in which we can reposition the enigmatic figure of Clemente, the *paje/poeta* who writes verses for Preciosa and pays court to her in Madrid, and who later appears as a potentially threatening rival for her affections in the gypsy camp. Criticism has identified him as some kind of double of Don Juan/Andrés, and considers that his function in the story is to reinforce the positive values presumably represented by the male protagonist. Although no critic I can think of makes a point of it, Clemente states that his real name is Don Sancho. He is in fact an aristocrat himself, the relative of an unnamed Conde, and he was a participant in a typically aristocratic *capa y espada* imbroglio that has resulted in the death of two other gentlemen and necessitated his flight from Madrid (114–15). The fact of his aristocratic lineage, and the fact of its suppression, as well as the common activity of assault with a deadly weapon and murder, indeed identify Don Sancho/Clemente as a kind of double of Don Juan/Andrés.

Don Sancho also inserts himself into an economic system, in this case the world of international finance. He is on his way to Sevilla, where he knows a "'Genoese gentleman, a great friend of my relative the Count, who frequently sends great quantities of silver to Genoa'" (115). He plans to join a shipment of silver from Sevilla to Cartagena and thence to the safety of Italy. In short, Don Sancho identifies himself as an aristocrat engaged, albeit as a parasitic hanger-on, in the unproductive passage of precious metals from America through Spain to Genoa. His brief narrative evokes the extraction and exploitation of a form of wealth that was already there and already valuable and that is not subject to any operation of manufacture that would increase its value. Nevertheless, by the time it reaches Genoa it will have passed through who knows how many hands, each of which will have extracted a profit. This profit is not the result of any increase in the value of the metal but of a series of operations that repeat the primitive extraction of the metal from the earth. In short, a typical aristocratic-style operation: retrograde, parasitic, and unproductive. In 1956 Pierre Vilar characterized the conquest of America in just that way: "In Castile, the ruling classes carried out the conquest of the New World as they had the Reconquest in Spain, *in the feudal manner:* occupy the land, reduce the inhabitants to servituide, make off with the wealth. None of this prepares for investment in the capitalist sense."[14] The profit from precious metal depends on an initial act of extraction and exploitation. No value-adding transformations occur along the way. The various middlemen who extract a profit are parasites, and there is a veiled suggestion that one of them may be the count that Don Sancho is related to.

The aristocratic economic order comes into apparently abrasive contact with the gypsy order when the male protagonist, Don Juan de Cárcamo, slips away from his aristocratic family and joins the gypsies under the name Andrés Caballero. He arrives in the gypsy camp on a rented mule. He insists that the animal be killed and buried in order to efface all trace of his flight from home and his present whereabouts. The gypsies, however, want to alter the mule's appearance and sell it. Don Juan/Andrés brings a typically aristocratic mentality to this situation. For him the mule has only a use-value and is to be discarded after use. For the gypsies, the same animal is a commodity to be exchanged. Its value can be enhanced by the operations of disguise, and it can be placed back into circulation. One doesn't have to be an economic historian to observe that the use-value mentality is characteristic of primitive economic systems, while the concept of exchange value is the hallmark of more developed ones. Don Juan's aristocratic practice is economically backward in another sense, which has only recently emerged into our collective consciousness. Killing the mule not only removes it from circulation; it also creates a problem of hazardous waste disposal, which unfortunately prevails over the gypsies' futile attempts to recycle.

But this contrast between gypsies and aristocrats is less drastic than it appears. If we compare what we have just observed about the gypsies and the rented mule with what we know about Don Sancho and the American silver, we can observe a common element shared by both groups. In both cases the valuable object in question—the mule and the silver—is a good seized from another: not a product, but the result of an act of rapine. The gypsies have no more right to the rented mule Don Juan has gratuitously introduced among them than Don Sancho's aristocratic relative has to the silver extracted by someone else's labor. The fictional Guzmán de Alfarache, a keen observer of the financial scene, opposes stealing, begging, and receiving tribute, which he groups under the rubric of *ajena sustancia,* to working and manufacture. He concludes simply that "nobody can get rich from someone else's possessions."[15] This brings us back to Leblon's secret affinity between aristocrats and gypsies.

As a second example of this affinity let us consider the expository-admonitory lecture that provides Don Juan/Andrés's introduction to the gypsy ethos and lifestyle. A venerable old gypsy delivers Preciosa over to Andrés in a speech that recalls the patriarchal dominion over women that in fact obtained in the society and that was ritualized in hundreds of speeches by hundreds of patriarchs in the *comedia.*

> "We give you this girl, the creme de la creme of all the gypsies in Spain, to be your wife or your companion. Look her over carefully and make sure she pleases you, and if you see anything in her you don't like, pick another one that you find more appealing from the selection here, because we'll give you whichever one you choose. Among us there is no adultery, and whenever there is, whether it is committed by a wife or by a girlfriend, we don't go to the authorities to seek justice. We ourselves are the judges and the executioners of our women." (100–101)

Woman is a possession of man, a commodity that circulates among men. Adultery as a concept applies to women only. Husbands and boyfriends have the right to punish infidelity by death. There is an exact correspondence between this ethos and what we see enunciated and acted out as part of the official system of values so tirelessly reaffirmed in the propagandistic theater of Lope and Calderón. This correspondence was recently observed in a thoughtful reappraisal by Alban Forcione: "If the reader looks closely at Cervantes's gypsies, he discovers that their perverse social order, with its institutionalization of thievery, its patriarchal repression of women, and its authoritarian mentality, resembles the real world of gypsies or any other 'threatening other' a lot less than it does the socio-political establishment of Spain."[16]

When Don Juan first meets Preciosa and offers her a hundred escudos, she refuses the offer on the grounds that she is not for sale. In fact she is for sale, or her virginity is for sale, but she will insist on setting her own price on it. Her grandmother is first incredulous and then furious with her for turning the money down. She explicitly relates the possession of "'a hundred gold escudos which could be sewn into the lining of a dress'" with the forms in which wealth is held by the aristocracy: "'and having them there is like owning a government bond on the pasturage in Extremadura'" (88). The gold coins are perfect, she says, for bribing the ministers of justice when one has fallen into their hands. She even offers an example drawn from her own experience, with explicit reference to the amounts involved in the transaction, including the commission charged by the *cambio* (banker). She concludes her diatribe with a metaphorical transformation of the royal coat of arms stamped on the coins into the armed might and protective power of the state: "'there is nothing that can come to our aid faster than great Filipo's royal arms: one can't get beyond their *plus ultra*'" (88). She thus announces the power of wealth, now identified with the power of the state itself, to thwart the rule of law and to unite the lowest elements of society with the highest: the gypsies are united with the aristocracy in that secret sympathy uncovered by Leblon.

In this context we can consider an episode that doesn't appear to be particularly well integrated into what we used to call the organicity of the work. While the gypsies are in Madrid they perform at the house of the Teniente de Asistente. What is most striking about this household is its genteel poverty. The Teniente's wife, Doña Clara, has no money to pay Preciosa for telling her fortune. Nor does her elderly *escudero*. None of her female servants does either, although one offers a silver thimble. Nor does any of her social peers, the other women present in her house as her guests. When her husband arrives we learn that he too is broke. Besides their lack of funds, what the people in this house have in common is their social status. They are members of what elsewhere in Europe would be the emerging urban middle class. The house belongs to a middle-level municipal official whose income is supposed to be derived from the honorable discharge of his duties. The other husband mentioned is a physician, who is supposed to live off fees for services. Both are types pilloried in traditional social satire: the official who takes bribes as Preciosa's grandmother has insinuated, and the unscrupulous doctor who milks his patients for all they're worth and ends by killing them. But these two are nothing like the stereotypes. The doctor is present simply to establish the social parity of his wife with Doña Clara, and the Teniente himself is characterized as a victim of his own probity. It is because he refuses to take bribes that he is so poor. Preciosa counsels him, "'take bribes, Mr. Teniente, take bribes, and you'll have money, and don't do anything out of the ordinary, or you'll die of hunger'" (81). This new middle class, which embodies what Preciosa calls *usos nuevos,* (things out of the ordinary), and which Leblon would consider bourgeois values, is economically sterile because in contrast to the gypsies and the aristocrats it is unwilling to pervert those values.

A similar failure by a middle-level official to participate in the corruption Preciosa recommends occurs near the end of the story, and it involves another Teniente. This is the Teniente Cura who is summoned by Preciosa's father and ordered to marry the happy couple now that their true identities have been revealed. He refuses to break the procedural rules adopted by the Council of Trent to minimize the abuses associated with clandestine marriages, specifically the requirement that *amonestaciones* (banns) be published on three consecutive feast days before the marriage (132). The father, now identified by his title of Corregidor as the top man in the civil hierarchy, simply turns to his ecclesiastical counterpart, the archbishop, who allows the marriage to proceed after only one amonestación (134). Like the gypsies, the aristocrats refuse to be bound by the rules that apply to the rest of the people. Their abuse of power here is totally gratuitous; the marriage can't take place until the groom's parents arrive in Murcia from Madrid, which would have allowed plenty of time to publish the required number of banns. There is no need to frustrate the law, except to demonstrate that it doesn't apply to the ruling class.

It turns out that, in broad terms, the gypsy and the aristocratic economic orders are slightly different variants of late feudalism. They stand in opposition to any form of bourgeois capitalism. Leblon's thesis is confirmed. But before concluding that gypsies and aristocrats are more or less equal and ascribing this conclusion to Cervantes's maddening ambiguity we should consider that all the foregoing observations are based solely on the behavior of men: gypsies and aristocrats. It is time to get some women into this chapter, especially since they represent the only progressive element in this fictional society.

The text begins with Preciosa and her grandmother, both enveloped in a web of associations and references to economics. To begin, the name Preciosa designates its referent as a valuable object. Joan Ramon Resina observes that the grandmother considers Preciosa as investment capital.[17] The text states that the old woman has a "tesoro" in Preciosa, and that she wants to "acrecentar su caudal" (grow her capital) and "vender su mercancía" (sell her merchandise) (62). Preciosa herself possesses capital in the form of "villancicos, de coplas, seguidillas y zarabandas," her repertoire of poems (62). She also has more important capital in the form of her virginity. Francisco Márquez Villanueva has offered exhaustive documentation of the semantic relationships among "preciosa," "joya," "joya preciosa," and the hymen, drawn from Proverbs, Erasmus, Vives, Fray Luis de León and, from a different perspective, from Freud and Robert Scholes.[18] Preciosa's own testimony is even more eloquent: "'I have a single jewel I hold dearer than life, which is my virginity, and I'm not going to sell it for promises or gifts, because it would be sold, after all, and if it can be bought it can't be worth very much. If you, sir, have come only for that article, you'll not have it except at the price of the ties and bonds of matrimony. If virginity must succumb, it should be to that holy yoke, for that would not be to sell it, but to invest it in fairs which hold out the happy promise of profit'" (85).

Preciosa could not be clearer nor more explicit. She identifies her virginity as a commodity and places it on the market. She refuses to sell it for "promesas ni dádivas," but that doesn't mean it isn't for sale. It means simply that the price will be higher: the price tag on this particular joya is "the ties and bonds of matrimony." Not only is her virginity a commodity to be sold, but selling it to a husband in exchange for matrimony is explicitly likened to investing it (*emplearla*, 'put it to work') in "fairs which hold out the happy promise of profit." Preciosa turns her own body into a commodity, she sets the price, and she displays an admirably advanced understanding of economic practices, an understanding beyond the grasp of any of the men in this story, in her offhand reference to the profit to be made at the merchant-banking fairs. This precocious fifteen-year-old has in mind the fairs of Medina del Campo, Medina de Ríoseco, and Villalón, which dominated the Castilian economy, where both merchandise and money were exchanged and profits were made on the exchange transactions. Her grasp of the distinction between a one-time sale and a long-term investment, and her apparent knowledge of the workings of the money markets, place her in the company of economic theorists in the line of

Martín de Azpilcueta's *Comentario resolutario de cambios* (1566) and Tomás de Mercado's *Suma de tratos y contratos* (1571). It might even be argued that Preciosa's offhand reference to "felices ganancias" skips over the thorny moral issues raised so insistently by the sixteenth-century theorists and simply assumes the legitimacy of increase resulting from trading at the fairs.[19]

It is apparent that Preciosa and her grandmother are involved in a progressive economic system that recognizes the force of the market and the profits to be made from operations of speculation and exchange. Preciosa certainly is in the forefront of late-sixteenth-century economic thought. But these two are not the only women in our story. In fact, all the gypsy women are inserted in a system based on notions of manufacture and added value. While the aristocratic men are busy practicing their *otium cum dignitate* and their *liberalidad*, and while the gypsy men are busy with what Dr. Carlos García called "la desordenada codicia de los bienes ajenos" (the unrestrained craving for other people's property), the gypsy women are busy working, as we shall see.

All these women are employed in show business. The text observes simply that the grandmother "looked for verses everywhere she could, and she got some from many poets; for there are poets who deal with gypsies and who sell them their poems, just as there are those who deal with blind men, who invent miracles for them and who always look for profit" (62). Outlined here is a chain of operations of manufacture, sale and resale, that reproduces, or rather anticipates the system of industrial capitalism we still live under. A raw material, language, is transformed by a poet into a manufactured product, a poem. Whereas the language belonged to everyone and was free, the poem is a commodity with a use- and an exchange-value. The poet sells his product to the gypsy women, as the text notes. But no money changes hands. This is a modern sale, made on credit, against the promise of a future profit, the "felices ganancias" already evoked by Preciosa. The gypsy women in turn perform an operation on the poem that increases its value again. They transform a linguistic artifact, a text, into a spectacle with music and dance, which they retail to the final consumers: in the streets, in the plazas, in the gambling houses, and in private residences. At this point the money begins to move. Every time the troupe performs, the text records the cash value of the transaction: "the quarters and the pieces of eight rained down; the quarters came down like hail, and the old lady's bucket caught thirty reales." The poet cannot be paid for his product until the cash is taken in at the final point of sale, the performance, at which time the money will begin to flow back along the chain. Preciosa makes this clear when she says: "'and look here, sir, do not fail to deliver the ballads you've promised. And if you want me to pay for them, let's do the accounting by twelves: a dozen sung, a dozen paid. Because if you think I'm going to pay in advance, you're thinking the impossible'" (72). At each stage in the process the value of the commodity is increased thanks to an operation of transformation effected by a human agent. Consequently, it can command a higher price each time it is resold. This chain also involves another feature of developed economies, the extension of credit. This is the economic wave of the future elsewhere in Europe, but in Cervantes's Spain it is relegated to the least prestigious segments of society, doubly marginalized as gypsies and as women.

Raymond Williams faults Marx for not considering performance as a sub-category of capitalist forms of production. "There is a footnote in the *Grundrisse* in which it is argued that a piano-maker is a productive worker, engaged in productive labour, but that a pianist is not, since his labour is not labour which reproduces capital. The extraordinary inadequacy of this distinction to advanced capitalism, in which the production of music . . . is an important branch of capitalist production, may be only an occasion for updating. But the real error is more fundamental. . . . Production is then work on raw materials to make commodities, which enter the capitalist system of distribution and exchange."[20] It is apparent from Cervantes's text that Marx's distinction is inadequate not merely to advanced capitalism.

It will be instructive to return for a moment to Don Sancho/Clemente, in his capacity as poet. He writes poetry for Preciosa, but instead of sending her a bill for his product he encloses money with it. He thus subverts the chain of production to sale to consumption. His largesse is a version of the *liberalidad* of the idle aristocrats in the gambling house; it fits into the pattern of conspicuous and gratuitous spending that identifies the aristocrats as such. Furthermore, the poems he sends Preciosa are not performed for profit. The first is read aloud by an aristocrat at the gambling house, and the second is also read aloud—over Preciosa's protests—by another aristocrat at Don Juan's father's house. The poems are transformed from a commodity into a gratuitous entertainment for aristocrats, the second time at Preciosa's expense. And it is Clemente who offers the frequently anthologized description of poetry as a *joya preciosísima,* thus converting Preciosa herself into a living allegory: Poetry/Preciosa is a "'beautiful damsel, chaste, discreet, clever, retiring, who holds herself within the limits of the strictest discretion. Solitude is her companion. The fountains entertain her, the meadows console her, the trees revive her spirits, the flowers make her glad, and finally, she delights and instructs all who commune with her'" (91).

On three counts, then, Clemente's participation in the process of production and consumption of discourse (in this case poetry) subverts or offers a polar-opposite alternative to that process as practiced by the gypsy women.

And when Preciosa, Don Juan, and Don Sancho all get together under the stars to sing amoebean songs, they are only superficially celebrating the order and harmony of the cosmos. They are simultaneously celebrating a specifically aristocratic form of the production of poetic discourse, the whole constellation of courtly, pastoral, and platonic commonplaces in the context of *otium cum dignitate,* which brings them together as aristocrats and separates them from the real gypsies.

It is in the context of the gypsy women engaged in productive labor that depends on the notion of increase that we return to the distinction between two economic systems characterized in terms of sterility and fecundity respectively. This opposition is at the core of modern economic thought. Capitalism's master trope of fecundation, birth, and growth is clearly derived from biological increase. The analogy has been around for just about as long as western civilization, figured in the Greek *tokos,* which simultaneously denotes biological offspring and material increase. The notion of biological fecundity and its association with women suggests the possibility of a metaphorical relation of women to capitalism, and *La Gitanilla* exploits that possibility. We might begin to explore it by considering Preciosa herself. Although she is not fecund as yet in the biological sense, we have already seen how she fits into the new protocapitalist mentality. She is immediately fecund in another figurative sense, however, and that is her control of the generation of discourse. What everyone remembers, and what criticism celebrates, is her quick wit and her singing and dancing. As we have seen, the text identifies her "villancicos, coplas, seguidillas y zarabandas" as capital (62). This web of relations invites us to consider the specific content of the discourse she generates.

This discourse includes the ballad about Santa Ana and the birth of Mary, the ballad about Queen Margarita and the birth of Felipe IV, and the verse *buenaventura* of Doña Clara, the Teniente's wife. Forcione notes that the "poems which dominate the first quarter of the tale . . . form a striking emblematic prologue, announcing the principal themes and introducing the central imagery."[21] He further considers that these themes and this imagery all revolve around the institutions of marriage and the family, and offer a vision of the Erasmian ideal of Christian matrimony that will subsequently be realized in the union of the two protagonists. Forcione sees a whole hierarchy of families, literally "the Great Chain of Being of families," represented in the text, "from the divine order, to the ideal social order of the court, redeemed as it is by a prince-savior, and finally to the ordinary urban world where most of the action unfolds. Here we discover a marriage in which both partners exhibit a good deal of violence and lust, frequently scold and beat one another, and appear to be yoked until death in a conjugal relationship plagued by tyranny, fear, mistrust, jealousy and adultery."[22]

There is another way to characterize the various families that avoids dividing them into an angelic and a demonic order, and that in fact renders such a division irrelevant. We can begin at the bottom of Forcione's ladder, with Doña Clara and her anonymous Teniente.

We have already noted the general economic sterility of the household. The prognostication so subtly analyzed by Francisco Márquez Villanueva makes much of the Teniente's expertise in "arrimar la vara," identified as sexual activity.[23] Forcione seizes upon this "ocupación constante y virtuosa" to demonstrate the Teniente's violation of the sacred vows of matrimony.[24] What is also demonstrated is the curious fact that the profligate husband has been unable to impregnate his wife. Biological sterility, specifically the Teniente's inability to procreate, joins the economic sterility overt in the text. The family is really focussed through Doña Clara and not through her husband. She has a name; he is only an office. The evocation of her future fecundity, even at the price of identifying and stigmatizing her as a conversa whose son will be excluded from the Toledo cathedral, is what attests to the husband's sterility. Doña Clara, in contrast, will be the founder of a matrilineal succession.

We can proceed to observe that the families evoked so positively in Preciosa's songs are also headed by women. Taken together, Preciosa's songs in fact constitute a celebration of womanhood, motherhood, and matriliny.

The first song is addressed to Santa Ana and performed on Saint Anne's day (63). Preciosa begins by assimilating herself to the mother of Mary first with a pun on her own name: "'Arbol preciosísimo / que tardó en dar fruto'" (Most precious tree, that waited to bear its fruit). She follows this with the existing association of herself to money. As she has been variously described as "tesoro" and "mercancía," so Ana becomes the "'the mint, where the die for the coins was cast.'" The forty-eight verses of this poem contain only two fleeting allusions to Ana's husband. The text is instead a celebration of her fecundity and of the chain of matrilineal succession that begins with her: Ana the mother of Mary, Mary the mother of Jesus. This brings us finally to the most notorious case of the marginalization of the father, that of Mary and her husband Joseph, alluded to here and in the next poem as well.

The song about Queen Margarita and her newborn son insists even more strongly on the assimilation of the queen to Preciosa. There is a linguistic connection between them. Margarita and Preciosa both mean "pearl." Covarrubias, s.v. perla: "the margarita or precious union." Probably this is where Joaquín Casalduero got the idea that Preciosa is an allegorical representation of the biblical Pearl of Great Price.[25] The more specific phrase "margarita preciosa" occurs in *Don Quixote,* part I, chapter 34, which Rodríguez Marín elucidates in a footnote, citing Matthew 7:6: "neque mittas margaritas vestras ante porcos" (do not cast your pearls before swine); and 13:45: "simile est regnum coelorum homini negotiatori quaerenti bonas margaritas" (the kingdom of Heaven is like the precious pearls businessmen seek).[26] Before we ever get to Preciosa's song and its multiple points of contact between her and Queen Margarita, the language has already established an absolute equivalence.

Like Preciosa, Queen Margarita is "esta perla" (70). Like Preciosa, she is a "rica y admirable joya" (67). Like Preciosa, she "se lleva las almas todas" of those who see her (68). Like Preciosa, she is the subject of a variety of exclamations of praise from the men who observe her. It is to be noted that not all of these comments are in tune with the solemnity of the occasion, and some of them appear to call into question the official values being celebrated. For example, the last bystander says of the newborn king: "'How many hopes he instills! How many desires he foils! How many fears he increases! How many pregnancies he aborts!'" The new king's ability to act on the world to the advantage of his realms, in the role of redeemer evoked by Forcione, would appear to be compromised to the point of counterproductivity.

In this poem of 119 verses, exactly four are devoted to the father: "'I commend you to his father, that human Atlantis who curves under the weight of so many realms and such remote climes'" (70). The father is not old but is evoked as though he were, and one doesn't need to be Freud to relate that curvature to problems of masculine impotence.

In these songs men are either absent altogether, as Mary's husband, or evoked as old, weak, and impotent, or potent only by divine intervention. Women, in contrast, are powerful, fecund, and united by their common fecundity in a kind of loose confederacy that begins to approach matriarchy. As we have seen, Preciosa assimilates herself to all these avatars of womanly superiority, or them to her. We should also recall that she appears at this point in the text to be the product of a matrilineal succession, in the person of the old gypsy woman who claims to be her grandmother, raises her, and names her Preciosa. In addition, the union of the two lovers appears at this point to involve the allied custom of matrilocality, as Juan/Andrés forsakes his father's house and prepares to move in with his gypsy bride.

The text offers a new way to consider lineage. In Cervantes's society lineage was generally reckoned according to the variables of blood—either pure or impure, noble or plebeian—and the identity of the father. The property handed down from one generation to the next is the *patri-*mony, as we noted in the preceding chapter. At this point in Cervantes's text what is being proposed instead is a system of matrilineal succession, extending from the earthy Doña Clara, passing through Preciosa herself and upward to the royal and the heavenly spheres. The text repeatedly depicts the marginalization, if not the total exclusion, of the father.

Matriliny and matrilocality, however, do not necessarily imply matriarchy. We have already seen that the gypsy society is if anything an intensified version of the patriarchy that prevails in general. When Don Juan/Andrés is received into the gypsy company he hears what amounts to a public reading of the Law of the Father. Preciosa's lengthy and impassioned response to the patriarch's speech is the culminating moment in her production of discourse, and consequently of her empowerment in general. It brings her into the company of the strong women she has already celebrated in song, and it situates her, at least for as long as she keeps talking, outside the law of the father.

It is significant that Preciosa does not receive her father's name until the end of the story, when she is incorporated into the patriarchal order and silenced. The process by which this is accomplished is instructive for the thoroughness with which it documents how Preciosa is stripped not only of her gypsy identity, but of her status as adult as well. First the women are separated from the men: "They took Preciosa along with her grandmother so the Corregidor's wife could see her" (125). It is worth observing in passing that this lady, who will shortly be revealed as Preciosa's mother, doesn't have a name. Her identity is a function of her husband's, which in turn is a function of his place in the hierarchy of political power. When the Corregidor enters the room he finds his wife and Preciosa engaged in the womanly exercise of crying. Preciosa, because at this point she is still Preciosa the gypsy, takes control of the discourse. She makes an impassioned plea for clemency for Juan/Andrés, which is reproduced in the text. The Corregidor "was astonished by the little gypsy's reasoned speech" (126). This is her last speech, for at this point the patriarchal-aristocratic order begins to assert itself.

The gypsy grandmother kneels before the Corregidor and produces the signs of Preciosa's aristocratic identity: the baby jewelry she was wearing when she was kidnapped, and a written statement, a kind of *ejecutoria de hidalguía* (certificate of nobility) stating the infant's name and lineage together with the date of her kidnapping. This document is directly incorporated into the text, displacing Preciosa's own speech about herself, which figures so prominently in the first part of the story, and brusquely relocating her identity outside herself, in her aristocratic parents and in the quasi-legalese of a written text.

Her mother's first reaction (a woman after all) is to faint, but she revives quickly and charges off to take possession of her daughter. When she finds her she demotes her back to infancy, to precisely that moment when she had earlier lost control over her. She first examines her daughter's body for defects and identifying marks, and then presents her to her father, as she had done fifteen years before. But although the force of this sequence is to render her *infans* (speechless), Preciosa is not an infant but an adult. She is subjected to a demeaning display of her woman's body. She is undressed and her left breast exposed in search of a birth mark. Her right foot reveals two webbed toes. Preciosa's body ought to be the final reduct of her individual identity, but it is no longer hers.

The march backward from adulthood has only begun. The mother's next act is to gather Preciosa up in her arms and present her to her father, exactly as though she were a newborn baby. "She came, finally, with her precious cargo, into the presence of her husband, and passing it from her arms to his, said: 'Receive, sir, your daughter Costanza'" (128).

The father now takes control of the discourse by imposing silence on the three women present and reserving to himself the right to make the news public. "The Corregidor told his wife, his daughter and the old gypsy that the case would remain a secret until he divulged it" (128).

Preciosa's speech appears in the text one last time, in the form of three lines in which she informs her father that Andrés Caballero is not really a gypsy. After that she is reduced to indirect discourse. "Her parents asked Preciosa a hundred thousand questions, which she answered with grace and discretion. She said she would remain content with whatever her parents desired" (129); "Preciosa told her mother the story of her life. She told her that she had already said that she had no other will than whatever they wanted" (131). Her father's response to this oblique display of filial obedience is, however, present in direct discourse: "'Be quiet, daughter Preciosa, for I, as your father, take it upon myself to find you a husband appropriate to your rank'" (129). And to his wife's suggestion that the wedding be arranged forthwith he insists on the parents' proprietary right: "'Let us enjoy her a little while longer, because once she is married, she will no longer belong to us, but to her husband'" (130). The one person Preciosa does not belong to is herself. She is transformed into the object of exchange between diferent generations of men familiar from the writings of Lèvi-Strauss and French feminism.

The text ends in a welter of discourse, attributed to practically everyone except the heroine named in the title. Like Zoraida when she shows up at Juan Palomeque's inn in *Don Quixote*, part I, chapter 37, Preciosa/Costanza becomes instead the subject of other people's discourse. "The news of the little gypsy's story and her marriage reached Madrid" (134). When the groom's parents arrive in Murcia, "they told each other their stories, and the poets of the city took upon themselves the task of celebrating the amazing case, as well as the little gypsy's singular beauty. The famous Licenciado Pozo wrote in just this way, and in his verses Preciosa's fame will last as long as the ages" (134).

We began with an opposition between two economic systems: gypsy precapitalism and aristocratic neofeudalism. One is fecund and productive and the other is sterile and ostentatiously unproductive. One is marginalized and the other is in power. But this opposition is functional only inside another one, between women and men, or more precisely between matrilineal succession and matriarchal authority on the one hand and the patrilineal system and the patriarchy that in fact prevailed on the other hand. The distributed middle term that unites these two sets of structural oppositions is the notion of fecundity and generation. The economic system presided by Preciosa's gypsy grandmother generates wealth by transforming raw materials into commodities and adding value at each stage. Preciosa is a protagonist in this process, and her product is discourse that celebrates women and matriliny. It is important to observe, nevertheless, that this economic fecundity takes place within a social order characterized, in the speech of the old gypsy patriarch who welcomes Andrés into the company, as just as patriarchal as the aristocratic order that prevails at the end. The difference between the two ultimately resides in the respective participation of women in economic activity. The gypsy women work outside the home. They speak, they sing, they dance, they handle money.[27] The aristocratic women are barred from economic activity outside the home, just as they are silenced. The text seems to be suggesting that the emancipation of women can only occur for economic reasons. Only as women enter the workforce can they achieve independence. The participation of women in the workforce is the real difference between the gypsy and the aristocratic social orders, both of which are officially patriarchal. The aristocratic economic system, the only protagonists of which are men whose identity is a function of patrilineal succession, substitutes consumption for generation and authority for fecundity.

As so many readers have noted, the patriarchal-aristocratic order prevails. William Clamurro claims: "Triumphant love and the comedic restoration of social harmony require that the fantasies of spirit give place to the concrete realities of social definition and limitation. . . . The world of *La Gitanilla* is, then, more conservative than the opening scenes suggest. In the orderly world that Cervantes creates in his *Novelas ejemplares,* recovery of identity requires that the precious free spirit, Preciosa, be removed from the unorthodox and beguilingly subversive gypsy world and restored as Constanza [sic], the conforming and *constant* woman."[28]

Theresa Ann Sears observes that "Preciosa's loss of spirit has proven difficult for recent criticism to justify," and cites Clamurro as an example.[29] Sears attributes this loss of spirit to Cervantes's unambiguous embrace of the sexist norms of his society, leaving nothing to explain or explain away. Sears is right about readers' uneasiness with this ending. Julio Rodríguez Luis was probably the first to call attention to the now famous loss of spirit and to simultaneously to explain it away. Preciosa's silence is necessary and for the best, he says, since she has now been transformed into Doña Costanza de Acevedo, who "doesn't need a voice of her own," presumably (and tautologically) because her social role assumes her silence.[30] Alison Weber offers perhaps the most nuanced attempt to reconcile the discrepancy between the "witty, outspoken and autonomous Preciosa" and her "submissiveness and silence at the end." According to Weber, Cervantes "imagines an impossibly 'unbound' woman—free from class, from family and from fetishized notions of chastity, but when he returns Preciosa to her patriarchal/aristocratic family, she is again bound up by the prescriptive values of her class." In the end, says Weber, "the paradoxical achievement of Preciosa's *desenvoltura honesta* is reduced to pentimento."[31] In a more strictly literary vein, Thomas Hart observes somewhat elliptically that "the world of aristocratic privilege celebrated in sentimental romance shows signs of strain in *La Gitanilla*."[32] Cervantes's ironic overturning of the conventions of sentimental romance has been most cogently and profitably exploited by E. Michael Gerli, who shows how this generic subversion extends to the official social values so that the apparently celebratory ending of reintegration and reconciliation must be read ironically.[33] I am inclined to agree with Gerli. As I read this text, paying particular attention to the economic dimension of the women's existence, the ending is not the celebratory resolution of problems typical of romance, but something much darker, an ironic meditation on women's place in the patriarchal/aristocratic order that approaches tragedy.

# Part 3

## Ideological Antagonism and Commerce

# ~ 6
## *El amante liberal* and the Ottoman Empire

The Mediterranean world in the late sixteenth century was divided into two spheres, Christian and Muslim, dominated by the Spanish and the Ottoman empires respectively. We know that the Spanish ideal is racial, ethnic, religious, and even linguistic purity. The Ottoman/Muslim sphere is characterized by every commentator as multicultural, multiethnic, multireligious, and multilingual.

In this chapter I want to follow Cervantes's fictional exploration of these two spheres of power and influence in *El amante liberal*. Two young Sicilians, Leonisa and Ricardo, are captured by Muslim pirates from North Africa and turned into merchandise. They are separated while at sea. Leonisa is taken to Cyprus and becomes the object of the sexual desire of the three most important men on the island: the cadi, and the outgoing and incoming pashas. Ricardo, who has desired her from the beginning, also turns up on Cyprus, where he becomes the object of the desire of the cadi's wife. The story tells how Ricardo and Leonisa, joined by another Sicilian, a renegade or convert to Islam named Mahamut, retain their chastity and return in triumph to Sicily, where Ricardo finally wins Leonisa's hand in marriage. *El amante liberal,* along with *La española inglesa,* has traditionally been considered in terms of literary genre, as a Byzantine romance in miniature rather than a verisimilar representation of life within the two competing sociopolitical orders in the Mediterranean.[1] It is this latter avenue that I wish to pursue here.

The boundary between the multicultural Ottoman world and the Christian-European sphere is unstable. *El amante liberal* takes place on two Mediterranean islands, Sicily and Cyprus. The former is an outpost of the Hapsburg monarchy headquartered in Madrid, the latter had recently become an analogous outpost of the Ottoman sultanate based in Constantinople. The setting of *El amante liberal* on Cyprus, with early and insistent evocation of its recent transfer from the Christian to the Muslim sphere, is significant in this respect. Cervantes uses the unstable boundaries to sabotage the official version of the confrontation between "our" world and "theirs," between "us" and "them."

The Ottoman fleet transported the first units of an expeditionary force to the Venetian possession of Cyprus in the spring of 1570 as part of a grand strategy to seize coasts and islands that dominated trade routes in the eastern Mediterranean. The invasion and capture of the island more or less coincided with the rebellion and defeat of the Spanish moriscos in the Alpujarra (1568–1570), with the temporary pacification of the Protestant rebellion in the Low Countries (1567), and with the consolidation of Ottoman power in North Africa across from Sicily (1569). This last fact bears on the action of Cervantes's story, which begins with a raid on Sicily.

The Cyprus that passed into the Ottoman sphere in 1570 was a multicultural society, with the majority being Greek by ethnicity and Greek Orthodox Christian by religion. There was a small colony of Jews, a few Armenians and Maronites, and a very few Latin Christians. The relations between these groups are discussed by Ronald C. Jennings. Non-Muslims living under Ottoman rule are known as *zimmis,* from Arabic *dhimmi* (protected people). "The Law knows no Turk, Arab, or Kurd, only those who have come to God and are true believers, i.e. Muslims; likewise it knows no distinctions between old believers and new converts. All non-Muslims who had submitted themselves to the authority of the Ottoman state and paid taxes were as a consequence entitled to protection of their lives and property and the right to practice their own religion. . . . Protecting their interests was one traditional charge to kadis."[2]

It is important to note that very few Greek Orthodox Christians had full legal rights or economic opportunities in Cyprus under the authority of the Roman Catholic Lusignan dynasty, nor in the Venetian empire. The judicial records on which Jennings's study is based indicate that all zimmis had extensive opportunities to use the court legally. Absolutely no restrictions were placed on the Orthodox majority, nor on the small Armenian and Jewish communities. Everyone had the same opportunities. There were no restricted crafts or trades. Anyone could become a farmer, butcher, silk weaver, or moneylender. Jennings considers that this freedom was probably a result of the Ottoman conquest. "The frequency of intercommunal land and property transfers points to the close proximity in which Muslims and Christians lived in Lefkosha [Nicosia] and indeed over much of the island. . . . Generally speaking, selling land or property to adherents of another faith did not cause any social stigma. . . . Often the neighborhood was already integrated. . . . the Christian and Muslim people of Cyprus in that period lived by their own preference in the greatest intimacy—as neighbors."[3]

Following the Ottoman conquest of Cyprus, many of the island's Christians converted to Islam. Contemporary observers and modern scholars have usually attributed that conversion to official compulsion, but Jennings finds no contemporary local sources to substantiate this view, and in fact it was the duty of the court to make certain that the conversion was voluntary. Sometimes economic incentives were offered. "Several instances occurred where only one spouse converted. Usually divorce followed. In fact, that may have been a way for zimmiye women to find relief from an unbearable marriage. . . . A few cases suggest that sometimes a zimmiye woman might have converted in order to be able to marry a Muslim she already had her heart set on."[4] Finally, reversion from Islam to the former faith was absolutely forbidden.

It was widely believed in the West that the converts to Islam were insincere and would welcome an invasion by Christian forces. A philosophy instructor from Perugia named Fray Jerome Dandini spent some three months incognito on Cyprus. He believed most of the Muslims were renegades who converted "'to make their lives more easy and supportable; so that it seems an easy task to recover this isle . . . for the renegadoes could no sooner see the Christian soldiers, but they would throw off their turbans and put on hats instead, and turn their arms against the Turks.'" Jennings observes dryly: "That theme is a common one not just of foreign visitors to Cyprus but all over the Ottoman empire, although for centuries it remained a naive and self-deluding idea, dangerously ethnocentric and religiocentric."[5] Precisely the same "naive and self-deluding" mistake was made with respect to the people of Cuba by the CIA in 1962. I also want to call attention to Dandini's reference to the semiotics of clothing (turbans off, hats on), because the same semiosis comes up in Cervantes's text.

Apparently Cervantes never spent time on Cyprus. Luis Astrana Marín reports that he was a member of an expeditionary force sent to relieve Nicosia that was disbanded in late September 1570 before reaching the island, apparently due to a power struggle between Doria and Colonna.[6] He certainly could have availed himself of any of several *relaciones* that began to circulate soon after the events. Ottmar Hegyi also suggests that "Greek refugees from the island must have been equally instrumental in filtering information to the western European public."[7]

Besides the shifting spatial boundary between Christian and Muslim domains represented by transfer of power in Nicosia, the difference between the two spheres is further eroded by the frequent explicit analogies established in

*El amante liberal* between Muslim/Turkish and Christian/Spanish hierarchical structures and imperial administrative practices. The *cadí* is defined as "the same as their bishop" (163). The *bajá* is "viceroy or pasha, as the Turks call viceroys" (164). The presentation of an official report "at court before the Grand Turk" is explained by analogy to the protocol of imperial Spain: "which, having been seen by the vizier-pasha and four lesser pashas, or as we would say by the president and the members of the royal council" (165). These insistent analogies suggest that what in the text are identified as Turkish practices may be standing in for imperial Spanish practices it would otherwise be impossible to criticize.

The foregoing springs from the observation of a textual anomaly. Why should Mahamut, a Sicilian, explain the Ottoman practices to his fellow Sicilian Ricardo by reference to the Spanish system and to the court of Felipe II? For one thing, Sicily is part of the Spanish system. For another, Cyprus is to Constantinople as Sicily is to Madrid, an outlying province, in both cases also incidentally an island, governed by a viceroy-pasha on behalf of an absent sovereign. This suggests that the observations made concerning the qualifications, the probity, or corruption of the pashas might be equally applicable to their imperial Spanish counterparts, and that Cervantes might therefore be offering some kind of meditation on various aspects of imperial administration, including the pool from which and the process by which officials are selected, and their accountability for their administration as they prepare to turn over their charge to a successor.

It seems probable that the two Ottoman governors in *El amante liberal* are the two pashas Cervantes knew best, but in different ways, from his Algerian captivity. Cervantes knew Hasán Pasha (Veneciano) personally, if we are to believe his own *Información de Argel* (1580) and Dr. Antonio de Sosa's account in the *Diálogo de los mártires de Argel* (1612). But Alí Pasha (Ochalí) had come and gone before Cervantes arrived in Algiers; he was by then the sultan's admiral. The two pashas are characters in Ruy Pérez de Viedma's autobiographical account of his captivity (*Don Quixote* I, 39–41), and what Ruy Pérez has to say about them is clearly derived from Diego de Haedo's *Epítome de los reyes de Argel* (1612).[8] They enter *El amante liberal* already as textual products, whose genealogy reaches back from *Amante* to *Cautivo* to Haedo's *Epítome*. The fact that the latter was not published until 1612, well after Ruy Pérez' account in *Don Quixote*, part I (1605) and too close to *El amante liberal* (1613) to have been of much use, suggests that Cervantes derived his knowledge of Alí Pasha from conversations with Sosa and/or readings of Sosa's manuscript in progress. The Alí Bajá in the story is almost certainly Aluch Alí, a.k.a. Ochalí, who "is known only as Alí Pasha."[9] He was king of Algiers from 1568 to 1572, when he became the sultan's admiral. In all probability the Hazán Bajá in the story is Cervantes's master Hasán Pasha Veneciano, who was Ochalí's protégé. The transfer of power in El amante liberal from Alí to Hasán Pasha is probably a fictionalized version of the transfer of power in Algiers from Ramadán Pasha to Hasán Pasha Veneciano. This occurred in June 1577, and it was the only such transfer that Cervantes actually witnessed during his captivity. Cervantes's fiction eliminates the intermediate pasha Arab Amat altogether, and substitutes Ochalí for Ramadán Pasha. In the fiction, the torch is passed directly from Alí to Hasán, and in fact Hasán was Alí's protégé.

Alí Pasha or Ochalí was born Dionisio Galea in a village in Calabria. He was captured along with his widowed mother, Pippa de Chicco, and a younger brother who took the name Juseli Mayumet and made his life in Constantinople. The mother returned to Italy where she died in 1567, just as her son was rising to eminence in Algiers.[10] "Aluch Alí, whose name we corrupt into Ochalí, is a native of the province of Calabria in the Kingdom of Naples, the son of poor and humble parents. In his youth he was a fisherman, until he was captured by Alí Amet, who put him to rowing in his *galeota,* where he spent many years, and since he had a fungus or tinea which made his head bald, the other captives mocked him, and refused to eat with him or row on the same bench. Because of this he was called 'fartax,' which in Turkish means 'tineous.'"[11]

His rise began when he converted, in order to avenge a blow dealt him by a Muslim, an Italian renegade named Hasán Zuhri. Alí Amet made him his *cómitre* (boatswain), a job in which "he made a lot of money in a little time. He put his money into a brigantine or frigate in Algiers, along with other investors. With this boat he made enough to outfit a galeota, and became one of the foremost corsair captains or arraeces in Algiers."[12] A primitive accumulation of capital ("a lot of money in a little time") allowed him to outfit a corsair ship and go into business for himself. He then came to the attention of Dragut Raez, the governor of Tripoli. When Dragut was killed in battle in 1565 the sultan's admiral, Piali Pasha, named Ochalí to succeed him in Tripoli, and in two and a half years he became very wealthy. Ochalí always cultivated the friendship of Piali Pasha, sent him costly gifts, and in due time Piali interceded with the sultan and Ochalí was named king of Algiers. This is the story of a self-made man who rose to eminence by a combination of talent, ambition, and the favor of influential men.

[Hasán Pasha], when he was young, served as an accountant's assistant on a Ragusan merchant ship. His Christian name was Andretta. He was captured and taken to Tripoli, where he became the property of an ordinary corsair who converted him to Islam and kept him until he died. Because his master had no children, Andretta (or Hasán, as he was now called) was inherited by Dragut Raez. Dragut died in 1565 and was succeeded by Ochalí, a Calabrian renegade. He took everything Dragut had left for himself, so that Hasán came to be Ochalí's property, and since Hasán was astute, assertive, audacious, and licentious, with these qualities and other Muslim hanky-panky, he came to be dearly loved by Ochalí. And so, when Ochalí became governor of Algiers, he made Hasán his *elami* [treasurer and paymaster]. He continued to serve in this office when Ochalí went to Turkey and became the sultan's admiral.[13]

It is interesting to compare Haedo's narratives with stories of patrilineal succession in the European manner. There is no bond of *linaje,* although there are relationships between older and younger men built on affect and mentoring. The "fathers" are all surrogate, and there is a homosexual subtext that Haedo plays down. Dragut Raez takes a fancy to Ochalí, Ochalí then inherits Hasán upon Dragut's death, Hasán becomes Ochalí's protégé, and so on. What is repeated in both of Haedo's narratives is a combination of religious conversion, native talent and ambition, and the favor of an important man.

In Ruy Pérez de Viedma's story, Cervantes insists on the analogies between Turkish and European practices of inheritance through patrilineal succession. But like Haedo, he also calls attention to the absence of real blood ties and to the absence of family names that would signal those blood ties or linaje. I must confess, though, that I miss what Paul Julian Smith describes as Ruy Pérez's "wonder" at the lack of patronymics among the Turks.[14] Ruy Pérez contrasts Ochalí, whom he values positively, with Hasán. Ochalí is exonerated from the charge of submitting to homosexual domination by his master, while Hasán is a "regalado garzón" or *bardaj,* the passive subject in a homosexual relationship. The fact of homosexuality is incidentally revealed as a negative marker of character for Ruy Pérez, who shares the typical Christian/Spanish homophobia. Cruelty is a less relative standard. Ochalí "was, morally speaking, a good man who accorded his captives humane treatment" (484), while Hasán is "the cruelest renegade anybody has ever seen" (485).

We usually hear about Hasán Veneciano's proverbial cruelty, but Haedo also emphasizes his expertise as an accountant, an expertise he shared with his captive Cervantes. Haedo also dwells on Hasán's greed and how he enriched himself in office. Among other things, Hasán cornered the market on wheat, "which was very scarce at that time in Algiers," meat, and other basic foodstuffs, to the point of being accused of monopolizing everything "except onions and cabbages." He insisted that the tribute owed him by the farmers be paid in grain, which he then sold back to them for food, "doubling his money twice over." He melted down Algerian silver coins, recast them in Turkish molds, and shipped them to Constantinople "because silver is worth much more there." He then recast the remaining silver into heavily alloyed Algerian coins. He monopolized the sale of hides to Christian merchants. He bought their merchandise at prices set by himself, for resale on the Algerian market. He levied taxes on tax-exempt Turks.[15] He brought some of his still-Christian relatives from Italy so they could share in his lucrative business ventures while he was in power.[16]

The fictionalization of these real but already textualized pashas from Cervantes's Algerian past is complex. Perhaps the most important aspect of these two pashas within the fiction of *El amante liberal* is the simple fact that they, like the Christian protagonists, are Italians. The text gives us a Calabrian Muslim (Alí Pasha), a Venetian Muslim (Hasán Pasha), a Sicilian Muslim (Mahamut), and three Sicilian Christians (Leonisa, Ricardo, Cornelio). The symmetrical religious antagonism of the three Muslims who oppose three Christians is undercut by their common Italian ethnicity.

The institution of the *residencia,* which the text describes in such detail and identifies as an Ottoman practice, is in fact a Spanish one, and as we shall see, the possibilities for corruption the text attributes so insistently to the Turks are more typical of Spanish than of Ottoman administration.

The residencia is the accountability for the previous administration, taken by the successor and written up as a report, which is then presented at court and according to which the outgoing official is either rewarded or fined, or neither. Mahamut explains:

> "Once the residencia is completed it is given to the outgoing pasha in a closed and sealed parchment, and he presents himself with it at the Porte of the Grand Turk. When it has been examined by the vizier-pasha and four lesser pashas, he is either rewarded or punished according to the tenor of the residencia, although if he comes with money he can buy his way out of the punishment. If he is neither punished nor rewarded, which is what usually happens, with bribes and gifts he secures the position he wants most, because there the government positions are not given for merit, but for money. Everything is for sale, and everything is bought." (165)

Covarrubias clearly has the Spanish context in mind when he defines *residencia* as "the accounting a governor, *corregidor* or administrator gives of himself, before a judge appointed for that purpose, and because the judge must be present and reside there while the accounting is being taken, it came to be called the *residencia.*" In *La Gitanilla,* fifteen-year-old Preciosa considers the residencia and the subsequent bribery and sale of offices to be normal practices in Madrid.

> "Take bribes, Mr. Teniente, take bribes and you will have money, and don't try anything different or you'll die of hunger. I've heard it said that an official has to get enough money out of his present post to pay the penalties on the residencia and to buy his next position."

"That's what unprincipled scoundrels say and do," replied the Teniente, "but the official who gives a good residencia won't have to pay anything at all, and his good performance will get him his next position."
"You talk like a saint, Mr. Teniente." (95)

Madrid also appears to equal Constantinople as a place where everything is for sale. Mahamut observes that "'everything is for sale and everything is bought'" (165), and in *La Gitanilla* it is "Madrid, where everything is bought and everything sold" (75).

Incidental corroboration of the corruption normal in the practice of the residencia at least since the mid-sixteenth century is provided by the Burgalese accountant and political economist Luis de Ortiz in his *Memorial* (1558): "All outgoing officials should be required to make a residencia as the *corregidores* do, but these residencias should not be taken as they are at present, by the incoming official, where the new one excuses the old one's malfeasance in office, and all to the detriment of the state. . . . The residencias should be taken by someone else, so that the new official cannot enjoy what the old one leaves for him."[17]

Bribery and corruption were in fact of epidemic proportions in Spain, to the point where Fray Juan de Mariana reports in 1609 that "it is said that for the last few years there is no government position which the ministers do not sell with gifts and bribes, even in the royal court and in bishoprics."[18]

Porras de la Cámara, who gets into Cervantes studies chiefly as the owner of alternate versions of two *Novelas ejemplares*, was moved in 1601 to write to his superior, Cardinal Fernando Niño de Guevara: "'No administration of justice, truth a rarity, little shame and fear of God, less confidence; no one receives justice except by buying it.'"[19]

Francisco Rodríguez Marín called attention to the "bitter memory of the penalties on residencias" in Cervantes's own family. It seems that Cervantes's grandfather, the licenciado Juan de Cervantes, was *teniente de corregidor* in Cuenca. When the residencia was being taken at the end of his tenure in office, two citizens made formal complaints against him, and he was fined.[20]

There is one reference to the residencia as an Ottoman practice, in Diego Galán, *Cautiverio y trabajos de Diego Galán* (1600). The year is 1592, the place is Algiers, and Herder Pasha is about to be succeeded by Shabán Pasha. Herder is hard-pressed to find the cash necessary to pay the janissaries the double salary advance due them on the occasion of the transfer of power. Although Herder Pasha has to sell off much of his wife's and his daughter's jewelry, he does manage to set sail for Constantinople with two galleys and 550 slaves.[21]

What about the truth of the assertion that offices are for sale in the Ottoman administration? According to the Turkologist I. Metin Kunt, the reverse was true.

Ogier Ghiselin de Busbecq, twice ambassador of Charles V to the court of Suleiman the Magnificent, made a . . . distinction . . . between the European rulers, dependent on their nobility, and the Ottoman sultan, master of his slaves in public offices. Busbecq commented that the lack of a blood nobility in the system allowed the sultan to pick his slaves and advance them according to their abilities; the system was a meritocracy where there was no impediment to the rise of any man to the highest offices other than his own capacity.[22]

At times the Turkish practices may offer a positive example to be profitably imitated by imperial Spain. The whole notion of a multicultural population living productively and in harmony under a monolithic government would be a general example. More specifically, the Ottoman regime provides equal access for all subjects to the judicial system. Jennings reports with respect to Cyprus during the period in question: "The official responsibilities of the kadis of Cyprus went far beyond merely making legal decisions. . . . [The kadi] was the final authority on every matter. He was also to help and protect the weak and the poor."[23] Cadis were specifically charged with protecting the legal and economic interests of non-Muslims (zimmis) and women. In *El amante liberal* the new pasha's first act is to make himself available to his subjects. The text dwells particularly on the cadi as judge.

> In a short time the cadi came out from the tent and announced in Turkish, Arabic, and Greek that all those who wished to ask for justice, or seek redress from Alí Pasha, could enter freely, that here was Hasán Pasha, sent by the Grand Turk as Viceroy of Cyprus, who would see that justice was done. . . . Several Greek Christians, as well as some Turks, went in and requested justice, and all in cases of so little importance that the cadi dispatched most of them with no legal formalities. . . . And among these barbarians, if they are barbarians in this, the cadi is the competent judge in all cases, . . . and there is no appeal to another court. (156)

A few pages later the two pashas, Alí and Hazán, bow to the authority of the cadi: "They obeyed the cadi's words instantly, and even if he had ordered them to do something more difficult they would have done the same, such is the respect in which the cadi is held by that damned sect" (159). The narrative voice describes a system in which no one, not even the viceroy, is above the law, a system clearly superior to the Spanish double justice system for *hidalgos* and *pecheros* and all its other exclusionary practices, and at the very end reclaims his own political-religious orthodoxy by attributing this superior system to that ironically described "damned sect."

The semiotic value of Ottoman society is destabilized. It can stand either for what our society is and should not be, or the reverse, what ours should be but is not. Georges Güntert ascribes this destabilization to the presence of two distinct but simultaneous levels of discourse in the text. He concludes that Cervantes's text panders to the expectations of the majority while simultaneously inviting the discerning reader to apply the criticism of Ottoman practices to the Spanish situation.[24] Güntert is in the line of Anthony J. Cascardi, who distinguishes between what he calls "exemplary" and "ethical" discourses,[25] and Francisco J. Sánchez, who invokes a dialectic between mass audience and individual reader.[26] Güntert, Cascardi, and Sánchez all posit an official discourse directed to the unaware reader, in harmony with society's norms and expectations, and a simultaneous subversive discourse directed at the more with-it reader that criticizes those norms and expectations.

The reversibility of Ottoman and Hapsburg institutions and practices in Cervantes's text invites us to consider a web of subsurface, mostly clandestine relationships between the two Mediterranean superpowers.

Braudel remarks that the 1580 Hispano-Turkish truce "is always presented as an isolated and exceptional agreement, when in fact it is merely one link in a long chain—and without the rest of the chain virtually incomprehensible."[27] He offers a detailed account of the various secret missions to Constantinople from 1577 to 1584, and the treaties that resulted from them. Most interesting is his evocation of the invisible army of shady characters who carried on these delicate negotiations: "Renegades hoping to be received back into grace, former captives claiming to be experts on the Levant, Greeks 'y es menester mirarles mucho a las manos' (as a Spanish report puts it), knights of Malta, Albanians, imperial envoys; and their interlocutors: Jews, Germans like Doctor Solomon Ashkenazi, dragomans [from the Turkish *turguman*, 'an official interpreter'] like Horem Bey. In the no-man's land between two civilizations, it was this strange army not always recognized by its employers which handled diplomatic matters."[28]

A certain Don Martín de Acuña left Venice in 1577 with a safe-conduct in order to ransom prisoners at Constantinople, but "his sole aim was to negotiate a treaty with the Turk, and indeed he obtained one for the space of five years." Acuña was characterized by the Viceroy of Naples as "'one of the most disreputable Spaniards ever to have come to Italy.'" He was a spendthrift, a gambler, and a drinker. In Constantinople he shunned the company of the respectable and sought out the most notorious renegades in the city. And he returned with a promise that the Turkish armada would not be sent out in 1577, over the protests of the sultan's admiral Ochalí.[29]

The Milanese Giovanni Margliani carried on the secret negotiations that led to the treaty of 1580. Margliani had lost an eye in the defense of Tunis in 1574, when he was captured by the Turks. In 1577 he was ransomed by the Ragusan merchant Nicolò Prodanelli and sent to Constantinople on the recommendation of the Duke of Alba. When he arrived in February 1578 he was practically snubbed by the Grand Vizier because he was not an official ambassador. Nevertheless, he managed to negotiate a one-year treaty. The great treaty, a three-year cessation of hostilities, was finally concluded on 4 February 1581, whereupon Margliani was able to return to Europe.[30]

Sola and de la Peña call attention to the participation behind the scenes of Aurelio Santa Cruz, "merchant, redeemer of captives, and Spanish secret agent in Istanbul."[31] Santa Cruz was a spymaster and money man. In particular he was responsible for paying various Christians and renegades who were recruited into the service of the Spanish king: his own son-in-law, the curiously named Mastras de Alfaro; the ex-captives Antón Avellán and Francisco Peloso; the sultan's interpreter Horem Bey; the Lucchan renegade Morat Aga (who was said to want to reconvert to Christianity); the Lucchan businessman Carlo Seminiate; and the Albanian double agent Bartolomé Bruti.

This was a time of feverish secret negotiating. 'Abd al-Malik's short reign in Morocco was marked by constant clandestine contacts, from Constantinople to London. In 1576, while he was negotiating for political advantage with agents of the king of Spain, he was simultaneously sending gifts valued at a half-million ducados to the sultan. At the same time he established commercial contact with England through the English merchant Edmund Hogan.[32] In 1577 he received a letter from Elizabeth I concerning the sale of African sugar and the purchase of English arms. This clandestine contact suggests a historical relation between the fictional worlds of *El amante liberal* and *La española inglesa,* which we shall examine next.

The five Gasparo Corso brothers were especially important as intermediaries. They resided strategically all around the western Mediterranean. Francisco was in Valencia; he would be named procurador general of the Order of the Holy Sepulchre for Spain, Portugal, and America in 1577. Andrea's residence is unspecified, although he appears in Marrakesh in 1577. Felipe was in Algiers and in close contact with Francisco and Andrea. Mariano was in Marseilles and similarly in touch, and the fifth brother was based in Barcelona.[33] They were also related by blood to one of the principal Algerian corsairs and trusted lieutenants of Ochalí, Mamí Chaya (a.k.a. Mamí Corso). In 1569 Felipe's government had attempted unsuccessfully to capitalize on this relationship in order to recruit Ochalí himself into the service of Spain. The Gasparo Corso brothers were also in constant contact with 'Abd al-Malik in the period following Lepanto until his death at Alcazarquivir in 1578.

Sola and de la Peña conjecture that Cervantes himself could have been an agent. When he first arrived in Algiers he was carrying letters from Don Juan de Austria and from the Duque de Sessa. These letters, at a time when the secret services controlled by those two were in constant activity, and when captives, ex-captives, and their redeemers all played important roles, made Cervantes a unique and an especially valuable captive. They further suggest that this presumed relationship with the directors of the Spanish secret service was what really saved Cervantes from execution following each of his repeated attempts to escape. In particular, they offer reasonable conjecture concerning Cervantes's possible employment as an agent of the secret service. The period leading up to his release from captivity toward the end of 1580 was marked by intense diplomatic activity: the culmination of Margliani's negotiations with the sultan leading to the treaty Ochalí opposed, the removal of Cervantes's master Hasán Pasha as king of Algiers, and the ultimately fruitless attempt by Ochalí to join the separate kingdoms of Morocco, Algiers, and Tunis into an anti-Spanish "greater Maghreb." To this end he had Morat Arráez in Tetuán with eight galleys, he called his protégés Ramadán Pasha and Hasán Pasha together at Algiers, and arrived there himself in May 1581. Spanish intelligence, at that time headed by the Duque de Medina Sidonia, had good reason to be apprehensive. Sola and de la Peña suggest that this is the context of Cervantes's mission to Oran in June of 1581 "for certain things in His Majesty's service." He spent a little over a month in North Africa and returned to Cartagena with some letters from a shadowy character known somewhat facetiously as "the warden of Mostagán." "That was all," conclude Sola and de la Peña: "an ex-captive like so many others, with five years' experience in captivity, sent on an information-gathering mission to an area he was presumed to know."[34] If this is true, and if Cervantes was to report to the Duque de Medina Sidonia, this episode might mark the beginning of Cervantes's lack of respect for the opportunistic Duque that culminates in the biting sonnet "Vimos en julio otra semana santa," written after Medina Sidonia had abandoned Cádiz to the English in 1596, which brings us back to La española inglesa. We shall explore the events of 1596 in detail in the following chapter.

〜〜〜

Piracy and the commodification of humans, so important to the plot of El amante liberal, were by no means limited to Muslim North Africa. Braudel summarizes: "In the past, western historians have encouraged us to see only the pirates of Islam, in particular the Barbary corsairs. The notorious fortune of Algiers tends to blind one to the rest. But this fortune was not unique; Malta and Leghorn were Christendom's Algiers; they too had their bagnios, their slave markets and their sordid transactions. For it was not merely in Algiers that men hunted each other, threw their enemies into prison, sold or tortured them and became familiar with the miseries, horrors, and gleams of sainthood of the 'concentration camp world': it was all over the Mediterranean."[35]

According to Godfrey Fisher, a close relationship existed between the European and African shores of the Mediterranean, "not only because of their historic economic interdependence but because of the existence in both areas of a large number of captives. The demands for the service of the galleys, which were many times more numerous at Christian than Berberesque ports," encouraged "French galley commanders' unwillingness to release Turks and Moors, . . . and the heartless cupidity of English captains in selling their captives into Spain."[36]

Braudel devotes several pages to the exploits of Christian privateers, especially the Knights of Malta and the Florentine order of Knights of St. Stephen. "A register of captives intending to pay ransom (their birthplaces range from Fez to Persia and the Black Sea), or a list of galley-slaves with their ages and place of origin gives an idea of the probable benefits of the operation to the pirate-knights of St. Stephen and their shrewd master." He also calls attention to "the specialized markets created by privateering, in particular the market in human beings which was the specialty of Malta, Messina and Leghorn."[37] Sola and de la Peña recall "Father Diego Marín, well versed in Arabic, since he served as an interpreter, with an ecclesiastical benefice from Bedar y Serena and a resident of Vélez Blanco, who in the months following the morisco rebellion in the Alpujarras was intensely involved in buying and selling Alpujarran slaves, especially girls." They conclude that Diego Marín's commercial activities permit his identification as a true slave dealer.[38]

Miguel Herrero García observes how difficult it is to believe that in a period of permanent hostility between Spanish Catholicism and Islam there should be Muslims in Madrid, but the documents demonstrate that this was indeed the case.[39] Some of these Muslims were slaves taken from Algerian pirate ships on the high sea or in the course of raids on the Spanish coast, some were taken by Spanish pirates raiding in North Africa, and some, according to Herrero García, were in Madrid to ransom the others out of captivity. Herrero García quotes from Jerónimo de Barrionuevo's *Avisos,* 8 November 1656: "'There are two Muslims from Algiers in the Half Moon Inn [where else would they stay?] who have come with a safe-conduct from Orán, to arrange the ransom of others who were captured by the galley *Santa Agata* when Don Juan de Austria was on his way to the Low Countries.'"[40]

The Sicilian port of Trapani, home base of Cervantes's protagonists in *El amante liberal,* played an important role in the Christian corsair activity. Salvatore Salomone Marino reports that in 1515 the "Palermitan" Don Luigi Requeséns, general of the squadron of royal galleys, encountered the flotilla of Solimán Arráez off the island of Pantellaria. After a battle in which Solimán Arráez was killed and seven of his ships sunk, Requesens returned in triumph to Trapani with five hundred Turks and four hundred Moors enslaved.[41] After pointing with pride to the Sicilian corsairs in general, Salomone Marino singles out "the daring mariners of Trapani, who prey on and defeat the Corsairs' galleys."[42] Braudel cites a reference from 17 November 1595 to a corsair brigantine from Trapani.[43] In addition, Trapani was an "interior" or behind-the-lines port for the Spanish fleet normally based at Messina.

Messina and Trapani were the sites of flourishing slave markets. In 1605 a group of slaves, all born in Algiers or Bizerte, attempted to flee Trapani and return home, guided by a Greek *passeur* (in my part of the world a *coyote*) specialized in smuggling human cargo from one side to the other.[44]

The staple of the Trapanese economy, more important even than official naval or corsair activity, was the export of salt. There was a regular traffic in Trapanese salt with Sardinia, Marseilles, and northern Europe. Trapani was particularly vulnerable to attack, being located in that *complexe sicilien* Bartolomé and Lucile Bennassar consider the second most dangerous area in the entire Mediterranean in terms of the statistical frequency of Muslim corsair activity and the capture of merchandise, human and otherwise. Barbary corsairs regularly lay in wait for Christian ships leaving port there. A fleet of four Flemish ships loaded with salt from Trapani was captured in the strait in 1630.[45]

There may not be a direct connection, but Cervantes's old bête noir the Duque de Medina Sidonia owned the salt flats of Sanlúcar de Barrameda, near the *almadrabas* of Zahara, which he also owned and which figure prominently in *La ilustre fregona*.[46] Antonio Domínguez Ortiz offers an interesting variation. It turns out that Felipe II had nationalized the salt flats in order to secure their income for the Crown. The Duque attempted to retain authorization to make all the salt needed for his fisheries, a matter of some twenty-four thousand *fanegas* per year. The Duque lost his suit, lost again on appeal, and was condemned to pay back two reales per fanega of salt for every year from 1564 to 1598. In 1612 the matter was still in the Sala de Mil Quinientas del Consejo de Castilla, and it was finally resolved when the Duque was allowed to pay back only half the original amount, or some seventy-four thousand ducados.[47] Probably Trapani salt competed with Sanlúcar salt, so that Cervantes's protagonists would be competition for the Duque. The Trapani salt flats appear in *El amante liberal* near the garden where Leonisa is captured by the pirates: "Leonisa and her parents, and Cornelio with his, had gone on a picnic with their relatives and servants to Ascanio's garden, which is near the harbor, on the road to the salt flats" (143). The salt flats reappear toward the end, when Ricardo recalls the pirate raid on the "jardín de las Salinas" (185).

Cervantes was in Trapani for about a month, beginning in late August 1574. He was a member of the expeditionary force commanded by Don Juan de Austria on its way from Genoa to relieve the garrison of La Goleta when bad weather forced the fleet to take shelter at Trapani. Unable to influence the disastrous outcome at La Goleta, Don Juan remained in Trapani until 29 September, when he departed for Naples. He left Cervantes's unit in Palermo, under the command of Don Lope de Figueroa.[48] A certain Don Juan Zanoguera wrote two reports concerning the fall of La Goleta.[49] Zanoguera was one of the principal defenders, and it was he who finally surrendered to Alí Pasha (Ochalí) on 14 September 1574, in return for the safe-conduct to Trapani of 335 Christians, mostly women, children, and merchants. Ironically, Zanoguera arrived in Trapani on the very day Don Juan de Austria departed. It is therefore possible that Cervantes met him on that occasion or heard from an eyewitness the story of the loss of La Goleta.[50] Zanoguera is among the brave Christian defenders of La Goleta mentioned by Ruy Pérez de Viedma in *Don Quixote,* part I, chapters 39–41.

Cervantes left Algiers on 24 October 1580, on a boat bound for Valencia. On 15 December of that year, Fray Juan Gil put a Trapanese named Brito and a Genoese named Benito on a boat bound for Sicily. Cervantes could have known the Trapanese Brito in Algiers.[51]

In 1614 the French renegade Guillaume Bedos (a.k.a. Xaban Arráez) recalled the case of a Trapanese Sicilian who reneged three times and each time succeeded in avoiding Inquisitorial justice.[52] One of the protagonists of the *Diálogo de los mártires de Argel,* a renegade named Morat, is introduced as "a Sicilian, born in the ancient and famous city of Trapani." He was shot to death with arrows along with his colleague Gallo in 1578, after both confessed to having stabbed to death a "mal cristiano" from Calabria who had been serving as guide for Algerian raiding parties around his home town.[53] Gallo, who was Morat's friend and fellow "turco de profesión" (convert to Islam), "was very friendly with a Christian, a Genoese like himself, who rowed at the same bench. And because they were from the same place, he did all he could for him and trusted him with all his secrets." This interfaith friendship recalls the two fictional Trapanese, Mahamut and Ricardo, in *El amante liberal.* Or, even closer to the fictional events of Cervantes's text, consider the case of the Calabrese Pietro Polimeno, whose Sicilian girlfriend had been kidnapped by Muslim corsairs and who embarked from Trapani to negotiate her ransom. Instead of liberating her, he converted to Islam himself. In 1580, serving on a corsair ship, he and the Venetian renegade Bernardino de Sforza instigated a mutiny, seized the ship, and returned to Sicily loaded with new captives.[54]

Especially reminiscent of episodes in *El amante liberal* is the following "classic trick of the trade": "'If one is bold enough to enter the Aegean 'alla turchesca, costeggiando terra firma,' it is sometimes possible to capture without a struggle passengers coming down to the quayside mistaking the Christian pirates for the galleys of the Grand Turk.'"[55]

The presence and the importance of Italian participation in all these events is truly striking. Although political sovereignty rested with Spain, many if not most of the men who crisscrossed the Mediterranean entrusted with carrying out Felipe's policies were non-Spaniards, mostly Italians, from leading players such as the Catalan-Palermitan Requesens and the Genoese Andrea and Gian Andrea Doria, to shadowy characters like Giovanni Margliani. The Sicilian protagonists of Cervantes's story, and their home base of Trapani in particular, are in this sense "historically accurate," and it would be a mistake to mentally transpose them into Castilians with improbable names. Their Sicilian specificity is functional.

At the same time, we have seen how many of the Muslim players are also Italian. Salvatore Bono claims that Italians from the *mezzogiorno* and the islands, former subjects of the king of Spain, were the "true protagonists" of the new cosmopolitan Algerian society.[56] We have seen that Ochalí himself was approached by the Spanish secret service through his still-Christian Calabrian relatives. Godfrey Fisher remarks on the "friendly relationship between Barbary and Sicily, whose inhabitants expressed their desire, about 1640, to be placed under Turkish rule."[57]

Many Sicilians divided their time between Sicily and North Africa, spending years in one place or another and crossing and recrossing the religious frontier as circumstances dictated. The Bennassars recall Salvador Morito, "whose double personality is evoked in his very name," a Muslim in Tunisia who requested baptism when he moved to Marsala, "without bothering to specify that he had already received it as an infant."[58]

There are family connections that overarch the border. Ciro Manca follows the fortunes of the family business of Guillaume Borgal, a native of Marseilles established in Algiers, and observes that his case is representative of a certain category of merchant-bankers—Spaniards, French, English, Flemish, and Italian—who did business in North Africa "so frequently with the aid of their renegade friends and relatives."[59] We have already seen Ochalí and his Italian relatives, some of whom convert to Islam and stay on; others, like his mother, who return to Christian Europe; Hasán Pasha and the Venetian relatives he brings to Algiers to share in the administration of his affairs; the five Gasparo

Corso brothers, strategically placed in Europe and North Africa, and their relative, the Algerian corsair Mamí Corso.

It seems that all the official dividing lines of antagonistic religions, ethnicities, national sovereignties, and international rivalries are systematically undercut by a close-knit, mutually interdependent economic system manned by individuals with ties on both sides of the divide, and who come and go in the pursuit of ends that transcend the official differences. The normal categories of identity become less and less relevant.

In literature, and in Cervantes in particular, the multicultural Ottoman world is the perfect setting for identities that won't stay constant, because multiculturalism implies many more categories or signifying systems in terms of which identification may be played around with.

Sexual practices are one such marker of identity. Homosexuality is widespread and socially acceptable among Muslims, in Algiers and elsewhere in the Ottoman domains, and is therefore considered to mark a distinction between the Christian and Muslim spheres. Sodomy in Algiers is condemned vigorously by Haedo: "They all live a bestial life of porcine animals, giving themselves over constantly to drunkenness and sex, and in particular to stinking and unspeakable sodomy. They use captive Christian boys that they buy just for this purpose and then dress Muslim style, or they use the sons of Jews and Moors from Algiers and other places, taking and keeping them in spite of their parents. They spend days and nights at a time with them, getting drunk on wine and spirits."[60]

The presentation of Turkish homosexual practices in the anonymous *Viaje de Turquía* (1557) is less judgmental and more matter-of-fact than what we see in Haedo. All Turks are simply presumed to be bi- if not homosexual, and they all seem to prefer boys to women.

> Pedro: They are the most jealous people alive, and with great reason, because since most of them are buggerers, the women have to look out for themselves.
> Juan: And do the women know that's what the men are?
> Pedro: Some are such great scoundrels that they keep their boys among their wives, and to show them who's boss they sometimes get in bed together with a woman and a boy, and spend the whole night with the boy and ignore the woman.[61]

Because homosexuality is normal in the Ottoman world, sexual identity and gender roles are open to problematization. Cervantes's text can play on the Christian European reader's expectations of at least the threat of homosexuality among the Muslims. There is an offhand reference to Muslim sexual practices when Ricardo's first captor, the Greek Yzuf, trades Ricardo and "six Christians, four for rowing and two pretty boys from Corsica" to another arráez named Fetala in exchange for Leonisa (149). But the sexual desire that dominates *El amante liberal* is in general resolutely heterosexual, and it is equally resolutely ascribed to the Muslims of both sexes.

Leonisa is the principal object of heterosexual desire. Yzuf had shipwrecked and been killed off Pantelleria and his crew had sold her to a Jewish merchant. He brings her to Cyprus to sell, whereupon the outgoing pasha (Alí), his successor (Hasán), and the cadi all burn with desire for her. This desire will spiral out of control and ultimately overcome the multicultural Ottoman social order.

It is worth noting that after Yzuf's death, when Leonisa is still in the custody of the Muslims but is no longer the property of any of them, they make no attempt on her chastity; she seems not to exist for them as an object of sexual desire. Leonisa's narration of these events, however, teases both Ricardo and the reader, whose stereotypical expectations of Muslim rapacity and sexuality are automatically mobilized only to be denied. Her sentence begins: "'I didn't come to until I found myself on land, in the arms of two Turks who had me turned face down to the ground,'" to conclude that they were only "'forcing out the great quantity of water I had drunk.'" She summarizes: "'We were on the island a week, and all that time the Turks respected me as though I were their sister, and even moreso'" (171).

In fact, the only sexually ambiguous character in *El amante liberal* is the Sicilian Christian Cornelio, the only principal character who never leaves Europe. Cornelio's father is Ascanio Rotulo. Their two names together may have a historical resonance, suggested by a certain Ascanio de la Corna, who was co-commander (along with Alvaro de Sande) of the troops that landed on 7 September 1565 on Malta to reinforce the garrison of the Knights of Malta.[62] The same Ascanio de la Corna was named *maestre de campo general* of the Santa Liga, so he and Cervantes were both present at Lepanto. It is a name Cervantes probably heard, and it is possible that he even saw or actually knew Ascanio de la Corna.[63]

The fictional Cornelio mocks the character and career of Ascanio de la Corna. He is described by Ricardo: "'Cornelio, the son of Ascanio Rótulo: a gallant youth, all dressed up, with soft hands and curled hair, with a mellifluous voice and loving words, all made of sugar and spice, dressed in fine cloth and adorned with brocade" (143). Ricardo describes Cornelio to Leonisa: "'Entwine your ivy around that useless trunk; comb that new Ganimede's hair into ringlets, he who courts you so tepidly, that boy, made haughty by his wealth, arrogant by his good looks, inexperienced by reason of his tender age, confident because of his lineage'" (144). He says to Cornelio directly: "'You won't stand up to defend it because you're afraid you'll mess up the perfumed elegance of your fancy clothes. Go on, go enjoy yourself in the company of your mother's maids'" (145). Ricardo draws his (phallic) sword, whereupon Leonisa faints and Cornelio runs away in the confusion. After Ricardo and Leonisa are captured, the pirates offer them for ransom. "Cornelio, the pretty boy, was watching from a distance" (147). Ricardo offers his entire estate as Leonisa's ransom, "and Cornelio didn't even move his lips to help her" (148).[64]

Paul Julian Smith calls Cornelio the "substitute figure onto whom is displaced the sodomitical spectacle of the Turkish empire." This is correct as far as it goes: homosexuality is normally associated with the Muslim, not the Christian world.[65] The question is why this "sodomitical spectacle" should be displaced onto, or relocated into, Christian Europe, where it becomes problematical. Making the effeminate character a European erases an official stereotypical difference between Christian and Muslim. But at another level it mobilizes a stereotype anchored in the Spanish sanctification of purity. Consider the anonymous "Diálogo entre Laín Calvo y Nuño Rasura" (1570),[66] which makes it abundantly clear that sexual practices are indeed a marker of identity. Conversos are defined in opposition to Old Christians, and Italians in opposition to Spaniards, by their presumed homosexuality. The text evokes "Genoa and Florence, and those steps of Naples, where they practice that little pecadillo and eat of that filthy sodomitical fruit."[67]

Cervantes's text is replete with references to national origin, ethnicity, and religion, with their distinguishing names, their specific signifiers of dress and language, and other identifying marks such as how people define "home," or "ourselves" and "the others." But names and other signs can be ambiguous. Sometimes *turco* means 'Turk' as opposed to *moro*, which means 'North African,' while at other times *turco* means 'Muslim' as opposed to 'Christian.' Sometimes Turks/Muslims masquerade as Christians (e.g. Alí Pasha's galley, 207). Sometimes Christians masquerade as Turks/Muslims by cross-dressing (e.g. the returnees to Sicily, 211). Sometimes they are forced to cross-dress (Ricardo, Leonisa). Sometimes Turks are really Christians in spirit (Mahamut, Halima). But Halima, in spite of her Turkish name, is a Greek, not a Turk. But she is also a Turk in the sense of 'Muslim.' And Mahamut, in spite of his name (which isn't Turkish but Arabic), is an Italian. And both of them, in spite of their Muslim religion, are "really" Christians.

Ottmar Hegyi observes that Cervantes's use of the adjectives *cristianesco* and *turquesco* in conjunction with language and clothing reflects "a vision of the world where distinctions as to language, nationality, dress, social customs, and religion become frequently blurred."[68]

We have already remarked that all Cervantes's principals, on both sides of the religious divide, are Italian. Besides the obvious fictional characters, the Sicilians Ricardo, Leonisa, Cornelio, and Mahamut, it is surely significant that the two pashas, the Calabrese Alí and the Venetian Hasán, are also Italian. There is no correlation between national origin and religion. Of the six Italian characters in question, three are sincere Christians, two are sincere Muslims, and one (Mahamut) teeters on the brink.

Ricardo is introduced as "a Christian captive" (137); Mahamut is introduced as "a Turk" (138). We learn from Mahamut's discourse that this Christian and this Turk are both Trapanese. In addition to his national origin, Ricardo has what might be termed an "imperial" identity. He recalls "'my father: you already know how diligent he was, how he always served the emperor Charles V in honorable positions in war, and you heard how the emperor honored him'" (164). This brief throwaway further identifies Ricardo in terms of another category, as a *caballero*, an aristocratic warrior whose family had been in the imperial service. This identity might begin to account for his counterproductive reflex bellicose impetuosity. Ruth El Saffar considers this a moral defect Ricardo must purge during his captivity in order to become worthy of Leonisa.[69] I shall argue that what in fact allows him to triumph is his evolution out of that aristocratic warrior mindset to a bourgeois mentality grounded in principles of commodification, exchange, and shrewd bargaining.

Halima and Mahamut are converts from Christianity (Greek and Roman respectively) to Islam. At the end they both reconvert to Christianity. Their status in this fiction is nothing if not verisimilar. In a section entitled "Clothes Make the Muslim," Bartolomé and Lucile Bennassar provide the following description: "Baggy cloth trousers, white shirt, fitted vest. Over the vest a kind of tunic or caftan with elbow-length sleeves, reaching to mid-calf like a dressing gown, gathered at the waist with a red silk cord. Yellow shoes, no stockings. The head, shaved except for the *chufo*, topped by a red fez." They further observe that: "For the Inquisitors, the eastern Mediterranean dress is 'Turkish,' and constitutes ipso facto proof of belonging to the religion of Mohammed."[70]

Mahamut addresses the matter of his religion and its signifier, his clothing:

> "Fortune has brought me by this circuitous route to wear this habit, which I detest. . . . My burning desire is not to die in this state I seem to profess. When my time comes I'm going to confess and loudly proclaim the faith of Christ, which I was separated from by my youth and deficient understanding, even though I know that confession will cost me my life, because I consider the loss of my life a light price for the salvation of my soul." (139–40)

> "Even though my youth and the folly of wearing this habit is screaming at you not to trust me. . . ." (154)

There is an ambiguity between the outward and visible signs, his clothing, and his invisible religious faith. He is a convert still true to Christianity; this means that it is safe and acceptable for Ricardo to trust him. This situation and attitude accord perfectly with case after case documented by the Bennassars. The vast majority (78.42 percent) of the converts to Islam in their database arrived in Muslim lands and were sold into slavery before age twenty.[71] They remark how zealously the Muslims proselytized young Christian captives, in a deliberate effort to insert these newly Muslim children into a social system ready to absorb them. This was how the cosmopolitan societies of the Maghreb were constituted.

As to the credibility of Mahamut's assertions regarding the sincerity of his Christianity, there was the whole gamut of possibilities, from apparent total sincerity to the most obvious cynical lying, as in the case of Gutierre de Pantoja of Segovia. Like Mahamut, he was captured and converted while still a teenager. He lived as a Muslim for half a century and made a brilliant career in the highest reaches of the imperial Ottoman administration, and when he was captured by Christians he swore up and down that he had been waiting the entire fifty years for the right moment to defect. He also happened to be married to a Russian convert to Islam named Halima.[72] Mahamut is by no means inverisimilar.

The Bennassars also relate some anecdotes of improbable reunions after amazing lapses of time. The Amabile family, wealthy merchants from Messina, were on their way to Naples in 1585 or 1586 when they were captured by corsairs. The parents ransomed themselves out of captivity, but the corsairs refused to sell their youngest son, aged four, who converted and was raised as a Muslim. When he grew up he became a corsair, and was eventually captured by Christians. His mother recognized him among the *forzados* on a Spanish galley in Messina harbor in 1619. She spent the next three years arranging his freedom. Or there is the story of Don Hernando Alvarez de Ribera, regidor of Tenerife, and his family. He was returning from Brazil in 1635 with his wife and their newborn daughter when their ship was captured by corsairs. The three of them were sold to a certain Mohammed. The young mother died soon after, and Don Hernando stayed with his daughter and instructed her in the Christian faith. When she was about six years old, however, she converted to Islam under pressure from their master. Don Hernando was offered ransom, but he refused on the grounds that his daughter needed to be included in the package. He tried everything to get her out, including lobbying the pasha of Algiers, to no avail. He finally converted in order not to be separated from her.[73]

The fictional Halima, a name identified by the Bennassars as one frequently bestowed on slaves constrained to convert, is married to the cadi. She is first mentioned by Mahamut as "'Halima, the wife of his master the cadi'" (163). She is identified as "la mora" (163). Then the cadi clarifies: "'I'll have Halima visit her parents, who are Greek Christians'" (167). She insists on the sincerity of her Muslim faith, even in the company of her unconverted Christian parents: "'It doesn't matter if Leonisa is at my parents' home and talks to them, since I talk to them all the time and I'm still a good Muslim [*buena turca*]'" (168). This is exactly the situation described by Jennings with relation to Cyprus. It might be that Halima converted in order to marry the cadi. Her story is also similar to the following anecdote related by the Bennassars. At Stena a Turk falls in love with a certain young Giosefina and marries her. This Turk is a cadi who refuses to transgress Koranic law. He demands his young wife renounce her Christian faith and she agrees, "to make him happy."[74]

Later Halima plans to reconvert to Christianity, driven by her sexual desire for Ricardo: "And this with the desire to flee to Christian lands and return to what she had been, and marry Ricardo. She reasoned that if she were once again a Christian, and wealthy besides, he could not fail to marry her" (176). This recalls the case of a certain María de Tinos, who converted to Islam when she married a Turk on Chios. They were married nineteen years, until she ran away with a young Greek to the island of Tinos, where they were married in the Church.[75]

An anonymous *Relación de la gran presa que hicieron cuatro galeras de la Religión de San Juan* (1617) recounts an episode that evokes the multicultural Mediterranean world of *El amante liberal* in its various aspects: ethnicity, religion, clothing and language, the commerce in human beings, and the workings of the international financial system. It is worth quoting *in extenso*.

"Among the captives was an attractive young woman. When they brought her before the general she told him in Spanish that although she was dressed Turkish style, she and her husband were from Lisbon. The husband (who was in chains) was brought immediately. When he was asked why a Spaniard was dressed that way, he responded that although he and his wife had been born in Lisbon, they were the children of Jews, and when their parents were arrested, his wife's uncle sent them to Sevilla with more than seven thousand ducados in a bill of exchange. After four months they received word from Lisbon to proceed to Italy because their parents had negotiated very poorly with the Inquisition. They gave their money to a Genoese who gave them a bill of exchange for Genoa, and the two of them, she with her hair cut and dressed as a man, embarked for Genoa at Alicante. In Genoa they took a bill of exchange for Venice, where they lived for two years, whereupon they moved to Constantinople to live with a cousin of his father. The Portuguese woman, who was young and pretty and had been crying the entire time, told her husband to quit mixing lies with the truth, and turning to the general, she said: 'Sir, I have been deceived, because although I am the daughter of Jews I have always lived as a Christian. My father forced me to marry this man, even though I wanted to marry an Old Christian. Once I was married to him I began to love him, and love made me leave

Spain in this habit and accompany him to Venice. That was where the traitor told me we were going to Constantinople. He became a Muslim as soon as we got there, and the cadi forced me to renounce my faith as well, but in my heart I have God and His mother.' The general ordered that she be treated well, and sent the husband back into chains. And with that, order was given to the galleys to return to the coast of Caramania."[76]

The Ottoman world is multilingual. Haedo mentions three languages current in Algiers: Turkish, Arabic, and *lingua franca*. The *Viaje de Turquía* mentions just about every language current in Europe and around the Mediterranean basin as spoken in Istanbul. In *El amante liberal,* with its Sicilian/Cypriot context, there are references to Turkish, Arabic, Greek, *lingua franca,* and Italian. Ottmar Hegyi observes Cervantes's sensitivity to the multilinguistic environment, "showing a remarkable awareness of the problem language barriers can cause, by carefully indicating how it is overcome, or occasionally suggesting the frustration of a particular monolingual character who is not able to understand what is being said around him."[77]

The language being spoken by the characters is either *marked* (noted and named) or *unmarked,* as our colleagues in linguistics say. Since the Christian characters are all from Trapani, Italian is presumed to be the "default language" of their speech, although the text is in Spanish. That is, the text does not usually identify the language spoken or refer to any difficulties of comprehension. At other times the language spoken is marked.

Ricardo recounts that when Leonisa is first captured, "One of the Christian oarsmen told her in Italian that the arráez had ordered that Christian (pointing to me) to be hanged, because he had killed four of the best soldiers on the galley while he was defending himself. When Leonisa heard that she told the captive to tell the Turks not to hang me" (147).

When he and Leonisa are finally divided between Fetala and Ysuf, Ricardo reports: "And although I was present at all this, I couldn't understand what they were saying, although I knew what they were doing, nor would I have understood the division of captives if Fetala hadn't come up and told me in Italian" (149).

The ceremonies of transfer of power from Alí to Hasán Pasha are marked: "The Janissaries shouted in their language. . . . A few moments later the cadi came out of the tent and announced in Turkish, Arabic and Greek that all those who wished to enter and seek justice . . ." (156).

Mahamut addresses Leonisa in Italian, to identify himself as her countryman even though his clothing identifies him as a Turk. "On the way into the city Mahamut was able to ask Leonisa in Italian where she was from" (161).

Although Ricardo was present when Leonisa was bid on by the two pashas and delivered by Mahamut into the cadi's custody, he didn't understand what was happening. "'Although I couldn't understand what the pashas were talking about in the tent, as soon as you took Leonisa away I found out, from a Venetian renegade who belongs to my master and who understands the Turkish language well'" (165).

At the end of their first conversation at the cadi's, Leonisa remarks to Ricardo: "'I'm afraid Halima overheard us, and she understands the Christian language, or at least that mixture of languages we all use to understand each other'" (174). Since Halima was raised in a family of Greek-speaking Christians, the "Christian language" she *may* understand must refer specifically to Italian. That is, "lengua cristiana" really means "our language," since Greek is also a language of Christians.

It is difficult to discern a pattern in the alternation of marked and unmarked speech. What we have instead is a series of sporadic reminders of the multilingual environment and the consequent necessity for brokering communication through intermediaries.

Clothing is not only a signifier of religious identity. The religious identity presumed to inhere in the clothing is presumed to contain certain attitudes toward sexual practices. When Leonisa is offered for sale by the Jewish merchant she is dressed Algerian style, the better to ignite the local dignitaries' desire. "Her face was covered by a gauzy veil of scarlet silk. On her insteps, which were uncovered, you could see two *carcajes* (which is Arabic for 'anklet'), apparently of pure gold, and on her arms, which were also visible through a thin gauze, she wore more golden bracelets, sown with pearls" (157). The price asked for her turns out not to include the clothes she is wearing. And in fact the body and the clothes remit to two different identities: "A beautiful Christian . . . dressed in a Barbary habit" (157). The officially presumed chastity of the Christian maiden is suggestively offset by the presumed seductiveness of the Algerian clothing.

The identity markers of language, clothing, and religion all come together on the high sea, where the social and political harmony of the Ottoman world is shattered by desire run amok. When Alí Pasha sets out in pursuit of Leonisa, who is aboard the cadi's ship, he flies Christian flags and his men are cross-dressed as Christians: "he had had his soldiers dress as Christians, in order not to be recognized and to cover his crime with that ruse" (179). His apparently "Christian" ship prepares to attack Hasán's, which in turn is preparing to attack the cadi's. But before the battle starts, "from the prow [of the 'Christian' ship] someone asked in Turkish what ship that was" (179). Upon learning that it is Hasán Pasha's vessel the Turk asks: "'How is it that you Muslims are attacking that ship, when we know it is carrying the cadi of Nicosia?'" (178).

The signifier of clothing is suddenly eclipsed by religion. Here and two paragraphs later the strange word *mosolimán* occurs. It is the only term that unambiguously designates the religion only, that doesn't include any reference to ethnicity such as *turco* or *moro,* which may mean 'Muslim' but refer first to national origin or to ethnicity. The text calls attention to this unusual word when the cadi shouts: "'What is this, traitor Alí Pasha? How can you, a *mosolimán* (which means Turk) attack me like a Christian?'" (179). The narrator interrupts Alí's speech to translate the unfamiliar term.

Alí attacks the cadi and almost kills him, whereupon the cadi throws up to him his status as convert. "'Oh cruel renegade, enemy of my Prophet! How dare you, accursed one, lay hands and weapons on your cadi, on a minister of Mohammed?'" (180). The Muslim side is suddenly using the same divisive kinds of identity markers as the Christians. The Ottoman sociopolitical order grounded in multicultural pluralism is melting away. The men's intense desire for Leonisa has literally rent the political and social fabric of their world. We shall return to this crucial episode.

When Ricardo, Leonisa, Mahamut, Halima, and company are approaching Trapani there is another instance of cross-dressing: "While this was going on Ricardo had asked Leonisa to dress as she had been when she walked into the pashas' tent. . . . She did so, and adding finery to finery, pearls to pearls, and beauty to beauty, which is usually heightened by happiness, she decked herself out so that once again she was a wonder and a marvel to behold. Ricardo also dressed Turkish style, as did Mahamut and all the Christian oarsmen" (183–84).

When the good citizens of Trapani see the turbans (synechdoche for 'Muslim dress,' standing metonymically for 'Muslims'), they go on alert. But when the ship reaches land, the gangplank is lowered, and the passengers disembark and kiss the ground, it is a "clear sign that it was Christians who had seized that ship" (184). And in fact, the coming ashore is suddenly transformed into a religious procession: "One by one, as in a procession, they all walked onto dry land, which they kissed over and over again with tears in their eyes. . . . Last off were Halima's parents and her two nephews, all dressed Turkish style, as we have said. And last of all came the beautiful Leonisa, her face covered by a gauzy veil of scarlet silk. She was flanked by Ricardo and Mahamut, and the spectacle stole the eyes of that infinite multitude that was watching them" (184).

Here we have a group of people dressed Turkish style coming ashore and acting out first a Christian religious procession, and then the cast at the end of a theatrical performance coming onstage in ascending order of importance to take a final bow. The clothing calls attention to Leonisa's beauty hybridized by her Moorish *galas,* and the reader is expected to recall the effect she had on the cadi and the two pashas when she was similarly attired. There is a contrast between that earlier effect—the eruption of sexual desire so powerful that it tears the sociopolitical fabric—and this one, all *muestras de alegría* and joyous but desexualized reunion. The same dress worn on the two different occasions indeed recalls the previous situation and the destructive effect of desire.

Theresa Ann Sears has written: "In the *Novelas ejemplares,* the loss of the truth of desire is the price of order, both social and literary. In *El amante liberal,* we can trace how the narrative overlooks the cost, and ratifies the imposition of order."[78] What happens in Sicily is an attenuated or corrected version of what happens on Cyprus and at sea. Desire is ubiquitous, acted out in tandem by Muslims and Christians. The Muslim men's desire run amok dissolves the order of their pluralistic sociopolitical order into violence. In the final scene among Christians, as Sears demonstrates, violence is avoided, and order maintained, by the sacrifice of the truth of desire. In a roundabout way, however, this tandem act demonstrates again how alike the Christian and Muslim spheres really are. The demonstration of this similarity is the result of Leonisa's appearance wearing her sexy Muslim *galas* as she steps off the ship in Christian Trapani.

<hr />

The differences between the Christian and Muslim spheres seem to lie chiefly in the realm of ideology and official rhetoric. Christian Europe, with Spain in the lead, is the champion of stasis and hierarchy embodied in patrilineal succession, and of purity in all its forms: racial, sexual, religious, and linguistic. The pluralistic Muslim side is openly what the Spanish side is only in secret and permanently attempting to deny. This rhetorical-ideological distinction allows Ottoman-Algerian society to proclaim its diversity as a virtue and become dynamic, while on the Spanish side the official denial of the same diversity is a perpetual obstacle to social harmony and material progress.

Let us heed the words of Fernand Braudel: "Islam and Christendom faced each other along the north-south divide between the Levant and the western Mediterranean, a line running from the shores of the Adriatic to Sicily and then on to the coast of present-day Tunisia. All the great battles between Christians and Infidels were fought on this line. But merchant vessels sailed across it every day. . . . The economy, all-invading, mingling together currencies and commodities, tended to promote unity of a kind in a world where everything else seemed to be conspiring to create clearly-distinguished blocs."[79]

It appears that men on both sides of the dividing line between Christians and Muslims were participants in the same economy, engaged in the same practices, and motivated by the same material considerations. Ciro Manca observes the mutual economic interdependence of the Christian and Muslim worlds, and considers it a function of the maturation of the corsair economy in North Africa simultaneous with the rise of mercantilism and banking in Europe.[80] The commodification of human beings was pervasive. The redeeming religious orders worked closely with merchant-bankers, through whose hands passed not only physical safe-conducts for themselves and their possessions but also authorization for all the long-distance financial operations necessary for the redemption of captives. Thanks to these same European merchant-bankers, the corsair economy of Algiers joined the circuit of European financial capitalism. The conditions governing the activities of professional redeemers of captives made specific allowance for trade in other commodities as well, in order to "facilitate the closest association of the sale of human and non-human merchandise."[81] The conditions of trade in other commodities between Algerian and European merchants described by Haedo, which we saw in our discussion of the captive captain's story, suggest that the official international political order, organized around national and religious antagonism, was undercut and in effect superseded by international commerce, which took precedence over the politico-religious oppositions. Manca remarks the "relative ease with which we can follow the routes that connect European and North African markets after Lepanto."[82]

Commerce in merchandise is minimal in *El amante liberal.* The stock of the Jewish merchant described by Leonisa is perhaps the only example: "'The Moors received us on their ship, on which a wealthy Jewish merchant was also travelling. All the merchandise on the ship, or most of it, was his: different kinds of textiles and other things they take from North Africa to the Levant'" (172).

What is particularly visible in the text is the commodification of humans, in particular our two protagonists. Ricardo is defined as a commodity in the traditional sense, in terms of exchange-value. It is actually Leonisa who commodifies him first. In an effort to save him from imminent execution she lets it be known that he has a high exchange-value: "She told the captive to tell the Turks not to hang me, because they would be losing a great ransom, and she begged them to return to Trapani, where I would be ransomed at once" (147). Ricardo is initially appraised at four thousand escudos (147), which his *mayordomo* manages to whittle down to three thousand (148), and is finally sold for two thousand (149). Much later he is presented gratis by Hasán Pasha to the cadi, although Hasán considered him worth two thousand escudos (175–76).

Ricardo is taken to Tripoli, where upon Fetala's death he is inherited by the viceroy, Hasán Pasha, who is then called to be viceroy of Cyprus, which accounts for Ricardo's presence there. "The viceroy of Tripoli and the sultan's warden of the dead divided my master Fetala's possessions, for the sultan is also the heir of those who die without heirs. I fell to the viceroy, and two weeks later he received the commission of viceroy of Cyprus. Since I had no intention of trying for ransom, he brought me here" (153). The same thing happens to Ruy Pérez de Viedma: "His captives, which at his death were about 3,000, were divided between the sultan, who is also the son and heir of all who die and shares in the inheritance with the other sons of the deceased, and his renegades" (*Don Quixote* I, 40, 271). Ricardo attempts to play down his value as commodity: "My master has told me many times to get myself ransomed, because I am an important man. I have never attempted to, and in fact I have told him that he was mistaken about my possibilities" (153). He prefers to remain in captivity and subject himself to constant suffering, in an effort to bring his life to a close (153).

The case of Leonisa offers something different. Marginalist economic theory, whose covert libidinous foundation has been excavated by Jean-Joseph Goux, offers a conception of value more closely attuned to the process of her commodification in Cervantes's text. In Goux's description of marginalist theory,

> *desire* is what opens and determines the economic register. . . . The element of labor plays no role. . . . Economic value . . . is no longer divided between exchange and use: there exists a single desire-value that is in principle subjective, variable, ephemeral. . . . To create value, all that is necessary is, by whatever means possible, to create a sufficient intensity of desire. . . . To define value by the intensity of desire or the anticipation of *jouissance* is, in the end, to reduce economic value to attraction value or libidinal value, to press one upon the other until they merge not structurally but substantially.[83]

This is what is at work in the commodification of Leonisa, including the rich, sexy clothing that intensifies the desire of the men who contemplate her. Leonisa is constituted as a commodity because she is the object of desire; her commodification obeys the logic of marginalist economic theory. Phrased another way, her price is a function of the testosterone level around her.

Marginalist theory would appear to be an evolved form of traditional "utility" theory, in which value is determined by *raritas* (scarcity), *virtuositas* (the ability to satisfy a human need or want), and *complacibilitas* (the appeal to the individual taste of a purchaser). Cervantes's contemporaries were debating in these very terms the question of how the just price of a commodity is determined, or in what its value consists. In 1547 Luis Saravia de la Calle offered what Marjorie Grice-Hutchinson calls "an extreme form of utility theory." He maintained that in order to determine the just price we need only consider three things: abundance or scarcity of goods, merchants, and money. This doctrine is founded on Aristotle's dictum: *pretium rei humana indigentia mensurat* (the price of things is measured by human need). Saravia denies that the cost of production can play any part in the determination of price. Like his medieval predecessors, he views the poor man not as producer but as consumer, and clearly fears that any relaxation of this tenet will give merchants an excuse for raising prices on the pretext of recouping their expenses.[84]

What this means is that it isn't necessary to give Cervantes credit for anticipating concepts that Goux, for one, considers a function of specific changes in modes of production and signification that occurred in the late nineteenth century. The basis of marginalist theory was already around long before Smith and Marx came into the world. One might say either that Cervantes makes explicit and conscious the connection between libido and market value, or, with a nod to the modern economists, that the connection that was conscious and visible to Cervantes and his contemporaries had gone underground and needed to be brought into consciousness by Goux's reading of marginalist theory.

In any case, Leonisa offers a conflation of the normal categories of use- and exchange-value into a libidinally determined "desire-value." She is repeatedly and relentlessly commodified by everyone else and by herself. Her commodification begins with the auction by Yzuf following her initial capture. The offers and counteroffers are explicit in the text, with the quantities always mentioned. First, Ricardo offers his entire estate for Leonisa's ransom, but Yzuf wants Leonisa for himself. "Yzuf asked 6,000 escudos for Leonisa, and 4,000 for me, adding that he would not sell one without the other" (147). He asked such a high price because he was supposed to divide all spoils equally with Fetala, the captain of the second pirate galley. He planned to give Ricardo, plus one thousand escudos in cash for a total of five thousand to Fetala, and buy Leonisa with the other five thousand. Ricardo's agent succeeds in bringing the price down—"after several offers and counteroffers my majordomo got him down to 5,000 for Leonisa and 3,000 for me" (148)—but the pirates are forced to leave before the cash can be assembled. This is only the first of a series of deals, all narrated with great attention to the details of pricing and haggling. The process of commodification is total; use-, exchange-, and desire-value are explicitly evoked in the text. Yzuf finally gives the other captain six male captives (four for rowing and two "muchachos hermosísimos"), plus Ricardo, in exchange for Leonisa, whom he intends to convert to Islam and marry. When he discovers that Leonisa still belongs to Yzuf, Ricardo tells Fetala to offer ten thousand for her, hoping to redefine her in terms of exchange-value, but she is no longer for sale (149).

When Leonisa shows up on Cyprus as the merchandise of "a venerable Jew" the price is set at "4,000 Algerian doblas, which are 2,000 Spanish escudos"

(158). Notice that Leonisa is worth three thousand escudos less on this market than she was back home. This time the price stays firm; the question is who offered it first. Alí gets his bid in first, whereupon Hasán invokes a ploy—he will buy her as a present for the sultan. Alí counters that that had been his plan too, because "as a man left without a job, I need to find ways of getting one." The cadi, who is also a bidder, but in secret, proposes that Alí and Hasán each pay two thousand doblas, or half the price, and then relinquish Leonisa to his custody. Underneath the discussion is desire-value. On the surface is a form of exchange-value, within the context of a presumably corrupt political system. Use-value surfaces, but displaced onto the sultan: "For the use of her is reserved for the sultan, for whom she was purchased. It is up to him to dispose of her" (159). The rhetoric of the text invites the reader, especially the Spanish reader of 1613, to apply the stereotypes and read these Muslim political and religious leaders as corrupt and venal. This invitation is enhanced by the narrator's observation that Ricardo was anguished to see "his soul on the auction block" (160). The juxtaposition of auction block with soul identifies Ricardo's interest as pure, in contrast with the Muslims' sordid commodification. And yet in the same sentence Leonisa is called Ricardo's *querida prenda,* a cliché that reifies the beloved and converts her into a possession. Leonisa narrates her own commodification at the hands of the Jewish merchant. "'The Turks took the same ship to Tripoli, and on the way they sold me to the Jew, who paid 2,000 doblas for me. It was an excessive price, except for the love the Jew revealed to me. Leaving the Turks in Tripoli, the ship proceeded on its way, and the Jew began shamelessly to importune me. I gave him the answer his disgusting desires deserved. Finding himself rejected, he decided to get rid of me at the first opportunity'" (172).

The merchant as narrated by Leonisa is the first *amante liberal* who appears in the text, and he is distinguished by his ability to separate desire- and exchange-value. Leonisa and her clothing are a single commodity as defined by desire, according to the logic of marginalism. The sexy clothing serves to intensify the desire of the prospective buyers: "'And knowing that the two pashas Alí and Hasán were on this island, where he could sell his merchandise as well as on Chio, where he had planned to sell it, he came here with the intention of selling me to one of the two pashas. And this was why he dressed me the way you see, to increase their desire to possess me'" (172). At the same time, she and her clothing can be uncoupled into two separate commodities. After getting his asking price for Leonisa, the merchant anounces that the price doesn't include her fine clothing and jewelry, "because all that was worth another 2,000 doblas, and that was the truth" (160). And in fact, the bystanders opine that "the price the Jew asked for the clothes was too low" (160). Leonisa's body retains its desire-value; the underpriced clothing is redefined in terms of exchange-value.

It turns out Leonisa was only worth two thousand doblas to this buyer. More importantly, she is such a mindless participant in her own commodification that she volunteers the opinion that the price was too high, that she isn't worth two thousand doblas: "'The Jew paid 2,000 doblas for me, an excessive price'" (172). This means that when Ricardo manipulates her into commodifying herself at the end, he is taking advantage of her preexisting autocommodification, as it is revealed here. He reads her just as Celestina reads Melibea.

An amazingly callous commodification is proposed hypothetically to Leonisa by Mahamut, who is attempting to ascertain whether she loves Ricardo. One of his gambits is to suggest that an unnamed Christian who was once "somewhat" in love with her would be willing to pay a pittance for her ransom. "He would be happy to find her and ransom her, if her owner had come to understand she wasn't as rich as he had thought, although perhaps because he had possessed her he held her in less esteem anyway. He would pay up to 300 or 400 escudos for her, because at one time he had been somewhat attracted to her" (162).

Instead of being offended, even when Mahamut drops the price because the merchandise is now used, Leonisa responds from within the discourse of the market. She does not question her status as commodity, only the price and the buyer. "It must have been a very little attraction if it was only worth 400 escudos. Ricardo is more generous, more gallant, and more courteous" (162–63).

The Muslim commodifiers are pikers compared to Christian Ricardo. At first he is willing to pay everything he has; later he offers a cool ten thousand escudos for Leonisa. The first price agreed upon is five thousand, but by the time she gets into the big leagues of Muslim buyers she is worth only two thousand. It might be argued that Ricardo's commodification of Leonisa is pure, that he doesn't want to sell her or use her sexually, only to help her, that he is willing to give his all in order to save her from a fate worse than death, and so on, and the text appears to support this interpretation. But if we recall that Leonisa is defined as a commodity by desire and that Ricardo has always desired her, we can relocate his apparently selfless efforts within the market economy, and in the process relocate him in the company of the merchant, the two pashas, and the cadi.

What happened on Cyprus was the commodification of Leonisa according to the logic of marginalist theory, specifically as an object of desire, and her being bid on by a series of men who desire her. As we shall see, the same thing occurs in Trapani, except that this time one of the bidders controls the auction by pretending to be disinterested. The sexy Moorish finery Leonisa wears on both occasions allows us to relate the commercial aspect of the two scenes, just as it recalls the desire present on both occasions.

Desire-value is not limited to physical objects such as bodies and clothing. The repeated expressions of a desire for narration, of narrative as the object of desire, and of offers to satisfy desire by narrating, suggest that narrative itself may be defined as a commodity with a desire-value.

Mahamut says to Ricardo during their first encounter, "'I beg you to tell me what the real cause is, and I offer you everything I have'" (139). Ricardo says to Mahamut on the same occasion: "'And so you'll be satisfied that this is the truth, I'll tell you in the fewest words possible. But before I do that I want you to tell me why Hasán Pasha has put up those tents and pavilions'" (140).

After Leonisa appears on Cyprus with the Jewish merchant, Ricardo asks him for a narration. He gets only a teaser, then the merchant is called away to narrate what Ricardo (and we) desire, but to someone else, offstage. The narration of these events finally falls to Leonisa herself, and the relation of desire to narrative becomes explicitly involved with exchanges and transactions. Ricardo agrees to play along with Leonisa so Halima can hear what she desires to hear, but in exchange he desires/demands the narration from her. His little speech is loaded with exchanges, payments, and gifts, all in the service of satisfying desire: "'I'll satisfy your desire and Halima's by dissembling, as you say, if by doing so I can gain the profit of seeing you. So you make up whatever answers you please, and from this day on my feigned will signs and seals them. And in repayment of what I'm doing for you, which is about all I think I can do, even if I were to give you again this soul I've already given you so many times, I beg you to tell me briefly how you escaped from the hands of the corsairs and came into those of the Jew who sold you'" (170). The subject of the desired narration itself will be a series of sales transactions.

A set of equivalencies or at least analogies begins to emerge here between desire and captivity, gratification and freedom. These correspondences are worked out in various ways. Gratification is first a reward for services. A *merced*, the opposite of modern economic practices, is offered by the cadi to both Mahamut and Ricardo/Mario if the seduction of Leonisa is successful. The proposal is to exchange the cadi's sexual desire (for Leonisa) for Mahamut's and Ricardo's desire (for freedom).

Leonisa tells Halima that Ricardo desires her even more than she desires him, but he must wait two weeks before he can gratify her, because he needs to pray to God to grant him liberty. Halima would grant Ricardo liberty before the "término devoto," if he would only grant her her desire, and she offers whatever the cadi was asking for his ransom (174).

The parallel relations of Halima-Leonisa-Ricardo and Cadi-Ricardo-

Leonisa, with Leonisa and Ricardo reciprocally brokering their masters' interest in the other, acts out at the level of sexual desire the pattern of exchange through intermediary that is typical of the general economy. Ricardo's summary brings these elements together. The rhetoric of sensual desire and gratification alternates with the discourse of brokerage and exchange:

> "I now hold dearer this glorious instant of looking at you than any other good fortune my desire could grant me in life or death. My master the cadi's desire for you is the same as Halima's for me. He has given me the job of brokering his intentions. I accepted the commission for the pleasure I would gain in being able to speak to you, so that you can see, Leonisa, the end to which our misfortunes have brought us: you to be the mediator in an enterprise you know is impossible, and I to be the middleman in one I would give my life not to succeed in." (172–73)

The libidinous desire of Halima and the cadi is not only parallel, but one "recompenses" (another economic technicism) the other: "Halima was locked in her room, praying to Mohammed . . . . The cadi was in the mosque recompensing his wife's desires with his own" (174).

We have seen that the three Muslim men experience gut-wrenching sexual desire for Leonisa, which results in violence and death, and finally in the disintegration of the multicultural values of Ottoman society. Hasán Pasha, "whom love had not allowed a moment's rest, was trying to think what he could do to avoid dying at the hand of his own desire" (176). The cadi "wanted only to get it over with quickly, to be rid of his wife and to put out the fire that was consuming his belly" (177). Alí Pasha is so "in love with Leonisa" (179) that he actually attempts to kill the cadi: "Only Alí closed his eyes and his ears to everything, and charging at the cadi, gave him such a knife thrust to the head that, had it not been for the hundred yards of turban wrapped around it, would have sliced it in two" (180).

In the ensuing battle the desires of the three Muslim men for Leonisa cancel each other out with almost mathematical precision, whereupon a settling of accounts occurs. Halima is offered a return trip to Cyprus and only half the riches she had brought with her. But she, who still desires Ricardo, chooses instead "to go with them to Christian lands, which pleased her parents no end" (181). The text effaces the financial advantage of her choice, insisting instead on its religious-erotic aspect and on the approbation of her still-Christian parents, but by mentioning the unfavorable terms of the return to Cyprus, allows the reader to do the arithmetic.

The cadi is offered captivity in Sicily or a return trip to Cyprus. He chooses his freedom, and decides to proceed to Constantinople to denounce the two pashas' scandalous behavior to the sultan. But when he discovers he has lost

Halima "he practically lost his mind" (181). It is difficult to reconcile this with his plan to murder her and the earlier statement that "he wanted to be free of her more than of death" (175). And he finally sails not for Constantinople but for Cyprus. He is suddenly transformed from a politically ambitious, ethically unscrupulous old lecher into a sympathetic cuckold, who "with tears in his eyes, stood watching as the wind carried away his property, his pleasure, his wife and his soul" (182). I am reminded of the sympathetic portrayal of Hajji Murad, left alone on the beach when Zoraida "escapes" to Christian Spain in the company of Ruy Pérez de Viedma in *Don Quixote,* part I, chapter 41. Both episodes seem to point up the ambiguities and the price, in human terms, of what is presumed to be the goal of all those trapped in Muslim lands, the triumphant return to "tierra de cristianos."

The presumed Muslim practice of commodification of people turns out to be the key to the dénouement once everyone has returned safely to Christian Sicily. Leonisa is manipulated into commodifying herself, and her marriage to Ricardo is presented as a fair-exchange business deal. Ricardo begins by attempting to commodify her in the normal way, as an object of exchange among men, by offering her to Cornelio. Then comes the ploy. He publicly comes to the realization, the theatricality of which has been admirably analyzed by Gonzalo Díaz Migoyo, Georges Güntert, and especially by Theresa Ann Sears, that he cannot give Leonisa to Cornelio because she is not his to give.[85] And if she believes she has obligations to him (he did deliver her from captivity, after all), he declares, in the discourse of double entry bookkeeping: "'from this moment I erase them, I cancel them and I consider them null'" (186). He thus acknowledges their existence as debts, and he inscribes them in an imaginary ledger, where he can then cancel them. He also makes a public donation to her of his entire estate, which he values at approximately thirty thousand escudos, whereupon she declares herself his possession: "'My will, until now retiring, perplexed and in doubt, declares itself in your favor, demonstrating that I at least am grateful, so that men may see that not all women are ingrates. I am yours, Ricardo, and I shall remain yours until death'" (187).

Ricardo recognizes that he cannot give Leonisa to Cornelio because he does not own her, not yet. But he can buy her; he can manipulate her into commodifying and then offering herself for sale to him alone. The lesson Ricardo finally learns is that commercial acumen works better than either the effeminate passivity of Cornelio or his own former supermacho aggressivity. Pierre Bourdieu writes: "There are only two ways of getting and keeping a lasting hold over someone: debts and gifts, the overtly economic obligations imposed by the usurer, or the moral obligations and emotional attachments created and maintained by the generous gift, in short, overt violence or symbolic violence, censored, euphemized, that is, misrecognizable, recognized violence."[86] Exactly; Ricardo's act of apparent abnegation is in fact an act of "misrecognizable violence."

Gonzalo Díaz Migoyo and Theresa Ann Sears have seen that Leonisa's "choice" is illusory, as Sears points out, "since Ricardo's carefully constructed rhetoric allows her no other option than to choose him."[87] I would insist, within this general framework, on the specifically commercial nature of this rhetoric and the choices it permits: Ricardo offers Leonisa no choice but to commodify herself.

Sears observes that the happy ending does violence to what she calls "the truth of desire": "Cervantes writes to close the space of desire, to block its tendency to move beyond the order of the text. . . . The formula that 'todos quedaron contentos, libres y satisfechos' denies unsatisfied desire, and cuts off the possibility of further narrative."[88] It is not clear whether Sears believes that closure has finally been reached, that sexual and narrative desire have been brought under control by the omnipotent author's imposed fiat, or whether some residue of unsatisfied desire remains.

What is reported as satisfied at the end is something vague and unspecified. Desire is absent from the text: "Everyone, in short, ended up happy, free, and satisfied" (216). Ricardo's generosity, or *liberalidad,* assures the material well-being of Halima's parents and her nephews. The desire for narration is in some sense satisfied, both intra- and extradiegetically. Otherwise the characters would never find out about each other and be able to resolve their problems, and there would be no text for us to read. Ricardo's liberalidad is also the agent of the satisfaction of the reader's desire, in the sense that the conventions of romance (and we know that's what this story is) demand that Ricardo get Leonisa, that they marry and live happily ever after. And thanks to Ricardo's liberalidad he does get Leonisa and everything does turn out the way we wanted it to.

However, because the liberalidad is really only a ploy to manipulate Leonisa, by engaging not her desire but her sense of fairness and duty, our sense of narrative satisfaction, of closure, of everything coming out right, is not quite as full as it might be. And sexual desire too remains unsatisfied.

Halima's is forcibly displaced from Ricardo onto the available Mahamut: "Thwarted in her desire to be Ricardo's wife, she contented herself with becoming Mahamut's" (215–16). Halima's desire is still frustrated, in the sense that Mahamut is a poor substitute for Ricardo. And because the word *deseo* is present in the text, desire is (literally) still there, imperfectly satisfied.

Ricardo's desire for Leonisa, present at the beginning in his overtly phallic behavior, has been displaced onto commercial activity. For her part, Leonisa had already transformed herself into a commodity when she sold herself to Ricardo in exchange for his services and his money, that is, his *liberalidad*. Her subjectivity is effaced as surely as Preciosa's following her reintegration into the patriarchal order in *La Gitanilla*. What remains is Leonisa's use-value, in the form of her reproductive capacity, and in fact Ricardo "had many children in Leonisa." Seen metaphorically in terms of capitalism's master trope of investment as insemination, these *muchos hijos* are returns on Ricardo's investment.

Like *La española inglesa*, which we shall consider next, *El amante liberal* is frequently stigmatized as a Byzantine romance in miniature, with the implication that it has no referent other than a particularly artificial literary genre. We have seen that this is not entirely accurate. The shifts in place from Trapani to Nicosia by way of Tripoli and return, the improbable coincidences, the people who turn up in unlikely places after having been presumed lost, the commodification and exchange of human beings, the communication brokered across linguistic differences, the cross-dressing, the conversions to Islam and reconversions to Christianity, all turn out to be quite plausible in the late sixteenth century. It is only our ignorance of history that enables us to miscategorize Cervantes's text. Within this verisimilar circumstantial context Cervantes offers a meditation on the vagaries of national, religious, and ethnic identity, and on the respective value of Hapsburg and Ottoman institutions and practices, including the question of purity and exclusion as opposed to multicultural pluralism. He offers different models of masculinity: the overly aggressive Ricardo who contrasts with the effeminate Cornelio at the beginning, the destructively phallic pashas, the scheming cadi who also falls victim to his own libido, the Jewish merchant who has sense enough to distinguish between desire- and exchange-value, and the finally successful Ricardo who subordinates his inherited aristocratic warrior mentality to newly acquired business acumen as the means by which desire may be satisfied.

# 7

## *La española inglesa* and Protestant England

In *El amante liberal* Cervantes gives us ideological antagonism played off against commercial rapprochement in the Mediterranean context of Christians and Muslims, identified with the Hapsburg and the Ottoman empires respectively. In *La española inglesa* there is a similar set of relations, this time between Catholics and Protestants in Hapsburg Spain and Elizabethan England. In both stories the true faith exists clandestinely in a hostile environment, defined either as Muslim or Protestant. In both stories the happy ending will consist in the members of the true faith escaping from the hostile environment and returning in triumph to live happily ever after in the lands of the Roman Church.

Ruth El Saffar and Alban Forcione consider *La española inglesa* and *El amante liberal* as the two purest examples of cervantine "romance," in the sense of inverismilar, idealized fiction in the service of an accepted official ideology.[1] Rafael Lapesa and Stanislav Zimic read both stories as miniature versions of Byzantine romance in particular, with heavy indebtedness to Heliodorus.[2] And, in the unkindest cut of all, Manuel Durán has called *La española inglesa*, with its wealth of traditional motifs, its wild shifts in place, its improbable coincidences, and its unswerving insistence on Catholic virtue, a "Golden Age soap opera."[3]

In fact, like all the other texts we have examined, this story is immediately and profoundly concerned with real historical, social, and economic issues. It constitutes perhaps Cervantes's clearest statement of the dialectic of aristocratic and bourgeois values. Finally, the utopian happy ending of *La española inglesa* brings it back from the great socioeconomic issues of early modern Europe and relocates it within the genre of inverisimilar romance where El Saffar and Forcione had originally placed it. They attribute the happy ending to the perceived unifying force of Roman Catholicism and abstract notions of goodwill and true love that are presumed to flow from it. I divide the happy ending into two phases. In the first, realistic phase, ideological differences between Protestant England and Catholic Spain are overcome not by the universality of a religion that calls itself Catholic, but by international commerce and banking. The utopian aspect of the dénouement consists in the public recognition of the legitimacy of international commerce and the probably *converso* business community within the socio-ideological structures peculiar to Spain.

We can begin by situating the characters and action of *La española inglesa* within history writ large and small. The names of Cervantes's characters recall those of the principals in the great political-religious historical drama of the sixteenth century: the English schism and the evolution of Anglo-Spanish political relations that resulted from it. The heroine's name, "Isabela," is an anglicized version of the Spanish form of the name of the English queen with whom she interacts and who is also an important character in the text. "Isabel" is also the name of the wife of Fernando el Católico and mother of Catalina de Aragón, who is the mother of Mary Tudor and mother-in-law of Felipe II, but whose failure to produce a male child provoked the English schism in the first place. "Catalina" is the name of the fictive Isabela's adoptive mother in England, who by the end of the story has become her mother-in-law. This Catalina-Isabel relation is reflected or at least refracted in that of Cervantes's wife Catalina de Palacios and his natural daughter Isabel de Saavedra.

This connection was observed by José María Asensio y Toledo.[4] It was elaborated by Norberto González Aurioles,[5] but debunked by González de Amezúa, who concludes: "I do not believe Cervantes had them in mind at all as he wrote this novel."[6] This gratuitous and undocumented observation is lodged within a series of coincidences between Cervantes's and Ricaredo's liberations from captivity, whose "autobiographical reminiscences" Amezúa is happy to point out. Even making maximum allowance for coincidence, it seems safe to conclude that Cervantes knew at least as well as Juliet what's in a name, and that the names of his characters evoked for the Spanish reader of 1613 a half-century of conflictive relations with England.

The fictional text in which these significantly named characters exist begins with a real historical event, the sack of Cádiz by the English under Essex and Howard in 1596. Ricaredo serves at sea under a certain "barón de Lansac," and indeed there was at Queen Elizabeth's court a Seigneur de Lansac, whose duties remain unclear but who is known to have been friendly with Howard and other notables.[7] Surely this is enough to enable us to conclude that *La española inglesa* is concerned at least in some way with real history. With this in mind it seems worthwhile to consider the raid on Cádiz as the historical and fictional starting point.

The Cádiz expedition was a major undertaking, one of the great naval operations of the early modern period. The fleet that set sail in June 1596 was, in Robert W. Kenny's words, the "largest ever sent from England on a mission of aggression—some 120 ships in all."[8] Luis Cabrera de Córdoba puts the number at 140.[9] The great armada of 1588, by comparison, was composed of 130 vessels.

The attack was announced beforehand, in a proclamation dated 25 April 1596, signed by Essex and Howard and published in English, Spanish, Dutch, French, Italian, and Latin. I quote briefly from the English version:

> To all Christian people . . . greeting. We Robert, Earle of Essex . . . and Charles Lorde Howard, Baron of Effingham, Lord High Admiral of England, having charge of a Royall Navy of ships, prepared and sent to . . . serve on the Seas, for defence of her Majestie's Realmes, Dominions and Subjects, against such mightie forces, as we are advertised from all partes of Christendom, to be already prepared by the King of Spaine, . . . to invade her Majestie's Realmes: as heretofore in the yeere of our Lord 1588 was attempted . . . with a greater Army than ever before in his time was sent to the Seas: though by God's goodnesse, and the valour and wisdome of her Noble and faithful Subjects, the same was notably made frustrate.[10]

The Cádiz raid was advertised as a massive preemptive strike. In fact, it is well known now and could not have escaped the English "intelligencers" at the time that no Spanish armada was being readied to invade England, and that the vessels in Cádiz harbor comprised the merchant fleet preparing to sail for America with some eleven million ducados' worth of merchandise on board, together with the customary military escort. Kenny suggests that the original idea for the raid "probably belongs to Antonio Pérez, who in 1595 convinced the Lord Admiral that the attack should fall on Cádiz, a city at once strategic and vulnerable."[11]

The contemporary chronicler and historian Luis Cabrera de Córdoba makes it clear that the raid was foreseen and what its objective was. His account begins to raise questions concerning the wisdom of the defensive tactics employed, but curiously stops short of indicting the Duque de Medina Sidonia, who bore final responsibility: "In the month of June, 140 vessels set sail from England, under the command of Admiral Charles Howard, and of the Count of Essex, the general on land. Their aim was to plunder the riches the fleets were bringing from the Spanish and Portuguese Indies, and the ships ready to sail for New Spain under the order of the American-trade merchants, and if time permitted, to attack and sack Cádiz. This was already known to the king's chamberlain Francisco Sermite, a Fleming, who had been notified in order to prepare the defense of Cádiz."[12]

Cabrera further states that before they could begin the attack, the English had to show themselves on the horizon and wait for a favorable wind, thus giving the defenders some hours' warning at least. He also insists that if the Spanish fleet had sailed out and engaged the English on the open sea, the battle would have gone the other way.

None of this happened, however, and the battle was lost. Our interest centers on the sack of the city and the treatment of the civilian population. The detailed eyewitness account of Fray Pedro de Abreu offers a corrective to the generally held impression of English magnanimity and good manners. Things began well enough, it is true: "The English generals promised safe conduct to all the townspeople without holding any for ransom. All the friars, nuns, and other women were also to be allowed to leave without offense to their person, until they were safely away. To this end it was announced that no one was to dishonor or mistreat the women nor take from them what they were permitted to carry, on pain of death."[13]

This is corroborated from the English side by the eyewitness account of Sir William Slingsby: "Order was given to put forth the inhabitants of the town of all sorts. Those of the meaner quality were sent over the Puente de Suazo with good guard, to pass over into the mainland. Those of the better sort, and especially the gentlewomen, were by commandment from the Lords Generals honourably entreated and conducted to the waterside to be embarked for St. Mary Port, which course continued until there were no Spanish inhabitants left in the town."[14]

Abreu reports that on the first day sacking was reserved to the aristocrats among the English, "a courtly and well-mannered group, who if they were not infected with heresy would have merited the thanks of their victims, on whom they declined to inflict a thousand injuries they might have." The second day, when the ordinary soldiers participated, was very different:

> The sacking proceeded with so much impiety and ferocity that it seemed all the infernal legions had conspired against Cádiz. They stole everything they could find in the houses, they knocked down walls, they threatened men and women, holding naked swords to their throats and tying them with cords as though they were about to hang them. They undressed the women to see if they were hiding anything of value, and if their clothes were of good quality they took them as well, leaving some in their undergarments and some completely unclothed.[15]

From the first moment confusion had reigned among the inhabitants. Abreu's account is graphic, and some of its details bear directly on Cervantes's story: "Everyone was frightened seeing such a powerful enemy at their doors. Young women were running here and there, undressed and bareheaded, without the reserve that chastity demands. High-ranking women were running along with the common crowd. Parents had lost track of their children, and children of their parents."[16]

Another eyewitness, Francisco de Ariño, describes the stream of refugees seeking the safety of Sevilla. "It was the most piteous sight to see so many boats filled with women crying and tearing their hair, some from Cádiz and others who had been on their way to America, husbands without their wives, wives without their husbands, looking for their children."[17]

The foregoing eyewitness accounts of the events at Cádiz demonstrate that, contrary to what has been generally accepted, the English were not uniformly polite and chivalrous to the citizens, they did not necessarily respect the persons of the women, and confusion was such that there was ample opportunity for a little girl to become separated from her parents and spirited off. Slingsby identifies by name some forty-one hostages who were taken to England and held for ransom. Abreu's list brings the total to fifty-two. Needless to say, there were no children named Isabel (or Isabela) among them, a fact surely as noteworthy as González de Amezúa's inability to locate a Clotaldo among the English.[18] Both eyewitness accounts, and Abreu's in particular, demonstrate the historical possibility of the fictitious kidnapping.[19]

Other facets of the events at Cádiz remain to be explored, chiefly the role played by the Duque de Medina Sidonia, who was charged with the defense of the entire coast. As we know from Cabrera de Córdoba, the English attack did not come as a complete surprise. The Duque could have organized an aggressive defense but apparently chose not to. His actions are recorded by various contemporaries. Abreu for example reports that "as soon as the news reached the Duke of Medina at his seaside town of Conil he immediately set out for Cádiz with as many men as he could muster, and when they reached the bridge at Suazo he ordered the troops that had been assembling there to make for Sanlúcar de Barrameda."[20] After the naval battle, but before the English put any troops ashore, reinforcements arrived from Jerez (two hundred horse and 150 foot), Chiclana (forty horse and two hundred foot), and forty horse from the Duque de Arcos, all of whom "remained at the bridge, on orders from the Duke of Medina." From his post upriver at Sevilla, Francisco de Ariño reports that a certain Captain Bernardino de Noli "received permission from the municipal authorities to set fire to the English fleet, and he set out with six boats filled with fireballs, but the Duke of Medina refused to allow him to proceed toward Cadiz without a written order from His Majesty."[21] The Duque's failure to counterattack did not escape the English either. Slingsby observes with amazement that "in all of which time of the stay of the English armies (notwithstanding the great levies made of Spanish soldiers in sundry places thereabouts under the command of the Duke of Medina, to the number of thirty or forty thousand), yet there was never so much as any alarm given by sea or land to interrupt or annoy them."[22] It is clear that, for whatever reasons, the Duque chose to abandon Cádiz to the English and to contain them there. He established garrisons at other places—Sanlúcar, Rota, Chiclana, Jerez—in order to prevent the raid from turning into an invasion. This conservative, even timid, strategy seems to have been successful, and the immediate damage was in fact limited to Cádiz and its harbor. Cabrera de Córdoba concludes that "in order to avoid putting his victory at risk, the Count of Essex embarked his men and set fire to the city after two weeks." Various Spanish subordinates, including don Juan Puertocarrero (teniente general de las galeras de España), Luis Alfonso Flores (general de la flota de Nueva España), and other lower-ranking naval officers were punished by Felipe II for the "loss of Cádiz."[23]

The Duque de Medina Sidonia did perform one positive act, however. He burned the fleet of some "thirty-six good merchant ships laden for the West Indies, with 6,000 pipes of wine, 2,000 pipes of oil, 5,000 kintals of wax, and other merchandise, of cloth of gold, silks, linen, broadcloth and quicksilver estimated to the value of eleven or twelve millions of ducats." Slingsby insists that the fleet was burned on the direct orders of the Duque, and that Essex and Howard were in consequence "utterly defeated of that infinite riches."[24] The economic historian Jacob van Klaveren reports these events and especially their consequences in greater detail. He points out, first of all, that the quicksilver bound for America was the property of the king, but that all the textiles—the great bulk of the merchandise—belonged to foreign merchant capitalists, especially English and Dutch, who did business in Cádiz through local intermediaries. The owners of the fleet had struck a deal with the raiders, to pay two million ducados and be left alone. "The Duke of Medina Sidonia did not agree to this arrangement, however, and allowed the ships to be set afire." It is clear, he continues, that the Duque would never have ordered the burning unless he knew that the actual losses sustained by the Spaniards would be minimal. The king's quicksilver could be recovered with little difficulty, but the textiles—the property, as it turns out, of the enemy—were gone forever. Lawsuits were brought in Amsterdam and other Dutch cities, and even in England, in a vain attempt to gain compensation for the disastrous losses sustained. The Dutch, it seems, had only reluctantly accepted the English invitation to participate in the raid because they were conscious of what van Klaveren calls the "boomerang effect," and their intention was probably to limit the loss of Dutch property as far as possible by their presence on the scene. It follows from this, van Klaveren concludes, that the Spanish merchants held title to the merchandise on credit, against payment after sale in the colonies, so that the risk during the voyage to and from America belonged to the foreigners.[25]

All this suggests that the Duque's action was brilliant and patriotic, and that by appearing to burn up Spanish merchandise he was in fact dealing the enemy a severe blow. The Spanish merchants did not escape without injury, however. If the Dutch lost real property, their Spanish surrogates suffered a devastating loss of credit. It is in this sense that Mariana can write that when the merchant fleet was burned "many merchants all across the country suffered and went bankrupt."[26] It is in this way that the nameless father of little Isabela in Cervantes's story is destroyed economically by the events of July 1596. By his own reckoning, his credit comprises the vast bulk of his total worth. And it is for this reason that Cervantes, who must have been aware of the effects of the Duque's action on the Dutch economy, can omit reference to it from his famous sonnet and depict him as a pompous, blundering coward who gave away Cádiz and its riches to the English:

> Vimos en julio otra Semana Santa
> atestada de ciertas cofradías,
> que los soldados llaman compañías,
> de quien el vulgo, no el inglés, se espanta.
>
> . . . . . . . . . . . . . . . . . . . . . .
>
> Y al cabo, en Cádiz, con mesura harta,
> ido ya el conde sin ningún recelo,
> triunfando entró el gran duque de Medina.

> (We witnessed, in July, a second Holy Week procession, complete with certain confraternities the soldiers call companies, and who only scare the people, not the English. . . . And at the end, in Cádiz, when the Count [Essex] had departed at his leisure, the great Duke of Medina came marching in in triumph.)[27]

We have already met the Duque and observed some of the facets of his administration, especially his ambiguous relationship to the local merchant community, in our discussion of *Rinconete y Cortadillo* in chapter 3. Now we have an opportunity to expand our knowledge of his policies and their probable motivations. Despite his good work against the Dutch, the fact remains, frozen forever in Cervantes's sonnet, that the Duque sat by and allowed Cádiz to be destroyed physically as well as economically, while he chose to protect surrounding towns such as Sanlúcar de Barrameda. The question of why he refused to mount a counterattack remains unanswered. Before we leave our examination of these events we must consider the economic rivalry between Cádiz and Sevilla, and the Duque's stake in that rivalry. The two ports had always been complementary alternatives. Cádiz offered a deep-water port with direct access to the sea, but it was vulnerable to attack. Sevilla offered total security from attack, but required a time-consuming passage upriver some ninety kilometers. If cargo was lost in the river, at least part of it could be recovered; cargo lost to an attacker at Cádiz was gone forever. Sevilla had the legal monopoly on trade with America. As we have seen, the technicism *monopolio,* so conspicuous in contemporary documents, is reflected in the Monipodio who controls organized crime in *Rinconete y Cortadillo.* Cádiz was oriented to a north-south axis, with trade to North Africa and up the coast of Europe as far as Norway. In 1519 the Sevilla monopolio authorized American shipping to load and unload at Cádiz as long as no precious metals were involved. Ten years later one of the judges from the Casa de Contratación (i.e. the Sevilla monopoly) began to spend four months each year at Cádiz. In 1535 this "circuit judge" was replaced by a full-time resident magistrate whose presence was supposed to assure Cádiz its fair share of the American trade. This provoked hostility in Sevilla, where all arrivals from Cádiz were considered suspect and strictly monitored. In 1561 the presence of a special category for Cádiz shipping in the *Libros de Registro* demonstrates that Sevilla had given up trying to force its rival out of the trade. The English attacks on Cádiz of 1587 and 1596 had the effect of weakening Cádiz with respect to Sevilla and thus lessening the tension between them. The seventeenth century witnessed the progressive decline of Sevilla, brought on in part by the silting-up of the river near Sanlúcar de Barrameda, until the Casa de Contratación itself was finally transfered to Cádiz in 1717.[28]

There is a curious connection to be observed between the presence of English merchants in these parts, their relations with the Duque de Medina Sidonia, and the relative prosperity of Cádiz and Sevilla. Albert J. Loomie reports that "the Brotherhood of Saint George of Sanlúcar de Barrameda had been formed by Englishmen trading in the area early in the [sixteenth] century to protect their interests commercially and to afford them a chapel for worship and meetings. The patron of this merchant colony was the Duke of Medina Sidonia, who had first given them a choice site of land near the Guadalquivir."[29]

When the embargo of English shipping and the expulsion of British subjects was decreed in 1586 many English merchants secured permission to stay on in Sanlúcar de Barrameda. Most of them had lived there for some years, and this in combination with their Catholicism commended them to the Duque de Medina Sidonia. The Duque seems to have had a special affection as well as a commercial attachment to the English. In 1594 the English Jesuit Henry Walpole wrote that "'the Duke of Medina Sidonia . . . hath not spared to say that in his port town of Sanlúcar he would be content to break traffique with all nations so he might have it with England only.'"[30] His preference for the English contributes to the explanation of the burning of the merchant fleet at Cádiz in 1596, which had such profoundly adverse effects on the Dutch economy. As van Klaveren observes, the English, not the Spanish, were the worst enemies the Dutch had.[31] This does not explain, however, why the captain-general of the Andalusian coast was willing to sacrifice Cádiz in the process.

As we have seen, Cádiz and Sevilla were locked in a deadly commercial struggle for preeminence in the American trade, and as we have also seen, Cádiz was gradually but steadily strengthening its position during the sixteenth century. The Duque de Medina Sidonia was the feudal lord of Sanlúcar de Barrameda and therefore chief financial partner on the side that was losing the competition, the Sevilla-Sanlúcar nexus. His financial stake in the Cádiz-Sevilla rivalry and his use of his office to protect it was made clear by Albert Girard in 1932.[32] His reluctance to come to the aid of Cádiz, and his curious willingness to consider the city lost before the battle had fairly started and to sit by and witness its sack and destruction while simultaneously taking care to fortify his own strongholds of Medina Sidonia and especially Sanlúcar with its English merchant colony under his protection, becomes readily comprehensible. The population of Sanlúcar decreased from 1,440 *vecinos* in 1588 to 968 in 1591, a sure sign of the growing importance of Cádiz.[33]

The Duque de Medina Sidonia's failure to defend Cádiz, then, is a function of his personal vested interests. By burning the merchant fleet he struck a blow at the Dutch economy in favor of the English, and by defending Sanlúcar while Cádiz burned he dealt a devastating blow to his commercial rival. His actions are doubly reprehensible, from the points of view of ethics and duty. It is interesting to observe that, of the contemporary chroniclers, only the Englishman Slingsby appears concerned with the economic infrahistory of the predominantly military events he describes. Abreu, Ariño, Cabrera de Córdoba, and Cervantes in his sonnet prefer to focus on the military and religious dimensions of the sack of Cádiz. Abreu and Cabrera stop curiously short of holding the Duque responsible for what was after all his responsibility, and Cervantes turns the affair into a simultaneous attack on the Duque's cowardice and on the meaninglessness of religious processions.

I insist on Cervantes's sonnet "Vimos en julio otra semana santa" because in *La española inglesa* he puts to use his insider's knowledge of the economic infrastructure and its relation to the political hierarchy and the official ideology. Cervantes was probably in Sevilla when the sack of Cádiz occurred. He had gone there in August 1595 carrying royal instructions regarding the bankruptcy of a certain Simón Freire de Lima, a merchant-banker to whom he had entrusted government funds. The money finally reached Madrid early in 1597. In the meantime Cervantes seems to have stayed on in Sevilla, "supporting himself by setting up, on the strength of his many contacts in the city, as a free-lance man of affairs."[34] His impression of the events at Cádiz was probably similar to that of Francisco de Ariño, who insists on the pathos provoked by the sight of the refugees streaming into Sevilla, "some from Cádiz and others who were on their way to America, wives without their husbands, husbands without their wives, looking for their children."[35] His knowledge of the economic rivalry between Sevilla and Cádiz, of the Duque's special relationship with Sanlúcar de Barrameda, facts that must have been common knowledge, cannot but have been enhanced by his own status as a minor member of the local economic infrastructure. It is indeed possible that Cervantes, like Isabela's father, suffered some financial loss as a result of the sack of Cádiz.

The foregoing dissertation on the sack of Cádiz, its causes, course, and consequences, is intended to insist on its importance to the business community there, of whom Isabela's father is a fictional representation. The magnitude of the loss, the treatment of the Spanish civilians at the hands of the English, and the double perfidy of the Duque de Medina Sidonia can only emerge from a reasonably detailed presentation of the historical events. Cervantes's presence in nearby Sevilla at the time, together with his involvement in business there, is crucial to his grasp of the magnitude and the meaning of the events at Cádiz, and hence of their suitability as the starting point for a fictional treatment of Anglo-Spanish relations in their two fundamental historical aspects of religion and commerce. To these he will add the love affair of Ricaredo and Isabela. It should be noted that the lovers embody different aspects of the historical themes. They share a common religion (which furthermore is the true one, as opposed to the Anglican heresy), but they are associated with two different and opposing economic systems. We shall return to these structural and representational considerations later. For the present we should follow Isabela from Cádiz to London, where she begins to grow up in a family of clandestine English Catholics.

The situation of English Catholics under Elizabeth I was complex. A cursory glance at Philip Hughes's history of the Reformation in England suffices to reveal that Catholics were considered a threat, Catholics were persecuted, and Catholics lived in a climate of insecurity and alienation.[36] In fact, their situation bears a striking resemblance to that of the conversos in Cervantes's own society, of whom Isabela and her family are a fictional representation, as Manuel da Costa Fontes and Pablo Virumbales have suggested.[37]

Cervantes's idea of the situation in England was probably derived from popularized versions of reports like this 1604 dispatch from Don Juan de Tassis to his monarch. We should keep in mind that this letter reflects the more "liberal" policies of Elizabeth's successor, James I.

"In England today there is one religion and two sects. The religion is the Roman Catholic Apostolic. There is a Protestant sect founded on the doctrines of Luther, and the Puritans, who follow Calvin. The Catholics can be divided into two kinds: first those called recusants, because not only do they refuse to recognize the king as the head of the church, but also to attend the king's church and hear the sermons. They are subject to a fee of £20 per month (more or less 70 gold escudos), and if they cannot comply, to a year in jail and the confiscation of two-thirds of their real estate and all their movable property. The second kind are also Catholics and known as such, but they are more politic, and willing to recognize the primacy of the king in order to be eligible for royal offices, gifts, and salaries. There are other, secret Catholics who do not dare to identify themselves as recusants for fear of losing their possessions and of the rigor of the persecutions of the Puritans, who are the Catholics' fiercest enemies. There is a fourth kind, who are Catholics in their heart but who profess one of the two sects in public in order to keep the property and benefits they have."[38]

In 1570 Pope Pius II placed Elizabeth under interdict and released all her subjects from their allegiance to her. English Catholics were with one stroke of the pen placed under suspicion of being actual or potential traitors. Catholics in the north had actually revolted in 1569. In November of that year they assembled a force of some one thousand infantry and fifteen hundred horse, entered Durham cathedral, tore up the Bible, and restored the Mass.[39] Early in 1578 Felipe II sent Don Bernardino de Mendoza to England to revive the embassy closed by the expulsion of the previous ambassador. In 1583 Don Bernardino was implicated in a Catholic plot, one of many known as "the enterprise," that involved Mary Stuart and a number of Catholic noblemen. For his part in these proceedings Mendoza was expelled. We might regard him with amused tolerance as the bumbling CIA agent of his day; an English document of 1589 is considerably more virulent. "Hee [Felipe II] hath oftentimes sent his messengers (you would rather say his fireflingers) into England, and of latest yeeres, two special persons, of all the rest the most eger and furious, Gerald Despes and Bernardine Mendoza, who ceased not to confound and perswade the minds of all those whome they coulde grow in acquaintance with, and were men given over to all mischiefes and diabolical practices, promising them and bestowing upon them extraordinary rewards, of purpose to stirre them up to more domestical conspiracies against her Maiestie."[40]

The simple existence of a plot involving prominent English Catholics and the representative of a Catholic foreign government demonstrates the level of religious and political tension, and documents the fact that plenty of Englishmen wanted their country to be Catholic. Elizabeth could ill afford to give them much leeway.

In terms of her age and physical appearance, and with respect to her relations with her Catholic subjects, the Elizabeth who emerges from the documents and histories stands in violent contrast to the beautiful and magnanimous queen who graces Cervantes's pages, who fails to punish Clotaldo for his willful disobedience to orders at Cádiz and who congratulates Isabela for her steadfast resistance to Protestantism. From the English side, E. Allison Peers has observed that "Queen Elizabeth, so recently the Spaniards' *bête noire,* is idealized to such a degree that one might suppose the author to have been deliberately working for an Anglo-Spanish understanding."[41] On the Spanish side, Américo Castro remarks that "Queen Elizabeth of England, the defender of Protestantism, tolerates and even favors Catholic Isabela."[42] For Castro, this presentation of Queen Elizabeth forms part of a series of visions of tolerant foreigners throughout Cervantes's works, visions intended to remind the reader of the corresponding lack of tolerance in Spain. Ruth El Saffar considers that "the lack of bitterness shown in the characterization of Elizabeth can be explained by the abstract conception of her role." She acts as the author's agent, setting up an obstacle Ricaredo must surmount in his quest for Isabela.[43] I must confess that the logic of this explanation escapes me. The English queen would have been much more effective as a blocking character had she been violently anti-Catholic, or had she locked Isabela in the Tower and confiscated Clotaldo's property, actions much more appropriate to the historical Elizabeth.

The foregoing attempt to ground *La española inglesa* in Elizabethan history has netted surprisingly little in the way of immediately useful correspondences. If anything, we have been led to a fuller appreciation of the radical unhistoricity of Cervantes's presentation of the English queen. But we have been able to document the general accuracy of his evocation of the human situation of English Catholics during her reign, and our lengthy excursion to Cádiz has also produced several useful facts and suggestions. The attack in the story is clearly the great expedition of 1596, which Cervantes experienced from nearby Sevilla. Eyewitness accounts describe the totality of the physical destruction, the devastating loss of property, the psychological devastation of the experience of invasion and violation, the chaos and separation of family members, and demonstrate that an action such as Clotaldo's kidnap of little Isabela was by no means impossible. We are also led by the same accounts to speculate on the attitudes and motivations of one of Cervantes's "favorite" aristocrats, the Duque de Medina Sidonia, whose decision to sacrifice Cádiz is open to the most ungenerous interpretations. Finally, the hitherto overlooked participation, as architect of the plan and co-commander in the field, of Lord Charles Howard is of crucial importance, for Howard links the generally sterile and antagonistic Elizabethan phase of Anglo-Spanish relations to the much more fecund and hopeful period that followed. Paradoxically, *La española inglesa* and the Elizabeth-Isabela pair only become possible after the historical Elizabeth had left the scene.

It is well known that upon Elizabeth's death in 1603 and the accession to the English throne of James VI of Scotland, Anglo-Spanish relations took a decided turn for the better. The peace, negotiated in London in the fall of 1604 between the two traditional rivals and confirmed in Valladolid in the spring of 1605, ushered in an era of good feeling that persisted to some degree until 1612, when English hopes for an Anglo-Spanish dynastic marriage were dashed.

Writing in 1916, Francisco Icaza was the first critic to situate the composition of *La española inglesa* in the period of Anglo-Spanish rapprochement following the accession of James Stuart.[44] Icaza's thesis is the only one that plausibly explains the warm-hearted portrayal of Queen Elizabeth, a portrayal certainly unpublishable and probably unthinkable during her lifetime. Some thirty-four years later, Rafael Lapesa similarly insisted that such a "placid vision" of an enemy country would have been impossible during Elizabeth's lifetime.[45] Lapesa considers that the repercussions following the Gunpowder Plot of 1605 would have had the effect of postponing the beginning of truly warm relations until perhaps 1609, when British hopes for a dynastic alliance with Spain were running high, and concludes that Cervantes must have written his novella during the period 1609–1611. As we shall see, the chronology of events suggests that the era of good feeling—good enough to effect the conception and composition of an *Española inglesa*—began suddenly and dramatically in 1604–1605, and had cooled considerably by 1609.

In an important but unfortunately brief study Thomas Hanrahan identifies the English mission to Valladolid in 1605 under Lord Charles Howard as the riveting occasion on which the Spaniards, Cervantes among them, actually saw sizeable numbers of Englishmen and experienced them not as devils but as surprisingly honorable gentlemen.[46] From the English side, Lee Bliss has suggested that the peace mission to Valladolid was the ocasion on which several English *literati* and their friends came into contact with the most recent Spanish writing, including *Don Quixote*.[47] In this context it is worth noting that Luis Astrana Marín makes a suggestive if wholly circumstantial case for the presence of William Shakespeare in Howard's retinue. He maintains, however, that Shakespeare and Cervantes probably did not meet.[48]

Hanrahan's is the third major critical statement to locate the composition of our text in the euphoria following peace with England, and the one that insists most strongly on the importance of the English presence in Valladolid from 26 May to 18 June 1605. I want to document in as much detail as is practical what is known about these festivities and the events in England that preceded them, using Hanrahan's sources and others, in an effort to establish a plausible human context for the genesis of Cervantes's text, including the question of the author's particular relationship to the great affairs of state and what access he might have had to information about them.

The English College of St. Albans at Valladolid played a role in the general rapprochement. Founded in 1589 to train fugitive English Catholics for the priesthood with the eventual goal of smuggling them back into England to minister to the Catholics there, it formed part of a network of English Jesuit colleges on the continent. Best known to English-speaking Catholics is the college at Douai. Another was located in Sevilla, and its proximity to Cádiz provoked the fury of the English invaders in 1596, according to Fray Pedro de Abreu.[49] In Valladolid the college generally maintained a low profile, but its presence did not go unperceived in the circles that mattered. Felipe III and Queen Margarita visited in August 1600, and in 1605 Lord Howard also paid a visit. It is known that Fray Joseph Creswell, the Jesuit administrator of St. Albans, frequented Howard's residence while the admiral was in Valladolid. It is more than probable that if Cervantes was not already aware of the English college, its frequenting by Howard and his men—some of whom were clearly Catholic—must have brought it abruptly to his attention.[50] During the period in question, most of the priests trained at Valladolid were sent back to England, where many were martyred.

Lord Charles Howard is undoubtedly the most important among the leading players in this historical-political-religious drama. Lord Admiral of England since 1585, he commanded the fleet opposing the Gran Armada. As we have seen, he was the architect and co-commander of the expedition to Cádiz in 1596, following which he was made Earl of Nottingham. When James I was casting about for someone to lead the mission to Valladolid, Howard was the ranking Earl in England, as well as a man whose name would generate respect in the memory of 1588 and 1596.[51] Perhaps more important for our purposes, he was a member of a family that had suffered for its Catholic faith and, although at least nominally an Anglican, he is thought to have been sympathetic to efforts to have Elizabeth succeeded by a Catholic. He finally supported James Stuart, probably in large measure because the Scottish king had picked a relative of his, Lord Henry Howard (who had been raised a Catholic), to be his man in London and oversee his efforts to secure the English throne.[52]

As early as two months before Howard's arrival, Valladolid was abuzz with news and rumors concerning the English admiral and his retinue. Cabrera de

Córdoba notes on 19 March that arrangements were being made to lodge Lord Howard in the home of the Conde de Salinas, "and it is said he is going to be regaled and fêted with great formality the fifteen or twenty days he is here, so he can return content to England." When the English arrived at La Coruña, Cabrera again refers to the lodgings prepared for Howard and his gentlemen, who "will be spread around in aristocrats' homes, and their servants will be lodged in houses on Calle Imperial, near the admiral, which are being vacated for that purpose."[53] The length of the visit was now reported to be an entire month.

Lord Howard was an imposing figure. His physique and attire were the subject of considerable commentary. A contemporary *Relación* reports that "the Admiral wore a hat with feathers and a diamond band, a woolen cape with gold clasp, orange coat and breeches and an amber-colored doublet. His body is large and well-formed. His hair is gray, his countenance grave. He appeared to be about seventy years of age, a very figure of authority and grandeur."[54]

On the occasion of the formal ratification of the peace treaty by Felipe III, the same document reports: "The Condestable Don Juan Fernández de Velasco, Duque de Frías, had Lord Howard on his right, dressed all in white. Around his neck he wore the chain of the Order of the Garter, and the Garter itself, of hammered gold garnished with diamonds, around his left leg. Even at his age he cuts a dashing figure." The same correspondent also remarks that Howard "understands the Castilian language well and speaks it reasonably."[55]

We have observed already that Howard and other members of his family had Catholic sympathies at least with respect to dynastic politics. Robert W. Kenny suggests that these sympathies might have reflected personal inclinations.[56] Howard's teammate, Sir Charles Cornwallis, who had accompanied him to Spain and who would stay on as resident ambassador, presents a slightly different picture. Ambassador Cornwallis had become increasingly upset by the behavior of the English Jesuits in Valladolid, who under the leadership of Fray Joseph Creswell, "'bestirred themselves here in conference and persuasion of young gentlemen . . . and do secretly brag of their much prevailing.'" Two members of Cornwallis's staff, in fact, converted to Catholicism and were summarily dismissed. Although many Spaniards believed he was a Catholic, Cornwallis presents himself as the champion of Anglicanism and hints repeatedly that Howard had "'dishonoured the English religion.'"[57]

Perhaps most interesting is the testimony of the Portuguese chronicler Thomé Pinheiro da Veiga, whose *Fastigimia* is surely the most entertaining and perceptive account of the events and atmosphere at Valladolid during the period in question, a worthy precursor of the best society journalism. Pinheiro reports cautiously, but report he does: "They tell me, but I don't believe it, that the admiral's eldest son told the king he is a Catholic. With the same uncertainty, I repeat that I have been told that the admiral himself told the Duque de Cea that he has written to the pope about reconciling himself with the Catholic Church."[58]

Finally, resident ambassador Cornwallis wrote that he had heard from reliable sources that Howard had accepted from Felipe III an annuity of twelve thousand escudos which, he added piously, "I assume myself not to be true." As a matter of fact, the admiral and several other prominent gentlemen had been on the Spanish king's payroll since the preceding spring, when Don Juan de Tassis had enlisted them in the cause of toleration for English Catholics.[59]

In short, the figure of Lord Howard dominates the English presence at Valladolid. His son was reputed to be a secret Catholic, he himself was possibly considering reconciliation with the Roman Church, he had played an important role in the events at Cádiz in 1596, and his career spans and links the hostile Elizabethan period of Anglo-Spanish relations with the era of good feeling following the peace of 1605. In fact, Howard in a very real and public way personifies the coexistence of these contradictory possibilities. Rather than rushing to identify him as the *modelo vivo* of Clotaldo or Ricaredo, I want simply to conclude that his career, his personality, and what was suspected of his religion surely must have engaged Cervantes's creative imagination, always attuned to phenomena of paradox, duality, and their harmonious synthesis.

Cervantes and his compatriots must also have had occasion to observe the Catholicism of other members of the admiral's party. As the English were making their way from La Coruña to Valladolid they stopped at the Benedictine priory at Villafranca. Our anonymous *Relación* reports that "many Englishmen went to see an exquisite miracle of the Holy Sacrament, some out of curiosity and others out of devotion, because it happened that, through Divine mercy, the wine was turned visibly into blood and the host into flesh, and those who were edified by this great miracle demonstrated an exquisite devotion."[60]

When they reached the outskirts of Valladolid the English halted to await the official welcoming party and escort.

> While the admiral and his party were waiting in the garden for their escort, they went up to the house and into an oratory, and the admiral and those who went with him were pleased to see how curiously it was constructed and decorated. But they paid no attention to the images, while others who came in afterward knelt and adored a crucifix, and bowed to the images, and began to read the books of devotion that were there and offered to buy them, and spoke like Catholics, but softly, so as not to arouse their comrades' suspicions. There are some Catholics among them who frequent the churches, and hear Mass, and confess and receive communion.[61]

Pinheiro da Veiga reports similar sightings of Catholics among the English party. When one of them discovered the truth about another, "he threw his arms around the other's neck and, both crying with happiness, they went to receive communion, revealing their hearts to each other. And they say others are doing the same, but in secret, and they pointed out two who planned to travel to Rome."[62]

At the baptism of the infant Felipe IV there was, naturally, a Mass. Pinheiro da Veiga reports that he was pleased to see many Englishmen in the church and in particular three of the most principal among them hearing Mass on their knees. Some of their servants told him that many had gone to the Holy Office to become reconciled with the Church. On Corpus Christi day "some of the Englishmen went along in the procession, as though they were curious, with great reverence."[63] We know enough now to be able to identify these *curiosos* as secret Catholics. In fact it becomes clear from the contemporary sources that Howard's retinue harbored a fair number of Catholic Englishmen—some in the highest echelons—who gratefully and joyously, but cautiously, began to engage in the exterior practices of their religion once they were safely in the capital of Catholic Spain. The fact that these coreligionists could have sailed together from England and traveled overland to Valladolid, all the while keeping their identity as Catholics secret from each other, is eloquent testimony to the tense and repressive atmosphere in which they were accustomed to living in England. The revelation of their precarious clandestinity must surely have impressed Cervantes.

The possibility of a dynastic marriage had been broached at the peace discussions held in London the preceding fall, and it came up again in Valladolid. It is documented from both sides, in a dispatch from the Duque de Frías to Felipe III dated 12 September 1604, and again in Howard's report to James I. It seems that everyone favored a marital alliance *española-inglesa*. There is even a curious reciprocity in the reports of enthusiasm for the project: the Duque de Frías attibutes it to the English queen, while for Howard it is Lerma's idea.[64]

Those were heady weeks in Valladolid. Lord Howard and his men conducted themselves in an exemplary fashion, several of them turned out to be secret Catholics, Spain officially took a hand in seeing to the welfare of the English Catholics, and talk of a royal Anglo-Spanish marriage was everywhere. The hostility so characteristic of the reigns of Felipe II and Elizabeth had seemingly melted away overnight. On both the Spanish and the English side we can observe genuine goodwill that permeates all levels of society. Pinheiro summarizes on 18 June: "On Saturday the English departed, without a single harsh word or any unpleasantness the entire time they were here. They conducted themselves with great modesty, respect, and courtesy in the presence of all our images and sacraments, as though they had been Catholics, so that the suspicions we harbored about them turn out to have been misconceptions based on ignorance. And in many of them our conversation was quite effective; may God will His dormant seed to flower once again in England."[65]

On the English side, a member of Howard's retinue named Robert Treswell offers the following: "Both in our going and in our return we might well observe how joyful our coming seemed to the common people, who, for that they found by experience the ill reports made heretofore of our nation altogether untrue, admiring our civility and good behaviour, being clean contrary to that which had been formerly preached into them. . . . The bounty of the King in gifts [and it was lavish] gave us not so good contentment in general as did the good esteem and behaviour we found in all, from the highest to the meanest."[66]

This general good feeling determined the immediate reaction in Valladolid to the Gunpowder Plot of 1605. Cabrera de Córdoba reports the event in his "column" of 24 December:

> On the fourth of the month news reached us of the treason attempted against the English monarchy by placing certain barrels of gunpowder with bits of metal under the Parliament, to blow up the room and everyone inside it. The plot was discovered and certain Frenchmen have been arrested as suspects. This news was transmitted to the English ambassador here, and he celebrated with a display of fireworks and a shower of coins from his windows. Don Diego Brochero has been sent to Lisbon to assemble an army of 8,000 men to offer the King of England if he needs them to punish the traitors.[67]

This text suggests that, contrary to Lapesa's belief, the negative effects of the plot to blow up Parliament on the course of Anglo-Spanish relations were not perceived, and that consequently the composition of La española inglesa need not have been put off until later. In Valladolid, Ambassador Cornwallis shared his personal sense of relief and joy with the local citizens by shooting off fireworks and scattering coins from his windows, and Felipe III responded by placing eight thousand troops at King James's disposal, should he require them to deal with the situation.

By the spring of 1612, however, relations between the two countries had seriously deteriorated. The Spaniards had decided against the matrimonial alliance with England that had figured so prominently in the gossip of 1605, and had arranged instead a double marriage with France. The future Felipe IV was betrothed to Princess Isabel of France, and his sister Ana to the future Louis XIII. The English naturally viewed with alarm this sudden rapprochement of the two Catholic continental powers, and Spanish diplomacy mounted a campaign designed to reassure them. Cabrera de Córdoba informs us on 7 April 1612:

> His Majesty has dispatched Don Pedro de Zúñiga to England to inform the English of the marriages that have been arranged. Because this was not done earlier, they now suspect some harm may come to them, and have taken defensive measures such as assembling a fleet and protecting their ports. They are reported also to have increased the persecution of Catholics. In addition, our ambassador is to attempt to convince them to discontinue the military expeditions from England to Florida because of the harm that results from them, which will only increase unless they stop.[68]

We are now worlds away from the euphoria of 1605, when Felipe and James and their courtiers outdid each other in the presentation of expensive gifts, when James seemed disposed to relieve the pressure on his Catholic subjects, when it appeared that England and Spain would be linked by royal marriage, and the concept of an *española inglesa* was a real possibility. In 1612 we have reports of renewed repression of English Catholics and England preparing to defend itself against invasion while preying once again on Spanish shipping in the New World; in short, a return to the situation of 1588.

I conclude from the historical evidence that *La española inglesa* had to have been conceived and written in the euphoric atmosphere generated by the peace with England and the presence of Admiral Howard and his retinue in Valladolid in the spring of 1605. The historical evidence is at variance with the textually inspired inference that our novella is a late work that transcends the peculiarities of history and individual experience in favor of a doctrinally orthodox presentation of universal themes and timeless values. *La española inglesa,* as I hope to have begun to show, is a text supremely concerned with the peculiarities of a historical moment, from the weightiest affairs of international politics to the only apparently trivial operations of the international economic infrastructure.

In this context it would be helpful to ponder Cervantes's role—as an actor, a professional observer, or a well-connected bystander—in the events of that "Valladolid Spring," and his relation to the other men who lived, observed, and wrote about them. It has been thought off and on for many years that Cervantes was commissioned to write an official relación of the events of 1605, and that either the text has been lost or is the anonymous *Relación de lo sucedido* to which we have already referred. Because of its aggressively Catholic tone, and because Astrana Marín considers it the work of another, I am content to conclude that Cervantes is not the author of the famous *Relación* that appears in the edition of his complete works published by Cayetano Rosell in 1864. However, the evidence brought forward by virtually all the scholars, namely a contemporary reference to a now-lost *relación* definitely written by Cervantes, leads to the conclusion that the author of *La española inglesa* was on the scene as a journalist, a professional observer whose business it was to get as close as he could to the protagonists of the events and to soak up as much detail as possible.[69]

We have had repeated recourse to the testimony of Luis Cabrera de Córdoba, who chronicled life in the Spanish court from 1599 to 1614. Although his *Relaciones* were not published until 1857, the unsigned prologue to the edition states that Cabrera was friendly with a number of writers, among them Cervantes. In the *Viaje del Parnaso* Cervantes praises Cabrera as a historian, the author of a theoretical work on historiography entitled *Historia: para entenderla y escribirla* (1611). E. C. Riley cites this work and assumes that Cervantes was familiar with it. Riley quotes several passages from Cabrera's treatise that seem to be in perfect consonance with Cervantes's view of history and historiography as a writer of fictions.[70] It is more than probable that Cervantes and Cabrera knew each other in Valladolid, engaged as they were in the common enterprise of reporting on the festivities, that they were friends, and that they exchanged concrete pieces of information—who went where, who wore what—as well as ideas concerning the relation of history to poetry.

Even more suggestive is the possibility that Cervantes was friendly with Thomé Pinheiro da Veiga, whose *Fastigimia,* as we have already observed, is the most witty, irreverent, and generally entertaining chronicle now extant of the events in question. Pinheiro describes an *entremés* presented on Corpus Christi in which there appeared a "Don Quixote digging the spurs into a poor gray horse, and Sancho Panza his squire, and the lady Dulcinea del Toboso."[71]

In short, it is not difficult to imagine Cervantes and Pinheiro, and perhaps Cabrera and other *cronistas* as well, sitting around after the day's festivities, sharing drinks and conversation as journalists are wont to do, alternating irreverent witticisms with serious talk about the English and the hopeful new course of Anglo-Spanish relations.

Astrana Marín takes for granted that Pinheiro and Cervantes were acquainted, and suggests that it was through Pinheiro that Cervantes was reminded of the sack of Cádiz in 1596. Coincident with the arrival of the English in Valladolid, the Duque de Medina Sidonia, whose "defense" of Cádiz had earned him Cervantes's ridicule, was restored to royal favor and named *general de la Armada.* Pinheiro was scandalized and devotes a full page to commentary on the event. To make matters worse, Medina Sidonia and Howard—the man of the hour in Valladolid—had been opponents in the debacle of 1588. The Duque was being raised to eminence in the very presence of the man who had twice humbled him in battle. Surely these ironies could not have been lost on Cervantes and Pinheiro. Astrana Marín further believes that Pinheiro and Cervantes must have frequented the same gambling house, because the Portuguese chronicler mentions the novelist in an anecdote concerning a banker named Lope García and his wife. Mrs. García insisted that her husband not interfere with her play because she was gambling with her own money. She called on Cervantes, who was apparently standing nearby, to hand her a candlestick, the better to illuminate the game. Astrana Marín and Pérez Pastor have both documented Cervantes's friendship with "that affluent banking family."[72]

There is substantial evidence, besides reasonable conjecture, that locates Cervantes within the journalistic and financial communities in Valladolid during the period in question. We shall return to the matter of our author's involvement in business and finance when we consider the text of *La española inglesa*. First I want to elucidate how close he might have been to the great events that bear on the theme of his story and in what company (and what spirit) he might have observed them.

We should begin now to move toward the text, noting first that Cervantes's story, like the various accounts of the festivities at Valladolid, is very concerned with clothing and fashion, frequently related to and a marker of national identity: "The next day they dressed Isabela in the Spanish style, with a full-length dress," whereupon one of Elizabeth's ladies remarks, "'the Spanish girl is all right, but I don't like the dress'" (248–49). On another day Isabela is "dressed English style, and she looked as good as she did in the Spanish style" (259). Or again: "Isabela's father and mother, newly dressed in the English style" (262). From this it seems clear that there was a definite English and a definite Spanish style, and indeed Isabela's Spanish outfit—"full-length dress of green stuff, slashed and lined in rich cloth of gold, the slashes closed with S's made of pearls, and the entire dress sewn with precious stones; neckline and waistband of diamonds, and with a fan in the style the Spanish women use"—is extraordinarily similar to one mentioned in 1606 by Cabrera de Córdoba, a gift from Queen Margarita of Spain to Queen Anne of England: "full-length dress of stuff the color of dried rose, embellished with amber and garnished with pearls."[73] And yet the national differences are not clear, for even in Elizabeth's reign there was considerable interpenetration of styles. Cervantes insists on the fan as a Spanish item, for example, yet Herbert Norris reports that in the inventory of Queen Elizabeth's wardrobe made in 1603, "no fewer than thirty-one beautiful fans of great worth are enumerated." The English queen is also depicted wearing "a surcote of a dark-coloured damask known as costume à l'Espagnole. It is made to be worn over a dress for extra warmth, lined with fur. This surcote, of Spanish origin, was very popular with great ladies in England and on the Continent."[74]

Men's fashions are similarly ambiguous, if not more so. Although there was a Spanish and an English style, in practice the gentlemen mixed and matched at will. Lord Admiral Howard and the Duque de Pastrana appeared in the same Spanish-style breeches with gold buttons.[75] Pinheiro da Veiga reports that on one occasion Howard appeared "half English, half Spanish."[76] Norris offers an opportune summary: "The garments clothing English men and women were a medley drawn from many nations: thus the same man might appear one day dressed entirely as a Spaniard, and on the next in a variety of garments each characteristic of a different country."[77] This certainly describes Ricardo's outfit when he returns to England from his maritime conquests: "Milanese armor, feathers Walloon style, breeches in the Swiss fashion" (259).

The internationalism we have noted in fashion may also be observed in social customs, for example in dancing. Various accounts of the festivities at Valladolid reveal that the English and Spanish ladies and gentlemen all danced the same dances to the same music and that partners could be changed at (royal) will. At a *sarao* held on 16 June 1605, the king "commanded the handsome young Earl of Perth to dance, and the young man chose Doña Catalina de la Cerda, and the two of them made such an impression that it was impossible to say whether the lady or the gentleman had danced more gracefully."[78] The categories of *española* and *inglés* are absorbed into *dama* and *caballero*.

The equality or interchangeability of national styles that we have just observed would seem to belie or undercut the organization of Cervantes's text, which takes seriously such distinctions as dressing "a la española" or "a la inglesa." Yet within the text examples of mixed or merged categories abound. Ricardo simultaneously frees Spaniards and "Turks" (i.e. Muslims from Algiers) who should belong to two mutually exclusive categories yet who are thrown together and identified as the *cautivos libres*. When his flotilla returns to London he displays conflicting signals. "He mixed signals of joy with signs of sadness: glad-sounding cornets, then rough-voiced trumpets; sad and lamentable fifes responded to happy drumbeats. From one masthead the crescent Muslim flag flew upside down; from another a long standard of black taffeta trailed in the water. In short, he sailed up the river to London in the midst of these contrary extremes, which held the innumerable crowds of onlookers in suspense" (258). When Ricardo enters the Queen's presence, "some compared him to Mars, the god of battles, while others compared him to Venus, who had dressed up that way to play some trick on Mars" (259).

At the structural level, the most idealistic and improbable kind of love story coexists with almost obsessive reference to the prosaic details of international commerce and banking. The text seems to be a gallery of irreconcilable opposites placed in paradoxical juxtaposition. Indeed, Guillermo Díaz Plaja has characterized *La española inglesa* as a "counterpoint," in which every positive value is opposed by a corresponding negative one.[79] This pattern of opposition is in itself in opposition to the harmony, goodwill, and easy patterns of international exchange I have tried to document historically in the preceding pages, and I seem at this point to have disproved my own thesis, which insists on the historicity of this text. Some explanation is surely in order.

Cervantes has worked a profound change on the raw material provided by the reality of Anglo-Spanish relations in the spring and summer of 1605. In general we might say that he has transformed raw data into members of a signifying system, into signs. He replaces a real historical signifier of 1605—James I (peace and goodwill)—with another, from the period just ended—Elizabeth (antagonism of every kind). In addition, he relexicalizes a series of signs—dress, language, and the like—which had in fact lost much if not all of their power to indicate differences. By performing these operations he mobilizes in his reader expectations and responses that were normal and appropriate during the reigns of Elizabeth and Felipe II. Having established a system of signifiers and a set of expectations, the text proceeds to undo both. The net result of this process is something like a return to the historical truth of 1605 and the possibilities of that moment, but expressed in the language of 1596. Furthermore, this text did not become public until 1613, when the signifiers and expectations of 1596 had again become valid. That is, the text subverts the attitudes and expectations of the reader of 1613 and, as experience has shown, those of succeeding generations of readers as well. This is what gives rise to the contemporary interpretations that ignore historical peculiarities of every type in favor of abstract notions of Catholic universality and virtue. I hope to have documented this text's dependence on history but in the process to have suggested a particular kind of relationship between historical fact and fictional text. In what follows I want to consider the presence of real history in the text, but now in relation to the reader's anachronistic expectations and system of reference.

Instead of considering the title *La española inglesa* as an unsettling oxymoron, and attempting to resolve the difference between its members, it is more productive to think of it as an equation, the principal characteristic of which, like all equations, is reversibility. The title, seen in this light, means "the Spanish woman who is also an English woman" and "the English woman who is also a Spanish woman." The Spanish heroine and the English queen have the same name. Properties commonly attributed to the historical Elizabeth are ascribed in the text to Isabela. Foremost among these is Elizabeth's bald head and famous collection of wigs. In the text it is Isabela who is disfigured by the loss of her hair. Elizabeth was the "Sun Queen," and in the text Isabela is "rayo de sol." These backwards coincidences between Isabela and Elizabeth cannot be the result of Cervantes's sketchy knowledge of things English. They are based on widely held beliefs whose truth or falsehood is irrelevant (and no one understood this better than Cervantes), pressed into the service of a kind of fictional algebra in which the women are interchangeable, as the title suggests.

With this in mind we can return, for example, to the matter of dressing "a la española" or "a la inglesa" and tentatively conclude that the two styles of dress are not meant to signal irreducible opposition and mutual exclusivity, but rather that "a la española" and "a la inglesa" are equivalent in the sense of being interchangeable without introducing any change in meaning.

There is a similar blurring of the doctrinal differences between Protestants and Catholics, differences presumed to be at the heart of Cervantes's religious thesis. The Protestant queen admonishes Ricaredo that he will have to earn Isabela by performing certain kinds of deeds. Her speech is top-heavy with references to the concepts of will and works. Her description of Ricaredo's expedition is in fact a secularized statement of the Roman Catholic theology of works endorsed at Trent. "'Ricaredo will not be betrothed to Isabela until he has earned her. By this I mean that his forebears' services are of no value; he must do something himself to serve me and to deserve this reward'" (250). Catholic Isabela, in contrast, renounces her own free will and declares it bound to that of Ricaredo's parents. Her speech is a paean to passivity. "'Since Heaven's rigor took my parents from me and gave me yours, I determined that my will would always be contained within theirs. Without their will in me I would consider the inestimable grace you are about to bestow on me as ill fortune. From this moment on I offer you the will that they give me'" (246). Read theologically, this text appears to go beyond even Luther's position in *de servo arbitrio*.

The same curious transposition may be more directly observed in a confrontation of Ricaredo with his rival, the conde Arnesto, when they meet in Italy. Arnesto offers an "economic" explanation of the events leading up to Ricaredo's forthcoming marriage to Isabela: "'My lady the queen commanded you to go and serve her, and to perform works that would make you worthy of the peerless Isabela. You went forth, and you returned with your ships loaded with gold, and with that you think you have bought Isabela'" (266). Ricaredo rises above this conception: "'I confess I not only do not deserve Isabela, but that no man alive today in the world deserves her. And so, confessing the truth of what you say ...'" (267). The language of this exchange appears to be that of commerce. Isabela is evoked by Arnesto as an object with a price on it, like the jewels so insistently evoked on the same page: a string of pearls appraised at twenty thousand ducados; a ring and a diamond appraised at six thousand (266). However, the repetition in Ricaredo's speech of the religious technicism *confesar* invites a theological reading of the passage. Accordingly, Arnesto's rhetoric of *comprar* and *merecer* via the performance of *hazañas* would place him within the conceptual framework of justification by works, with Ricaredo countering from the perspective of justification by faith and grace. What is of crucial importance here is the fact that the spokesman for works is the Protestant Arnesto, while Ricaredo, who speaks up for faith and grace, is a Roman Catholic committed by the Council of Trent to a theology of works. Positions have been interchanged. The doctrinal differences between Christians are thereby obliterated or at least rendered considerably less important than we might expect.

This phenomenon of interchangeability occurs within a general climate of exchange. Indeed, our last example was a verbal exchange, about courtship as a form of exchange, which dramatizes an exchange of theological positions. With this in mind we might profitably turn our attention once again to real commerce and exchange, and the real economy as it appears and functions within Cervantes's text and also outside and around it. We should begin by going back to Cádiz.

The raid on Cádiz was in fact a nationalistic commercial enterprise (and we have seen how the tables were turned by the "strategic incompetence" of the Duque de Medina Sidonia), based on and justified by political and religious antagonism, and with physical violence and rapine as its modus operandi. The first noun in Cervantes's text is *despojo* (243), and its referent is Isabela. Our heroine enters the text dehumanized, reduced to the level of an object, a spoil of war. It is also worth noting that this despojo is presumed to have value in and of itself. It is not taken, as were the forty-one individuals identified by Slingsby, to be exchanged later for something else. In opposition to what we saw so insistently in *El amante liberal*, Isabela as a commodity has a use-value, not an exchange-value. She is part of a retrograde economic order with respect to the thriving trade in ransomed captives that sustained Algiers in the same period.

Similarly, the expedition commanded by Ricaredo is also a commercial venture, although sanctioned and indeed instigated by Elizabeth and thus an instrument of national policy. Robert W. Kenny observes that "the two biggest prizes of Elizabethan times were taken by ships under the queen's commission. In 1587 Sir Francis Drake took the carrack *San Felipe* with a cargo—a major part of the year's pepper supply—valued at nearly £115,000. The *Madre de Dios*, taken in 1592 by Sir John Burroughs, carried quantities of pepper, cloves, cinnamon, cochineal and thousands of diamonds and other stones." Her cargo was worth £141,000, "even after indiscriminate looting."[80] Kenny further notes that under Elizabeth's policies, "any Englishman who could outfit a ship could have a go at Spanish commerce."[81] This practice was officially discontinued by James I even before his coronation, a manifestation of his desire for peace with Spain. Cervantes's text, however, offers a realistic and historically accurate portrayal of things as they were under Elizabeth. Even the cargo of the fictional ship seized by Ricaredo—"spices, and pearls, and diamonds worth more than a million in gold" (254)—is virtually identical with that of the historical *Madre de Dios.*

Ricaredo's expedition is, as we have already observed, at once an instrument of national policy and a primitive kind of commercial venture. It runs afoul of a similar, nationalistic commercial enterprise, that of Cervantes's old "acquaintance" and first master in Algiers, the Albanian corsair Arnaute Mamí, which had overpowered "a ship returning from the Portuguese Indies loaded with spices" (254). Pinheiro da Veiga notes that the English gentlemen in Valladolid were wearing in their hats "hatbands of gold, and medallions of diamonds and rubies, all paid for by our ships from the Indies."[82] With respect especially to the English corsairs, the economic system in operation here is a primitive one. It resembles the Algerian corsair economy in its idea that wealth is produced by taking it away from someone else, in its reliance on physical violence, and in that it is based on antagonism and fraud (the English ship flies a Spanish flag). However, the English version of the corsair economy, as it exists in this text and especially with reference to little Isabela, thinks first in terms of use- rather than exchange-value.

But the Portuguese ship captured first by Arnaute Mamí and then by Ricaredo and his band of English primitives belongs to a different economic order. This ship, on which Isabela's parents have coincidentally taken passage, is carrying spices from India to America by way of Spain. That is, Ricaredo and his men have interrupted a worldwide commercial network that, were it not for them and the Algerians, would function in an orderly and harmonious fashion beneficial to everyone involved. The captured ship belongs to an economic order in which wealth is generated by the process of exchange, an order based on cooperation and good faith, and furthermore one that spans the entire world. In a word, this ship is the representative of a *Catholic* economic order. The doctrinal differences among Algerians, English, Spaniards, and Portuguese are absent from the text, and have been replaced by the economic differences we have just noted. It would be more accurate to say that Catholicism has ceased to be a religious word, and that the concept it represents has been redefined in economic terms.

If we consider the families of Isabela and Ricaredo within their respective economic orders we can observe similar distinctions. When Ricaredo captures him, Isabela's father relates the loss of his daughter to the loss of his fortune.

"You know, sir, that in the loss of Cádiz I also lost a daughter the English must have carried off to England, and with her I lost the relief of my old age and the light of my eyes. The terrible depression that resulted from her loss, and that of my property, which I also lost, left me in such a state that I neither desired nor was able to engage in trade in merchandise, which had reputed me the richest merchant in Cádiz. And it was true, for besides my credit, which exceeded many hundred thousand ducados, the property I had within my house alone was worth more than 50,000. I lost everything, but I would consider it as nothing, if only I had not lost my daughter." (257)

Isabela is clearly not her father's wealth, yet in a sense she might as well be. Her loss and the loss of the fortune occur simultaneously. The lexicon and syntax of the father's speech push the two together: the repetitions of "loss" and "lost," the parallelism of "I neither desired nor was able," suggest something approaching identification, or perhaps interchangeability.

Furthermore, Isabela's father demonstrates his membership in a sophisticated economic order. The great bulk of his wealth, several hundred thousand ducados, is in the form of credit. This intangible wealth is far greater than his physical assets, which amount to only about fifty thousand ducados. He can be plausibly identified with those historical Spanish middlemen who stood in for international capitalists and who were ruined when the Duque de Medina Sidonia sent the merchant fleet to the bottom of Cádiz harbor. Finally, it was the father's *crédito* that enabled him to do business in the first place, which in turn gave him the reputation (*opinión*) of being the wealthiest merchant in Cádiz. The father's wealth is presented not as an empirically demonstrable fact, but as an opinion, a matter of belief, which is made possible by an initial act of faith, the granting of the first credit. There is an obvious semantic relation between *crédito* and *opinión,* trust and faith. The root of *crédito* is *credo,* after all. Emile Benveniste traces *credo* to a system of "economic obligations, a sequence linking a donation to a remuneration."[83] As in the case of the Portuguese ship captured en route to America, an examination of the economic order in which Isabela's father exists leads us back to the religious thematics of our text, and implies a kind of "small c" catholicism, divorced from the specifics of dogma but uniting and resting on the concepts of faith and universality. Cervantes is clearly not concerned here with the kind of Catholicism manifested, for example, by the English gentlemen at Valladolid who fell to their knees and commenced to adore the holy relics in the shrine.

In all respects, the family of Clotaldo offers a striking contrast to what we have just observed. We first see Clotaldo as a member of the military-economic expedition to Cádiz, bringing home booty in human form and participating thereby in a primitive and unproductive economic order based on antagonism, rapine, and deceit. Isabela, the spoil of war, is simply a physical economic asset. "Clotaldo arrived in London and turned the beautiful child over to his wife as a rich spoil" (244). Queen Elizabeth considers her similarly when she berates Clotaldo for "'keeping this treasure secret from me, but the treasure is such that I can understand what moved you to this greed. You are obliged to return it to me, for by law it is mine'" (249). The queen's choice of pronouns leaves no room for doubt; Isabela is not a female person, but *el tesoro*. Feminist critics might want to ponder this presentation of an infecund economic order, presided by a sterile woman, which systematically reduces women to the status of (infecund) commodities.

In the course of all this we learn that Clotaldo and his family are aristocrats. Like all aristocrats, they toil not, neither do they spin. And they have no idea how to make money except by the most primitive means. They bring home wealth in the form of a human captive, and they plan to marry wealth in the form of Clisterna, the rich Scottish girl. If Cervantes derived her name from the noun *clíster,* she becomes a deliberately vulgar and malicious representation of the notion of (financial) influx, for clíster is defined by Covarrubias as "an enema syringe."

To recapitulate, aristocratic Clotaldo and the old-order economic system to which he belongs conceive of wealth only in terms of physical assets held, and believe that wealth is generated by taking it away from somebody else (Isabela) or marrying it (Clisterna). Isabela's father, however, belongs to a system based on credit and believes that wealth is generated through investment of capital and operations of exchange.

When she returns to Spain, Isabela brings with her ten thousand escudos, which she turns over to her father, who uses the money to go into business. In the "catholic" system as we have defined it, this money is not an end in itself but is capital to be invested. We are thus reminded that in fact both Isabela's father and Clotaldo are Catholics, which renders the contrasts we have noted all the more striking. Clotaldo, however, is a Catholic who is forced to function in an un-catholic economic system that he, a victim of ideology, believes is natural and normal. He is what we might call a Catholic manqué, deprived and ignorant of an essential aspect of his Catholicism. It is for this reason that he is able to commit the un-Christian act of abduction that begins the narrative, which led Joaquín Casalduero, in search of an excuse for this reprehensible behavior, to call him "the lukewarm Catholic."[84] If Casalduero's assertion is transposed to the economic system, or broadened to include the economic dimension we have been considering, it takes on a new relevance, no longer apologetic but explicative.

The text is at great pains to inventory Isabela's capital and to narrate its transfer from England to Spain in detail. She had already been given expensive clothing, and jewelry valued at twenty-six thousand : pearls worth twenty thousand, and a diamond worth six thousand (266). The queen adds "other jewels and dresses" (270). When Ricaredo pretends to agree to marriage with Clisterna he entreats his father "to refrain from taking from Isabela any of the riches the Queen had given her" (271). As Isabela and her parents prepare to depart for Spain, the queen herself orders Clotaldo "to leave Isabela in possession of all she had given her, including clothing and jewelry" (272). Apparently, both his son and his sovereign fear that Clotaldo's acquisitive tendencies, the result of his active participation in a rapacious economic system, will tempt him to despoil Isabela as he and his colleagues had despoiled Cádiz years before. One is reminded of Abreu's descriptions of the English soldiers who "undressed the women to see if they had anything of value hidden on them, and if the dresses were of good quality, they took them too."[85] This detail, important enough to be mentioned twice, serves to estrange Queen Elizabeth from the primitive economic order over which she in fact presides, and to identify her with Isabela, with the economic order represented by her father, and with the forces of right in general. Finally, Isabela's capital is completed by an indemnity of ten thousand escudos in cash paid on Elizabeth's order by Arnesto's mother following the discovery of her treachery (272).

The transfer of Isabela's capital to Spain is narrated in great detail, provoking both critical censure and attempts to justify it on the grounds of Cervantes's eagerness to show off his knowledge of the inner workings of the banking business. Joaquín Casalduero, for example, observes that it would have sufficed to say that the queen handed him ten thousand escudos.[86] González de Amezúa faults Casalduero for forgetting that Cervantes loved to show off his expertise in the things he writes about.[87] Neither reaction addresses the function of this prosaic material in the text. Queen Elizabeth is estranged from the English economic system by her admonition of Clotaldo. She is next shown participating actively in the "catholic-international" system. There was in fact a clandestine English Catholic commercial and financial network in Europe, as John Bossy reports: "From Antwerp to Sanlúcar de Barrameda, English merchants and agents . . . arranged passage, gave directions, lent money, saw to its conveyance, cashed bills of exchange. . . . The fact that 'merchant' came to be used by Catholics as the conventional periphrasis for a priest is not entirely accidental or insignificant."[88] It is Queen Elizabeth who personally arranges the transfer of funds. She takes care of Isabela's capital as she took care of Isabela's health by sending her personal physician to attend her when she was poisoned.

What the queen arranges is a complex series of operations that transcends political and national barriers, and that involves the participation of several individuals presumed to be separated by those same barriers. The text is worth quoting *in extenso* because it insists on this complexity:

> The Queen called on a wealthy French merchant-banker established in London who had connections in France, Italy, and Spain, to whom she gave the 10,000 escudos, and she requested from him bills of exchange for Isabela's father on Sevilla or another Spanish financial venue. The merchant, after deducting his expenses and profit, told the Queen he would provide absolutely secure bills of exchange drawn on another French merchant-banker in Sevilla, in this way: he would have the bills of exchange drawn first in Paris by his correspondent there, so that they would appear to originate in France instead of in England, to circumvent the ban on communication between the two countries, and it would be sufficient to present a letter bearing his countersign for payment by the merchant-banker in Sevilla, who would have been advised by his colleague in Paris. (272)

The political and religious antagonism between Spain and England should render commerce impossible or limit it to the rapine practiced by Clotaldo and his fellow corsairs. But we discover through this text an invisible, but by no means unknown, economic order that transcends this antagonism, an order based on trust as opposed to deceit, cooperation as opposed to rivalry, and that functions through processes of mediation. The money does not make the trip; what travels from England to Spain is a series of letters that stand for the money and that pass through a series of human intermediaries. This combination of trust or belief in the certainty of things unseen (faith), and its manifestation in the form of written texts—the bills of exchange—suggests the presence of the Protestant *sola fides, sola scriptura* in the heart of the catholic economic order.

The chain is completed in Spain. "They were in Cádiz for a little over a month, then they went to Sevilla to see if the payment of the 10,000 escudos by the French merchant-banker could take place. Two days after they arrived in Sevilla they looked him up and presented the letter from the French banker in London. He recognized it, and told them that he could not make the payment until the bills of exchange and the letter arrived from Paris, but that he expected them any day" (273).

This news does not provoke any anxiety; the atmosphere of trust remains undisturbed. Forty days later the *avisos* duly arrive from Paris and Isabela receives the cash that never left London, from the hand of a French banker, in Sevilla. At the two extremes of this chain stand England and Spain, Elizabeth and Isabela, *española* and *inglesa*. Their linking is made possible, as we have seen, by an international network of bankers that exists underneath and in spite of the political and, insofar as religion is an instrument or a goal of national policy, the religious rhetoric of exclusivity and antagonism. This is analogous to what we observed in Algiers: the entire economy, based on the redemption of captives across religious and ideological barriers, is made possible by a network of international bankers operating on both sides of the Mediterranean.

Isabela's wealth, as we have already remarked, is capital to be invested. "The French banker gave the 10,000 to Isabela, which she turned over to her parents. And with that, plus some additional cash raised by selling some of Isabela's many jewels, her father began once again to deal in merchandise" (274). This is accomplished to the great astonishment of "those who knew how much he had lost." What is even more astonishing is the simultaneous recuperation of her father's credit and Isabela's beauty (274).

The losses suffered as a result of the sack of Cádiz have all been restored. Isabela is back, her beauty is back, and her father and his credit are also back. Things are *sicut erant in principio.* There is a clear identification of her beauty with his credit. The text is always careful to distinguish between credit, with all that it implies, and wealth in general. Credit is a signifier; it is not wealth but it stands for wealth. Beauty, as even the most conservative commentators of our text have observed, similarly stands for something else, in this case nobility of soul. Credit is not an end in itself but the beginning of a process. Beauty is also the beginning of a process, in this case the union of Isabela and Ricaredo.

Things are as they were, except that Isabela is no longer a child of six but a grown woman, who furthermore is in love with and betrothed to Ricaredo, and Ricaredo is absent. The story of his travels and fortuitous appearance in Sevilla just in time to claim Isabela as his bride turns out to be another tour through the mechanisms of international banking.

After he puts himself right with the Church in Rome and has visited "the innumerable holy places" there, Ricaredo sees to his finances. "'And of 2,000 escudos I had in gold, I gave 1,600 to a banker who made them payable to me here in Sevilla through a certain Florentine named Roque. I took the remaining 400 and set out for Genoa, with the intention of continuing on to Spain'" (279). There is no political or religious barrier to the transfer of funds from Italy to Spain; Ricaredo is moved simply by considerations of prudence and safety to divest himself of most of his cash before he makes the trip. Before discussing his adventures at sea we should pause to contrast the vagueness with which he recounts the religious dimension of his stay in Rome with the precision and detail he lavishes on the description of his financial arrangements.

When Ricaredo is captured by pirates he expresses less concern for the loss of his freedom than for the loss of the receipt for his money. "'Of course you can believe me if I tell you how much I regretted my captivity, and especially the loss of the receipts from Rome, which I had in a tin box'" (281). Again, the contrast is instructive. It is not the cash that is at issue, but the cédula that stands for it.

His liberation from captivity is not the result of a daring escape à la Ruy Pérez de Viedma and Zoraida, but of a rather complicated financial arrangement:

> "They took us to Algiers, where I discovered the Trinitarian fathers were ransoming prisoners. They arranged my ransom in this way, giving 300 ducados, the first 100 in advance and the remaining 200 when the ship with ransom money arrived from Spain to ransom the Trinitarian who had remained in Algiers in pawn for 4,000 ducados, because he had spent more than he actually had. As a final stroke of luck I found the tin box with the receipts and the cédula. I showed it to the good padre who had ransomed me and offered him 500 ducados in addition to the price of my ransom to aid him in his good work." (281)

Narciso Alonso Cortés and Agustín González de Amezúa have hastened to identify the facts of Ricaredo's narration with those of Cervantes's own life.[89] Fray Juan Gil, procurador general of the Order of the Holy Trinity, had three hundred escudos available to ransom Cervantes, but Hasán Pasha had set five hundred as the price. Fray Juan organized a loan from several mercaderes to make up the difference, and Cervantes then paid off the new debt with miscellaneous charitable contributions. Although it has the virtue of demonstrating the historical possibility of operations like the one Ricaredo recounts, analogous to our earlier demonstration of the historical possibility of Isabela's abduction from Cádiz, drawing attention to these coincidences runs the risk of confusing fictional text with biographical anecdote. If we consider this episode within the fictional structure of *La española inglesa,* it becomes clear that the precise and detailed description of these financial arrangements belongs in a series that begins with the transfer of Isabela's capital from England to Spain. We can conclude that this text is at pains to make visible the economic infrastructure on which the characters' happiness rests, and to make the relation of cause and effect equally visible. In addition, we are back in an economy based on the notion of exchange-value as opposed to use-value. Ricaredo and the good padre who ransoms him become commodities that can be exchanged for other commodities, in this case the "universal equivalent" or cash. This is the exact opposite, it need hardly be stated, of the system into which Isabela's abduction from Cádiz is inserted. Finally, we are again in the presence of what I have called the "catholic" economy, an advanced system of exchange based on credit, on mediation, on charity (that is, on love of one's fellow man), and on universality, and here at least involving the direct participation of the Roman Catholic Church.

The story of Ricaredo's arrival in Sevilla is also the story of the arrival of his money. When he finishes the narration of his adventures he produces his receipt for the funds he had entrusted to the banker in Rome, and "Heaven ordained that the Florentine banker to whom the cédula for the 1,600 ducados was addressed was present at all this. He asked to see the cédula, which he immediately recognized and accepted for payment, because he had been expecting it for some months" (282). The prompt payment of these funds allows Ricaredo to make good on his promise of five hundred ducados toward the ransom of the Trinitarian in Algiers. The narrative loose ends to be tied up are transformed into outstanding financial obligations to be discharged, and the catholic and Catholic aspects of the economic system that has produced this happy ending are specifically linked.

The Church is present and intimately related to the new economic order, but the relation is complex and needs to be explored in some detail. When Isabel and her family reach Sevilla they rent a large house across from the convent of Santa Paula, where a relative is a nun (273). Since this takes place while they are waiting for their money to arrive from Paris, the rental must have been arranged on credit. The family, their participation in a credit-based economy, and family membership in a religious order are all joined here, linking the economic system to the Church. The family waits forty days after their first inquiry before the letra de cambio arrives from Paris. The precise number of days in question relates these events to the liturgical sequence of Lent followed by Easter, fasting and scarcity replaced by abundance and a promise kept. While she waits for Ricaredo, Isabela gives herself over to a round of specifically Roman Catholic activities. She hardly leaves her home except to go to the convent, she earns jubilees with the associated indulgences, and she participates imaginatively in the stations of the cross (275). The letter from Catalina with its "greatly exaggerated" report of Ricaredo's death arrives fifty days after it was sent. If forty days are Lent, then surely fifty suggest Pentecost, ironically reversed here as the demonstration of Christ's life is transformed into the erroneous report of Ricaredo's death. Finally, the letter prompts Isabela to withdraw from the world in the most specifically Roman Catholic practice of all, entrance into a religious order, a celibate life and spiritual marriage to Christ. This series of practices—the jubilees, the stations of the cross, and especially the monasticism—constitutes the only reference in our text to the doctrinal aspects of Roman Catholicism, and they are presented in a manner that does not invite enthusiasm. In particular, Isabela's entrance into the convent is the one event that must not be allowed to happen if the story is to end happily. Phrased another way, Ricaredo's sudden arrival in Sevilla defines Cervantes's text as a story about human love with a frank sexual component (Ricaredo has desired Isabela since she was twelve) triumphing over a series of obstacles, and defines becoming a nun (which might be positive in another context) as the last such obstacle to be overcome. So the Church is present, but in a special way, not theologically, and with negative reference to the specific exterior practices of Roman Catholicism.

The Church is present along with other institutions in the crowded room in Isabela's father's rented house where Ricaredo narrates his tale of personal and economic redemption. At the conclusion of his narrative he "took the receipts out of a tin box and gave them to the *provisor,* who looked them over together with the *asistente,* and as a final confirmation, Heaven ordained that the Florentine banker was also present" (282). The *provisor* represents the Church, as the archbishop's vicar. The *asistente* represents the Crown and the Florentine banker of course represents the new international economic order. All three are present for the express purpose of validating Ricaredo's story and legitimizing his claim to his money and to Isabela.

Ruth El Saffar has written that *La española inglesa* contains "the most complete statement in the *Novelas ejemplares* of Cervantes's preoccupation with religion. . . . The joining of Ricaredo and Isabela is an example of Catholic generosity which transcends national boundaries. It is the resurrection of a dream of peace on earth and the recovery of faith in the unity of all things despite the presence of forces of disruption and disintegration."[90] All this is true and of good report. What it neglects to mention, however, is what the text hammers home again and again: all this personal and Catholic reconciliation and peace on earth is made possible only by the international financial network that transcends nations and religions. As we have seen, it is the English Protestant Elizabeth who sets the whole thing in motion by calling on the "French banker established in London." Similarly, El Saffar's assertion that in Cervantes nobility becomes the social correlative of "the elect of God who achieve union with Him after death" is undone by the text.[91] Indeed, one way to consider the paradoxical joining of the idealistic love story and the detailed descriptions of financial operations would be to consider *La española inglesa* as a reflection of the dialectic of history as conceived in classic Marxist theory. The idealized love story is or had been traditionally the province of the aristocracy, but Cervantes eliminates aristocratic protagonists in favor of the bourgeoisie. When Cervantes belabors the financial infrastructure of the bourgeois lifestyle he is insisting on the emergence of the bourgeoisie onto center stage in both history and fiction. The bourgeoisie displaces the aristocracy as the protagonist of history, and fiction mirrors this change.

This analysis, however, ignores some particular facts of Spanish history and therefore inevitably falsifies the relation between history and fiction. Michel

Cavillac has observed apropos of our text that "the entire novella, filled with the finest sentiments (the context of improved relations with England under James I is not absent), basks in an atmosphere of European concord held together by commerce, presented as one of the most honorable pursuits."[92] However, he also cites Enrique Tierno Galván to the effect that the failure of the *comunidades* in 1520 was "the first decisive blow that separated the middle class in Spain from the rest of western Europe." From that moment there developed what Tierno Galván calls an insidious process of absorption of the bourgeois mentality by the ideology of the aristocracy.[93] Bartolomé Bennassar has offered copious documentation of this absorption in the urban environment of Valladolid. It is difficult if not impossible to distinguish between a bourgeois and an aristocratic lifestyle. Bourgeoisie and aristocracy outfit themselves in the same luxury fabrics. Their households are similarly replete with liveried servants. This applies as well to the ownership of a coach, of a secondary residence, of a house with a carved stone façade, or even with a tower. This last feature was shared by the homes of the Conde de Benavente and the banker (mercader) Fabio Nelli.[94]

The social structure peculiar to Spain, the overwhelming importance of lineage in its two aspects of *hidalguía* and *limpieza,* simply did not allow for the independent development of the bourgeoisie. And yet this is not quite true either, for there were in fact dynasties of wealthy merchant-banker families in both Andalucía and Castile. Furthermore, the aristocracy was frequently heavily in debt to them. In Valladolid a few years before Cervantes moved there, for example, the Duque de Osuna (the father of Quevedo's friend) owed 1.26 million maravedís to Fabio Nelli of the towered house.[95] Other examples include the Conde de Benavente's debt to the chancelry lawyer and clairvoyant economist Martín González de Cellorigo. Bennassar and others have shown the extent to which the merchant-bankers and other monied classes—the *letrados,* for example—controlled the economic infrastructure, the visible superstructure of which is the national policy of war in Europe or peace with England, the ostentatious lifestyle of the aristocracy, and the kind of sumptuous festivities described by Cabrera de Córdoba and Pinheiro da Veiga: the clothing, the carriages, the ceremonies, the banquets, the bullfights, and the dances. But the Nellis, the Ruiz's, the Méndez's, the Maluendas, and their like never appear in the chronicles of the public events that their wealth in fact made possible. Both Cabrera de Córdoba and Pinheiro da Veiga offer list after list of the participants in this bullfight or that sarao, and every name on every list belongs to an aristocrat.

Cervantes's protagonists are definitely not aristocrats, and contrary to what we have just observed, Isabela's family does not seem particularly interested in adopting the aristocratic lifestyle with its characteristic conspicuous consumption. Their wealth, we recall, is mainly invisible, in the form of credit. In this they resemble those sober-sided Sevillian merchants Berganza finds so attractive in the *Coloquio de los perros*. They are opposed, for example, to Guzmán de Alfarache's Sevillian merchant father, who as soon as he has accumulated some wealth attempts to *arraigarse* (literally to sink roots into the earth, figuratively to identify with the class whose status is a function of its ownership of land, i.e., the aristocracy) by purchasing an opulent villa in suburban San Juan de Alfarache. Guzmán's father follows the pattern of behavior documented by Tierno Galván and Bennassar. The enriched merchant-banker class attempts to put its (dishonorable?) origins behind it, to cease to be what it is and to become indistinguishable from the landed aristocracy.

To understand why this was so, and to begin to appreciate the ideological message Cervantes's text conveys through its distortion of what appears to be historical fact, we need to return again to Cádiz in 1596. We have already mentioned Fray Pedro de Abreu's eyewitness account of what happened there, and it will now be instructive to consider his version of the causes of the catastrophe. Fray Pedro is in this respect a particularly articulate spokesman for the dominant ideology; he considers that Cádiz was lost basically on account of the greed of the financial and mercantile community. Their attachment to material things at the expense of the salvation of their souls had corrupted the common folk and robbed them of their will to resist, and there were too few aristocrats to rally the people and organize the defense.

> This calamity befell Cádiz because its inhabitants had forgotten the perpetual and eternal values and occupied themselves instead with ephemeral and perishable things. They were enjoying great prosperity and abundance, born of the great profits they were making in trade and merchandise; they pursued this lure blinded by greed, with their thoughts and concerns so occupied in profit that they forgot their conscience. This can be inferred from the presence of so many of humble and ill-born beginnings who had acquired great wealth and substance in a short time. In their arrogance they threw money into sumptuous clothing and grand houses, competing with the truly powerful whose grandeur and prosperity was inherited. This is where they put their happiness, their pleasure and their purpose, as if these material things could promise them eternal security and everlasting life. And the very cosmopolitanism of these people contributed to their weakness, because if Cádiz had been populated solely by natives who cared nothing for commerce and merchandise, raised in hardship to be tough, instead of being made effeminate by greed, they would have made a greater effort to defend themselves, their wives and children, and their homeland. And this is borne out by experience: they let the enemy in without making a stand, they retired to their homes expecting courtesy where none was to

be had. The aristocrats were alarmed to see the common people so timid and cowardly, because there were only six or seven families of noble lineage in the city, and although they did everything they could, calling on their ancestral courage, it was not sufficient to resist that force.[96]

We know that in fact Cádiz was lost not by the cowardly bourgeoisie but by an aristocrat, the Duque de Medina Sidonia, whose own business interests proved more powerful than his sworn duty to defend the place. He let the English destroy Cádiz in order to eliminate the competition to Sanlúcar-Sevilla. It is easy to dismiss Abreu's explanation as mere rhetoric, part of an official mythology based on the concepts of lineage and a racially inspired antibourgeois sentiment that boiled to the surface in, for example, the pogroms of 1391. It would be a mistake to dismiss Abreu, however, for his text bears witness in spite of itself to the gap between official rhetoric and socioeconomic reality that Cervantes's fiction brings to light.

In fact the Spanish economy was international, a form of mercantile capitalism, and was participated in not only by an urban bourgeoisie but by the aristocracy as well. We have made repeated reference in this connection to the role of the Duque de Medina Sidonia. The official rhetoric, however, depicts a feudoagrarian economy controlled by the aristocracy and stout Old Christian peasants, and suppresses all positive references to mercantile capitalism on the grounds that *tratos y mercancías* had historically been the province of Jews. This is manifested in Abreu's evocation of the spineless, effeminate mercaderes who refuse to fight, in opposition to the courageous but hopelessly outnumbered aristocracy.

The official rhetoric, that is, the ruling prejudices of the society, actually produced the second historical reality we have documented here, the efforts of the wealthy bourgeoisie to adopt the lifestyle of the aristocracy. This too is evoked by Abreu when he rails against the nouveaux riches bourgeois who "threw money into sumptuous clothing and grand houses, competing with the truly powerful whose grandeur and prosperity was inherited."[97] It is worth noting that for Abreu this is not a matter of adopting a kind of protective coloration, but an act of aggression, an affront to the aristocracy whose grandeur "was inherited."

Cervantes's fiction is a complex restructuring of reality and rhetoric. It brings to the surface certain important facts systematically suppressed by the official rhetoric and joins them paradoxically to other aspects of the sustaining national mythology. In the end his text is both truer to life and more fictitious—one might even say utopian—than any contemporary version I can think of. Cervantes subverts both history and fiction. He offers a wealthy bourgeois family, members of the advanced economic order that existed in fact but the record of which was relegated to the back pages of contemporary fiction and historiography. Isabela's family is ruined by the brutal incursion of another more primitive system turned into an instrument of national policy and backed by armed might. Here history and fiction coincide. Elizabeth's policies were in fact those evoked in *La española inglesa*. The English system is depicted the way the Spanish system was assumed to be according to the official rhetoric. In the great tradition of Castilian history, wealth was generated by a class of aristocratic warriors (*ricos omes*) who took it away first from the Moors and then from the Indians in the New World, as Pierre Vilar has explained.[98]

The official rhetoric maintained the superiority of feudalism over mercantile capitalism. Cervantes's text demonstrates the opposite, thus subverting the official rhetoric but not necessarily the historical facts. The text does subvert fact, however, in the matter of the assimilation of the bourgeoisie to the aristocracy. Nowhere do we read that Isabela's family is anything but bourgeois, and the heroine's marriage to noble Ricaredo is evoked in terms of his assimilation into her (bourgeois) family, not the reverse. She invites him to "'come to my parents' house, which is yours, and there I will surrender my possession'" (278). It is true that Queen Elizabeth is an aristocrat, and everyone has observed what a nice lady she turns out to be. She clearly belongs with the protagonists, not with the enemy. Of the many ways in which Elizabeth is identified with Isabela, the most important is her direct and personal charge of the arrangements attendant on the transfer of Isabela's funds from England to Spain, that is, her participation in the international economic order. This sets her apart from her subjects, in particular from Clotaldo. Secondly, her alliance with Isabela's mercantile family acts out the traditional "royal alliance" of urban Jewish business interests and the Crown who came together for mutual benefit and protection against the rapacious aristocracy and resentful commoners. In this sense, history and Cervantes's fiction offer a startling contrast to the alliance repeatedly depicted by Lope in his best-known plays, between the Crown and the stalwart Old Christian peasants against the rapacious aristocracy. In spite of the heroic rearguard action fought by more than one generation of prominent hispanists, it has by now come to everyone's attention that the aristocracy depicted by Lope is strongly suspected of (horresco referens) racial impurity, while the monarch and the peasants are united in limpieza de sangre. Lope's version of the official rhetoric joins aristocracy, greed, and impurity, and proceeds to ostracize them. Abreu's alternate but just as orthodox version joins bourgeoisie, greed, and impurity, and proceeds to the same conclusion. The constant in both versions is the nexus of greed and racial impurity.

This brings us to our final consideration of Isabela's family. If they were real, they would in all probability be the descendants of Jews who converted to Christianity at least a century before the attack on Cádiz. Cervantes does not go out of his way to identify them as Old Christians, from which we may infer that they are presumed to be conversos. Pablo Virumbales, for one, operates on this assumption, and calls attention to the approving presence of the ecclesiastical and temporal dignitaries at Isabela's profession and at the grand apotheosis following the lovers' reunion, "which proves the great social prestige enjoyed by merchants."[99] What this episode demonstrates is the fictionality of Cervantes's text. The "prestige" enjoyed by the wealthy merchants was in fact that described by Abreu, who unmasks their *nouvelle richesse* and their attempts to ape the aristocracy, and holds them responsible for the destruction of Cádiz.

When Cervantes groups together the asistente, the provisor of the Church, the archbishop's vicar, and "all the titled ladies and gentlemen" in the crowd that gathers to witness Isabela's profession, and when they are joined a few pages later by the Florentine banker, all of whom celebrate the union of Isabela and Ricaredo, joining the blessing of Church, Crown, aristocracy, and international business community, he is creating a scene of social reconciliation possible only in fiction. Cervantes's text affirms that the bourgeoisie need not attempt to assimilate into the aristocracy, that the bourgeoisie qua bourgeoisie can come forward with honor as a protagonist of history, that there is no dishonor attaching to the profession of merchant capitalist, that the wedding of a bourgeois family is a public event as worthy to be chronicled as the aristocratic festivities in Valladolid, and finally that these converso business types with their international connections are among the best Catholics. In short, Cervantes's text is a direct refutation of the official rhetoric.

This official rhetoric may be characterized as economically primitive, politically nationalistic, socially racist, and religiously divisive. Cervantes brings to the surface of fictional discourse some of the unspoken or unspeakable characteristics of the reality that existed beneath the rhetoric. There was an advanced international economy dependent on credit and goodwill largely in the hands of converso bankers and businessmen. This economic infrastructure is compatible with and inseparable from the ideal of Catholicism—not the dogma that divides Catholics from Protestants and Muslims, but catholicity in its broader, "catholic" sense. All this is present explicitly in the text and guarantees that the otherwise improbable and rather sappy love story of Isabela and Ricaredo resonates with deeper meanings. It is not for nothing that she is so insistently identified with Elizabeth, and it is not for nothing that the recuperation of her beauty coincides with her father's recuperation of his credit.

To distinguish again between catholic and Catholic, Isabela's final profession and entrance into the convent must not be allowed to happen if the story is to end happily. The contrast between the celibacy of the convent and the implied fecundity of matrimony enables us to conclude our consideration of how *La española inglesa* became possible and how it was produced. I say the implied rather than the actual fecundity of matrimony because, contrary to our expectations of what should constitute living happily ever after, there are no references anywhere in the text to Ricaredo and Isabela's children. This is doubly curious when we recall that, in a sense, the entire story has been the story of family relationships, in which legitimate and foster children have played important roles. The ending of *La española inglesa* offers a marked contrast in this respect with that of *El amante liberal,* for example, which celebrates "the many children Ricardo had in Leonisa" (188). Instead of biological increase, *La española inglesa* offers the other sense of the Greek *tokos:* restoration of wealth and the acquisition of property. "By these circuitous routes Isabela's parents regained their daughter and restored their wealth, and she found a noble husband, in whose company she is believed to be living today, in the houses they rented across from Santa Paula, which they later bought from the heirs of an hidalgo from Burgos named Hernando de Cifuentes" (283).

It is not people who are fecund here, but capital. We have already observed two implied equations in our text. The first is named in the title, according to which *Isabela la española* is identified with *Isabel(a) la inglesa.* The other relates Isabela to her father's capital. The term common to both is Isabela. In the first she is linked to physical sterility, in the second to economic fecundity. In the course of this operation the notions of sterility and fecundity are tranferred from one referential axis to another, from human generation to the generation of wealth.

The text suggests that fecundity can be defined in a new way while retaining its legitimacy and positive value. It also posits a utopian vision of the dialectic of history. The last sentence quoted involves two families with very different characteristics who may be considered as signifiers in a social code. Isabela's family has no name, and she and Ricaredo have no offspring. The family's activities are the recuperation of wealth that it uses to purchase urban real estate. This family defines itself, and redefines fecundity, in economic terms. The other family has a family name and is part of the aristocracy. Its activities as reported in the text are restricted to selling the urban property to the first family. The text insists—has always insisted—on the anonymity of Isabela's family. Their anonymity and their money cast them in opposition to the aristocracy, who are defined precisely by the possession of a name that passes from generation to generation, and by the ownership of real property. The family of the Burgalese hidalgo Hernando de Cifuentes and his heirs are the remnants of the old unproductive economic order. Scholars have labored mightily to locate this Hernando de Cifuentes in Cervantes's life.[100] The point is not *who* is signified by the name in the text, but *what*. The name means "an aristocratic family defined by the possession of a name and property." The change in ownership of the houses (the locus of prestige) across from Santa Paula (the locus of belonging) concretizes within the text the triumphant emergence of a new class, the urban bourgeoisie, to replace the aristocracy as the protagonist of history.

But this is the utopian vision I referred to earlier, for Cervantes surely must have realized that real history had already outflanked even this revolutionary overturning of the official rhetoric. By his calculated inaction at Cádiz in 1596, the Duque de Medina Sidonia had dealt a numbing blow to the local bourgeois capitalists and assured the continuation of the aristocracy as the real protagonist of history. These facts are recalled in the text by the simple presence of the fictional protagonists in Sevilla and not in Cádiz, to where it would have been natural for them to return if there had been a viable economy there. The text affirms the superiority of a capitalistic economic system in the hands of the probably New Christian bourgeoisie over a feudal economy in the hands of the aristocracy, as presented by the official rhetoric. But underneath this play of fictional text and official rhetoric lurks a historical reality of which Cervantes cannot have been unaware, namely that a capitalistic economy in the hands of the most powerful aristocrats is best of all.

It seems to me that Cervantes's quarrel is finally not with England or Protestantism or lukewarm Catholics or even with feudalism as opposed to capitalism, but with the aristocracy as opposed to the bourgeoisie. This quarrel exists on two levels. There is first the official rhetoric that associates the aristocracy with feudalism. The system resulting from this association is unmasked and attacked in the text of *La española inglesa*. More sinister is the reality that the official rhetoric served to sustain: the association of the aristocracy with capitalism, invisible but present in the (suppressed) facts of the destruction of Cádiz and the only apparently triumphant ending of the story in Sevilla.

# Afterword:
## On the Urgency of Materialist Studies

While I was working on this book during the summer of 1997, the business section of the *Santa Barbara News Press* (a New York Times company) reported: "Jobless rate drops to 4.8%; Wall Street worried." There it was: an unabashed, upfront statement of the fact that management requires a large pool of unemployed workers waiting to take the jobs of those employed, should they get it into their heads that they'd like a living wage. Full employment is bad for business. It turns labor into a scarce commodity and allows workers to demand higher salaries. Higher salaries mean less profit. Profits can be kept up by raising prices and passing the increase on to the consumer, but people don't like it when prices go up. It's better to keep prices low by keeping wages low, and this requires that pack of hungry unemployed circling around outside the campfire. Higher prices are called "inflation" because it appears that the consumer's money is worth less than it used to be. No consumer likes that, so it's easy to sell the idea that inflation is an evil to be avoided. Never mind that the rise in prices is management's doing, in order to keep those profits up, and is in fact not an unfortunate but inevitable consequence of full employment.

We live in a society where capitalism has gone mad, greed has run amok, where the gap between rich and poor is widening virtually by the hour, and where the middle class is threatened with extinction. We live in a society where the owners of the means of production actively and openly seek a situation in which a certain number of their fellow citizens go to bed hungry every night, because that is essential to keep profits at an acceptably high level. Recent political events are not encouraging. We are witnessing the resurgence of a pre–New Deal disregard for human values in a mad dash for profit. We see social programs gutted, while the poor are held responsible for their poverty and put on the street, and this is called "welfare reform." We export high-paying jobs in manufacturing to the Third World and replace them with subsistence-level McJobs in the "service sector," and this impoverishment of the labor force is called prosperity, a booming economy, "the envy of the industrial world." All this bodes ill for most citizens, and indeed, these conditions are the seedbed of revolution. It's happened elsewhere. But not to worry. Here in California we're making sure we have cells enough for the restive elements, even at the cost of spending more money on prisons than on higher education.

And what about higher education, for those of us who are in it? Where do we fit in? Most tenured academics live immune from the daily downsizings that affect our fellow wage earners in unprotected industries. Our nontenured colleagues are subjected to ever more rigorous demonstrations of intellectual achievement and, in at least one case known to me, to barely concealed political litmus tests, but at least many of them get into the club. And what shall we say of the growing pool of bright Ph.D.s who, since the mid-1970s, have formed an exploited underclass of ill-paid temporary workers whose job security exists nine or ten months at a time, who accumulate no retirement benefits, who are ineligible for research grants and sabbatical leaves, and who do all the tedious jobs we'd rather not: how to write grammatical sentences with some rhetorical panache, or how to drill your way through somebody else's language. Their job is to get by, and hopefully find something dignified and secure; they can't afford to be alienating employers. The job of the tenure-track assistant professors is to walk a perilous moral tightrope: to teach their classes and write their books with all the passion and intellectual integrity they can muster, and to try to steer clear of controversy while compromising their principles as little as possible. Only those of us who enjoy the security of tenured appointments can afford to actually act like scholars and educators, to "follow the search for truth wherever it leads," and to share unpopular truths with our students without fear of being downsized or eliminated for some unimpeachable-sounding reason like "poor quality scholarship." That is what the institution of tenure is for, and it is no coincidence that tenure is under massive assault today.

I am not an economist, only a hispanist and literary critic, so I can't speak about any of this with authority. In spite of my lack of credentials, the foregoing suggests to me that the academy participates in the same unequal distribution of wealth and the same growing gap betweeen rich and poor, the same growing reliance on an insecure temporary labor force, that we see in industry. We have a situation that cries out for some kind of dialogue and negotiation between labor and ownership, in the interests of the economic well-being and personal dignity of the workers, and the ultimate self-interest of the owners.

But we also live in a society where the labor movement has been emasculated to the point where we are the least unionized country in the industrial world. Not only that, and here is where we educators might come in, our young people don't seem to be able to formulate our problems—their problems—in terms of the opposing economic interests of workers and owners. A few years ago, in a class on various aspects of the Franco dictatorship in Spain (1939–1975), I remarked that the labor unions, to which all workers were required to belong, were official agencies of the government. Instead of gasps of disbelief or snickers of cynicism, I heard no reaction at all from the students. Upon questioning, it developed that none among the hundred or so bright young people in the class knew what a labor union is, or was. No wonder it doesn't occur to them to formulate their concern for their own future in terms of labor relations.

It is evident that we who call ourselves educators have a job to do. If our students don't know what a union is, we need to tell them. If they don't know what went on in the world before they got into it, we need to tell them. If we are living out a version of a social conflict that has existed many times before, our students need to know about it. And they need to know what analyses were made on those other occasions, and what solutions were tried out, with what consequences, for whom.

The obligation I perceive to educate our students is not entirely without self-interest. As I grow older certain clichés become more real to me: the one about "our kids are our future," for example. As I approach retirement, and my pension is going to be generated by the labor of young people like my students, I sure as hell don't want a labor force all making minimum wage flipping hamburgers and scanning bar-coded plastic shrink wraps. Give me some well-paid industrial workers whose labor generates serious wealth and who pay serious taxes. And as my daughter gets ready to enter the labor force, and begins thinking about getting married and starting a family of her own, that whole schtick about what kind of a world do I want to leave for them takes on not only relevance, but urgency. I have a compelling obligation to contribute, in my professional capacity as an educator and from within my particular area of professional expertise in Spanish Golden Age literature, to making their world better than mine.

Like all literature, the stories, plays, and poems written by Cervantes and his contemporaries are the products of, and engage in a living dialogue with, all the institutions and forces of the society in which they were produced and read. As an educator I have a responsibility to my students to make them aware of that dialectic of text and context, so they can have some idea of what the authors were doing and what the texts meant when they were produced. And this

obligation is the more compelling the more similarities I come to perceive
between that historical moment and ours, in terms of the problems confronted,
the remedies proposed, the choices made, and the results obtained. We also
need to explore the precise relations of text and context: how all of that in-
fluences literary production, how it shows up in literary texts, and how it is
influenced by those same texts. There is also an obligation to share one's dis-
coveries and ideas with one's professional peers, and to enter into a dialogue
with them concerning the goals of our collective enterprise. In my case this
means specifically a dialogue with my fellow senior professors of Spanish
Golden Age literature in American universities. This book is largely an attempt
to discharge both these obligations.

I have been concerned here with the representation of the material conditions of life, and the commercial operations necessary for it, in various texts
by Cervantes. Historical materialism is not a well-trod path of literary inquiry in the Anglo-American tradition in general, although notable exceptions
come readily to mind. It is still less traveled by Golden Age studies in the United
States, although, again, there are exceptions. I see among my colleagues first a
general unwillingness to discuss these subjects on the grounds that others are
sexier, and second a general ignorance of the facts when those subjects are
under discussion. Let me confess that virtually nothing in these pages is really
original with me. The analyses I offer of Cervantes's texts are grounded in the
published work of mostly European scholars in disciplines mostly other than
literature. This work has always been available for us to incorporate into our
own investigations, but for various reasons we have on the whole been loath
to do so.

Part of this indifference to materialist studies is determined by the economic infrastructure of our profession. We have eight years in which to produce
enough scholarly writings of sufficient quality to get us over the tenure hurdle.
In many cases, academic quality is defined as demonstrating familiarity with
the prevailing trends in critical theory and mastery of the discourse that goes
with them. If original thinking is encouraged, it is only within the paradigms
of established critical orthodoxy. In addition, unless you have an intellectual
background that most American-trained humanistic scholars lack (but which
our Latin American and European peers routinely command), you just don't
have time to start learning about philosophy, or theology, or psychoanalysis, or
political, social, or economic history. What we have time for in the race for tenure is some version of formalism, so we make a choice among what's available
at the moment from our particular mentors, in light of our personal inclinations. When we emerge into the sunlight of tenure, we tend, not illogically, to
continue to do the sort of thing that got us there. It is clearly acceptable, and

more importantly, it's what we know how to do. Most of us are disinclined to start learning now what we might (should?) have known before. We keep reading, we pick up bits and pieces of lore, we bone up on some topic in the preparation of a particular conference paper, but generally we do not subject ourselves to a lengthy second apprenticeship in some ancillary discipline.

Part of it is determined by the organizational structure of American universities, the definition of fields of study according to academic departments, and the practices of the job market. We belong to a *habitus* that defines literary study as separate from the "social sciences" of history, economics, sociology, and so on. At my university we belong to different divisions and report to different deans. Our departmental graduate curricula are established with an eye to securing a share of the market and then limiting our customers to our products. This is an example, by the way, of the same short-sighted monopolistic mentality that ruined the Castilian economy around 1600, and which Cervantes unmasks in *Rinconete y Cortadillo*.

What I remarked at the beginning bears repeating here. Américo Castro taught us to perceive the intercaste conflicts underlying behaviors as diverse as eating pork products and getting into the Order of Calatrava, and how an entire society was organized around those conflicts. Fernand Braudel has taught us to perceive the importance of commerce in spite of national antagonisms in early modern Europe, and José Antonio Maravall has produced and inspired massive documentation of the Spanish experience in particular. For reasons that differ in each case, none of these seminal thinkers has defined or even particularly affected the course of mainstream Cervantes studies in the United States. This is a pity and a disservice to scholarship, because their work places us in a position to identify the themes Cervantes deals with, in terms of their relation to the socioeconomic and political problematics of his time.

The question is always the relationship of that time to our time. Clearly they are not the same. The specifically early modern dialectic of feudalism and capitalism has been superseded by a new dialectic founded on the uneasy relationship between sovereign nation-states and transnational corporations. The ethnic division between Old and New Christians is not the same as that between whites and people of color, nor is the division between *hidalgos* and *pecheros* identical to that between rich and poor. It seems at the very least methodologically unsound to conflate the two epochs. And yet there are analogies that outweigh the theoretical consideration of possible anachronism. Like Cervantes, we live in ethnically diverse societies where notions of purity and exclusivity clash with diversity and pluralism. We inhabit societies characterized by an astoundingly unequal distribution of wealth and power. Our society is called upon to make choices similar to those that confronted Cervantes's.

In this book I have attempted to elucidate Cervantes's texts first and foremost in terms of their historical specificity. At the same time, the analogies with our own situation are so precise and so compelling on so many occasions—*juros* and tax-free munis, for example—that they cry out to be made explicit.

God knows there are plenty of ways of coming to grips with or attempting to elucidate Cervantes's texts. I passed some of them more or less facetiously in review at the beginning of this book. Every one of them poses certain questions and consequently can only yield certain answers. Like traditional humanism, the approach taken here situates the text within its relevant historical context and attempts to elucidate its meaning in consequence. It differs in that it foregrounds what humanism normally silences: the socioeconomic underpinnings of that relevant context. This shift in emphasis allows the text to respond in different ways, revealing aspects that normally remain invisible. For example, the characters' possiblities for action are discovered to be circumscribed by their economic situation, meaning both their relative affluence or poverty and the particular economic system within which their lives unfold. This in turn determines their attitudes, perceptions, and values: in a word, their character. At the same time, and paradoxically, historicizing Cervantes's texts within their own socioeconomic context has the potential to illuminate questions of compelling interest within our own time and place.

# Notes

## Introduction

1. Robert ter Horst, "'Une saison en enfer': *La Gitanilla*," *Cervantes* 5 (1985): 112.

2. *Lazarillo de Tormes* (1554), ed. Francisco Rico (Madrid: Cátedra, 1987). References to this text will be parenthetical. My translation.

3. George A. Shipley, "Lazarillo and the Cathedral Chaplain: A Conspiratorial Reading of *Lazarillo de Tormes,* Tratado VI," *Symposium* 37 (1983): 216–41.

4. José Antonio Maravall, *Estado moderno y mentalidad social,* vol. 2 (Madrid: Alianza, 1986), 448.

5. References to the *Quixote* are customarily to the part (I or II) in Roman numerals, followed by the chapter in Arabic numerals. The third number in my parenthetical reference is the page number in the Norton Critical Edition. Thus (I, 1, 13) stands for part I, chapter 1, page 13. Hereafter, all references to the texts of Cervantes's works will be parenthetical.

6. See Antonio Domínguez Ortiz and Bernard Vincent, *Historia de los moriscos: Vida y tragedia de una minoría* (Madrid: Revista de Occidente, 1978), 113n.14. See also Augustin Redondo, "Acercamiento al *Quijote* desde una perspectiva histórico-social," in *Otra manera de leer el Quijote* (Madrid: Castalia, 1997), 69.

7. See Charles V. Aubrun, "Sancho Panza, paysan pour de rire, paysan pour de vrai," *Revista Canadiense de Estudios Hispánicos* 1 (1976): 25. See also Javier Salazar Rincón, *El mundo social del "Quijote"* (Madrid: Gredos, 1986), 190; Redondo, "Acercamiento al *Quijote,*" 77n.66.

8. See Aubrun, "Sancho Panza," 26. See also Redondo, "Acercamiento al *Quijote,*" 78; and Augustin Redondo "La princesa Micomicona y Sancho negrero *(Don Quijote I,* 29)," in *Otra manera de leer el Quijote,* 363–82.

9. Francisco Rodríguez Marín decoded these names in his edition of Cervantes, *Don Quijote* (Madrid: Atlas, 1949), appendix 14.

10. Cervantes, *Don Quijote*, vol. 1, ed. Luis Andrés Murillo (Madrid: Castalia, 1978), 315n.59. My translation.

11. Ernest H. Templin, "Labradores in the *Quijote*," *Hispanic Review* 30 (1962): 48.

12. See Carmelo Viñas Mey, *El problema de la tierra en la España de los siglos XVI y XVII* (Madrid: CSIC, 1941), 54–65. See also David Vassberg, *Land and Society in Golden-Age Castile* (Cambridge: Cambridge University Press, 1984), 64–79.

13. Sebastián de Covarrubias, *Tesoro de la lengua castellana* (1611; reprint, Madrid: Turner, 1978). My translation.

14. The evolution of this line of reformist thought has been admirably studied by Michel Cavillac, *Pícaros y mercaderes en el "Guzmán de Alfarache"* (Granada: Universidad de Granada, 1995).

15. Lisa Jardine, *Worldly Goods: A New History of the Renaissance* (New York: Nan A. Talese–Doubleday, 1996).

## Chapter 1: The Drama of Sancho's Salary

1. R. M. Flores has shown that the rigid system of oppositions between Don Quixote and Sancho had been debunked as early as 1913, but that just about everyone—readers, critics, and other writers—generally continues to accept one version or another of the familiar symbolic polarization. See R. M. Flores, *Sancho Panza through 375 Years of Continuations, Imitations and Criticism, 1605–1980* (Newark, Del.: Juan de la Cuesta, 1982), 80.

2. Castro, "Como veo ahora el *Quijote*," estudio introducción a la edición de *Don Quijote* (Madrid: Magisterio Español, 1971).

3. Vicente Llorens "Don Quijote y la decadencia del hidalgo," in *Aspectos sociales de la literatura española* (Madrid: Castalia, 1974), 47–66; Noël Salomon, *La vida rural castellana en tiempos de Felipe II* (Barcelona: Planeta, 1973).

4. Eduardo Urbina, *El sin par Sancho Panza: parodia y creación* (Barcelona: Anthropos, 1991).

5. Francisco Márquez Villanueva, "La génesis literaria de Sancho Panza," in *Fuentes literarias cervantinas* (Madrid: Gredos, 1973), 20–94. Mauricio Molho, "Raíz folklórica de Sancho Panza," in *Cervantes: raíces folklóricas* (Madrid: Gredos, 1976), 217–336.

6. Augustin Redondo, "Acercamiento al *Quijote*," 55–100.

7. Javier Salazar Rincón, *El mundo social del "Quijote*," 161. My translation.

8. Cited in José María Díez Borque, *Sociología de la comedia española del siglo XVII* (Madrid: Gredos, 1976). My translation.

9. Cited in Noël Salomon, *Recherches sur le thème paysan dans la "comedia" au temps de Lope de Vega* (Bordeaux: Institut d'Etudes Ibériques et Ibéro-américaines de la Université de Bordeaux, 1965), 52. My translation.

10. Salazar Rincón, *El mundo social del "Quijote*," 181–92.

11. Earl J. Hamilton, *Tesoro americano y la revolución de los precios en España, 1501–1650* (Barcelona: Ariel, 1975), appendices 4 and 5.

12. See Bartolomé Bennassar, *Recherches sur les grandes épidémies dans le nord de l'Espagne à la fin du XVIe siècle* (Paris: SEVPEN, 1969).

13. Viñas Mey, *El problema de la tierra*, 32–48; David Vassberg, *Land and Society in Golden-Age Castile* (Cambridge: Cambridge University Press, 1984), 94–95, 204–7.

14. Cited in Viñas Mey, *El problema de la tierra*, 42. My translation. See Pedro de Valencia, "Discurso contra la ociosidad," in *Obras Completas*, vol. 4, bk. 1, ed. Rafael González Cañal (León: Universidad de León, 1994), 159–73.

15. Martín González de Cellorigo, *Memorial de la política necesaria y útil restauración de la República de España y Estados de ella y del desempeño universal destos Reinos*, ed. José L. Pérez de Ayala (1600; reprint, Madrid: Instituto de Estudios Fiscales, 1991), 20. My translation.

16. Pedro Fernández Navarrete, *Conservación de monarquías y discursos políticos*, ed. Michael D. Gordon (1626; reprint, Madrid: Instituto de Estudios Fiscales, 1982), 107. My translation.

17. Ibid., 108.

18. Cited in Viñas Mey, *El problema de la tierra*, 184. My translation.

19. González de Cellorigo, *Memorial*, 77.

20. Cited in Viñas Mey, *El problema de la tierra*, 184. My translation.

21. Cited in Salazar Rincón, *El mundo social del "Quijote,"* 169–70. My translation.

22. Cited ibid., 171. My translation.

23. Ibid., 163.

24. Cited ibid., 171.

25. Aubrun, "Sancho Panza," 21.

26. Hamilton, *Tesoro americano*, 417. My translation.

27. Aubrun, "Sancho Panza," 21.

28. Ibid., 24.

29. Ibid., 22.

30. See Carroll B. Johnson, *Madness and Lust: A Psychoanalytical Approach to Don Quixote* (Berkeley: University of California Press, 1983), 92.

31. Aubrun, "Sancho Panza," 24.

32. Redondo, "Acercamiento al *Quijote*," 77–78.

33. Redondo, "Acercamiento al *Quijote*," 55–100, and "La princesa Micomicona y Sancho negrero," 363–82.

34. Fr. Tomás de Mercado, *Suma de tratos y contratos, (1571)*, ed. Restituto Sierra Bravo (Madrid: Editora Nacional, 1975), 279. My translation.

35. Aubrun, "Sancho Panza," 25.

36. Redondo, "Acercamiento al *Quijote*," 79. My translation.

37. Salazar Rincón, *El mundo social del "Quijote,"* 307–8.

38. Fernand Braudel, *The Perspective of the World* (Berkeley: University of California Press, 1992), 621.

39. José Antonio Maravall, *Utopia and Counterutopia in the "Quixote"* (Detroit: Wayne State University Press, 1991), 48, 50.

40. Antonio Domínguez Ortiz, *Las clases privilegiadas en la España de los Austrias* (Madrid: ISTMO, 1973), 114. My translation.

41. See for example José Antonio Maravall, "La crisis económica de los siglos XVI y XVII interpretada por los escritores de la época," in *Estudios de historia del pensamiento español* (Madrid: Cultura Hispánica, 1984), 165.

42. Juan de Medina OFM, *De poenintentiae, restitutione et contractibus tractatus* (1550), cited in Marjorie Grice-Hutchinson, *Early Economic Thought in Spain, 1177–1740* (London: Allen and Unwin, 1978), 99.

43. Pedro de Valencia, "Discurso sobre el precio del trigo," in *Obras completas,* vol. 4, bk. 1, ed. Rafael González Cañal, (León: Publicaciones de la Universidad de León, 1994), 91, 97.

# Chapter 2: Guilds and Entrepreneurs in Sevilla

1. Julio Rodríguez Luis, *Novedad y ejemplo en las "Novelas Ejemplares" de Cervantes,* vol. 1 (Madrid: José Porrúa Turanzas, 1980), 171. My translation.

2. Joaquín Casalduero, *Sentido y forma de las "Novelas Ejemplares"* (Madrid: Gredos, 1962), 102.

3. Domingo Ynduráin, "*Rinconete y Cortadillo:* De entremés a novela," *Boletín de la Real Academia Española* 46 (1966): 321–33; José Pascual Buxó, "Estructura y lección de *Rinconete y Cortadillo,*" in *Las figuraciones del sentido: Ensayos de poética semiológica* (México: Fondo de Cultura Económica, 1984), 181–213.

4. Pedro Herrera Puga, *Sociedad y delincuencia en el siglo de oro* (Granada: Universidad de Granada, 1976); Mary Elizabeth Perry, *Crime and Society in Early Modern Seville* (Hanover, N.H.: The University Press of New England, 1980).

5. I translate from Harry Sieber's edition of Cervantes, *Novelas ejemplares,* vol. 1 (Madrid: Cátedra, 1980), 191. All further references will be parenthetical.

6. Rodríguez Luis, *Novedad y ejemplo,* vol. 1, 176.

7. Francisco López Estrada, "Apuntes para una interpretación de *Rinconete y Cortadillo:* Una posible resonancia creadora," in *Lenguaje, ideología y organizacion textual en las "Novelas Ejemplares,"* ed. José Jesús Bustos Tovar (Madrid: Universidad Complutense, 1983), 62. My translation.

8. Pascual Buxó "Estructura y lección," 197. My translation.

9. Manuel Criado de Val, *Teoría de Castilla la Nueva* (Madrid: Gredos, 1960), 349.

10. Rodríguez Luis, *Novedad y ejemplo,* vol. 1, 178; Pascual Buxó, "Estructura y lección," 198.

11. I translate from the text of the Porras version offered by Juan Bautista Avalle-Arce in his edition of Cervantes, *Novelas ejemplares,* vol. 1 (Madrid: Castalia, 1987), 294.

12. Rodríguez Luis, *Novedad y ejemplo,* vol. 1, 179.

13. For the relevant texts see *El sacrosanto y ecuménico concilio de Trento,* Sesión XXV (Barcelona: R. Martín Indar, 1847), 328–31, 346.

14. Antonio Domínguez Ortiz, *Orto y ocaso de Sevilla,* 2d. ed. (Sevilla: Universidad de Sevilla, 1974), 31. My translation.

15. Rodríguez Luis, *Novedad y ejemplo*, vol. 1, 188.

16. Ibid., 176n.5.

17. Pierre Chaunu, *Séville et l'Amérique aux XVIe et XVIIe siècles* (Paris: Flammarion, 1977), 32. My translation.

18. Domínguez Ortiz, *Orto y ocaso de Sevilla*, 55.

19. Michèle Moret, *Aspects de la société marchande à Séville au début du XVIIe siècle* (Paris: Marcel Rivière, 1967), 29–30. My translation.

20. Pierre Chaunu, *Séville et l'Atlantique*, vol. 1 (Paris: Armand Colin, 1955), 70. My translation.

21. Henri Lapeyre, *Une famille de marchands: les Ruiz* (Paris: SEVPEN, 1955), 488–89. My translation.

22. Moret, *Aspects de la société marchande*, 24–25.

23. Jean-Marc Pelorson, *Les "letrados": juristes castillans sous Philippe III. Recherches sur leur place dans la société, la culture, et l'Etat* (Poitiers: Université de Poitiers, 1980), 281n.2; 286–87.

24. Modesto Ulloa, *La hacienda real de Castilla en el reinado de Felipe II* (Madrid: Fundación Universitaria Española, 1977), 274–77.

25. Peter O'M Pierson, *Commander of the Armada* (New Haven, Conn.: Yale University Press, 1989), 1.

26. José Antonio Maravall, *Estado moderno y mentalidad social*, vol. 2 (Madrid: Alianza, 1986), 31.

27. This observation found its way into print in *Les parentés fictives en Espagne (XVIe–XVIIe siècles)*, ed. Augustin Redondo, travaux du "Centre de Recherche sur l'Espagne des XVIe et XVIIe siècles," no. 4 (Paris: Publications de la Sorbonne, 1988), 161.

28. Moret, *Aspects de la société marchande*, 94.

29. Cited ibid. My translation.

30. López Estrada, "Apuntes para una interpretación," 59–68.

31. Cited in Maravall, *Estado moderno*, vol. 2, 52n.70.

## Chapter 3: Ricote the *Morisco* and Capital Formation

1. Francisco Márquez Villanueva, "Leandra, Zoraida y sus fuentes franco-italianas," in *Personajes y temas del Quijote* (Madrid: Taurus, 1975), 77–146.

2. Leo Spitzer, "Perspectivismo lingüístico en el *Quijote*," in *Lingüística e historia literaria* (Madrid: Gredos, 1961), 173n.30; Helena Percas de Ponseti, *Cervantes y su concepto del arte* (Madrid: Gredos, 1975), 269.

3. Américo Castro, "La palabra escrita y el *Quijote*," in *Hacia Cervantes*, 3d. ed. (Madrid: Taurus, 1967), 359–419. See also Monique Joly, "Afición de los extranjeros al vino y al jamón," *Nueva Revista de Filología Hispánica* 22 (1973): 321–28.

4. Cited in Mercedes García Arenal, *Los moriscos* (Madrid: Editora Nacional, 1975), 163. My translation.

5. Fernand Braudel, "Conflits et refus de civilisation: Espagnols et Morisques au XVIe siècle," *Annales: Economies, Sociétés, Civilisations* 2.4 (1947): 397–410.

6. Cited in Francisco Márquez Villanueva, "El morisco Ricote o la hispana razón de estado," in *Personajes y temas del Quijote* (Madrid: Taurus, 1975), 267. My translation.

7. Cited ibid., 167n.91.

8. Cited ibid., 267n.91. My translation.

9. See Louis Cardillac, *Morisques et chrétiens: Un affrontement polémique (1492–1640)* (Paris: Klincksieck, 1977); Jeanne Vidal, *Quand on brûlait les morisques (1544–1621)* (Nîmes: n.p., 1986); Domínguez Ortiz and Vincent, *Historia de los moriscos.*

10. Spitzer, "Perspectivismo lingüístico," 173.

11. Joaquín Casalduero, *Sentido y forma del Quijote* (Madrid: Insula, 1966), 338–41. See also A. Ramírez Araujo, "El morisco Ricote y la libertad de conciencia," *Hispanic Review* 24 (1956): 278–89.

12. Fr. Felipe de Meneses, *Luz del alma* (1554), cited in Américo Castro, "Erasmo en tiempos de Cervantes," in *Hacia Cervantes,* 3d. ed. (Madrid: Taurus, 1967), 245. My translation.

13. Pedro Aznar Cardona, *Expulsión justificada de los moriscos españoles* (1612), cited in Márquez Villanueva, "El morisco Ricote," 275. My translation.

14. Cited in García Arenal, *Los moriscos,* 247. My translation.

15. Cited in Domínguez Ortiz and Vincent, *Historia de los moriscos,* 204. My translation.

16. Cited in García Arenal, *Los moriscos,* 167. My translation.

17. Cited in Márquez Villanueva, "El morisco Ricote," 297n.167. My translation.

18. Fr. Jaime Bleda, *Crónica de los moriscos de España* (1618), cited ibid. My translation.

19. Fr. Marcos de Guadalajara, *Memorable expulsión y justísimo destierro de los moriscos de España* (1613), cited in Julio Caro Baroja, *Los moriscos del reino de Granada* (Madrid: ISTMO, 1976), 216n.45. My translation.

20. Domínguez Ortiz and Vincent, *Historia de los moriscos,* 174. My translation.

21. Cited in Caro Baroja, *Los moriscos del reino,* 217–18. My translation.

22. Pedro de Valencia, "Discurso sobre el acrecentamiento de la tierra" (1607), in *Obras completas,* vol. 4, no. 1, ed. Rafael González Cañal (León: Universidad de León, 1994), 156–57. See also José Antonio Maravall, "Reformismo social-agrario en la crisis del siglo XVII: tierra, trabajo y salario según Pedro de Valencia," *Bulletin Hispanique* 72 (1970), 12. My translation.

23. Domínguez Ortiz and Vincent, *Historia de los moriscos,* 127.

24. Bernard Vincent, "Amor y matrimonio entre los moriscos," in *Minorías y marginados en la España del siglo XVI* (Granada: Diputación Provincial, 1987), 52.

25. Domínguez Ortiz and Vincent, *Historia de los moriscos,* 176, 192.

26. Caro Baroja, *Los moriscos del reino,* 212.

27. Cited in A. Huerga, ed., *Avisos para predicadores del Santo Evangelio* (Barcelona: Espirituales Españoles, 1959), 250. My translation.

28. Braudel, *The Perspective of the World,* 185.

29. Ibid., 187.

30. Fr. Jaime Bleda, *Crónica de los moros*, cited in Márquez Villanueva, "El morisco Ricote," 280. My translation.

31. Luis de Ortiz, *Memorial* (1558), in *Economía, sociedad y corona*, ed. Manuel Fernández Alvarez (Madrid: Cultura Hispánica, 1963), 382. My translation.

32. Cited in Domínguez Ortiz and Vincent, *Historia de los moriscos*, 210. My translation.

33. Julio Caro Baroja, "Los moriscos aragoneses, según un autor del siglo XVII," in *Razas, pueblos y linajes* (Madrid: Revista de Occidente, 1957), 96–97. My translation.

34. Caro Baroja, *Los moriscos del reino*, 237n.1.

35. Pierre Vilar, "El tiempo del *Quijote*" (1956), in *Crecimiento y desarrollo* (Barcelona: Ariel, 1976), 339–40. My translation.

36. Márquez Villanueva, "El morisco Ricote," 253.

37. Michel Moner, "El problema morisco en los textos cervantinos," in *Las dos grandes minorías étnico-religiosas en la literatura española del Siglo de Oro: los judeoconversos y los moriscos*, ed. Irene Andres-Suárez, annales littéraires de l'Université de Besançon, no. 588 (Paris: Diffusion Les Belles Lettres, 1995), 95. My translation.

38. Ibid., 95n.2.

39. Ibid., 95.

40. Cervantes, *Don Quijote*, vol. 2, ed. Luis Andrés Murillo (Madrid: Castalia: 1978), 540n.12.

41. Cited in Bernard Vincent, "La familia morisca," in *Minorías y marginados en la España del siglo XVI* (Granada: Diputación Provincial, 1987), 24. My translation.

42. Bernard Vincent, "Amor y matrimonio entre los moriscos," 64.

## Chapter 4: Women and Men, Christians and Muslims

1. E. Michael Gerli, "Rewriting Myth and History: Discourse of Race, Marginality and Resistance in the Captive's Tale (*Don Quijote* I, 37–42)," in *Refiguring Authority: Reading, Writing, and Rewriting in Cervantes* (Lexington: University Press of Kentucky, 1995), 42.

2. Ibid., 53.

3. Angel Rodríguez Sánchez, "El poder y la familia: Formas de control y consanguinidad en la Extremadura de los tiempos modernos," in *Poder, familia y consanguinidad en la España del Antiguo Régimen*, eds. F. Chacón Jiménez and J. Hernández Franco (Barcelona: Anthropos, 1992), 22–23. My translation.

4. Salazar Rincón, *El mundo social del "Quijote,"* 92.

5. Karl Marx, *Economic and Philosophical Manuscripts of 1844* (Moscow: Progress Publishers, 1977), 56.

6. Bartolomé Clavero, *Mayorazgo: Propiedad feudal en Castilla, 1369–1836* (Madrid: Siglo XXI, 1989), 261–62. My translation.

7. Ibid., 81.

8. Cited ibid., 56.

9. Cited ibid., 59n.56. My translation.

10. Cited ibid., 77. My translation.

11. Jerónimo de Baeza, *De non meliorandis dotis ratione filiabus* (1534), cited ibid., 231. My translation.

12. Clavero, *Mayorazgo*, 231.

13. Cited ibid., 265.

14. Subhi Y. Labib, "Capitalism in Medieval Islam," *Journal of Economic History* 29 (1969): 79, 81.

15. Halil Inalcik, "Capital Formation in the Ottoman Empire," *Journal of Economic History* 29 (1969): 99, 105.

16. Ibid., 138.

17. Ronald C. Jennings, *Christians and Muslims in Ottoman Cyprus and the Mediterranean World, 1571–1640* (New York: New York University Press, 1993), 293.

18. Inalcik, "Capital Formation in the Ottoman Empire," 123.

19. Ibid., 124.

20. Fr. Diego de Haedo, *Topografía e historia general de Argel* (1612), vol. 1, ed. I. Bauer y Landauer (Madrid: Sociedad de Bibliófilos Españoles, 1927), 93. My translation. The true author of this work is now considered to be Cervantes's fellow captive in Algiers, Dr. Antonio Sosa.

21. Ibid., 94.

22. Ibid., 85–87.

23. Ciro Manca, *Il modello di sviluppo economico delle città maritime barbaresche dopo Lepanto* (Napoli: Istituto Universitario Navale, 1982), 14.

24. Salvatore Bono, *I corsari barbereschi* (Torino: Edizioni RAI, 1964), 115.

25. Manca, *Il modello di sviluppo*, 14.

26. Ibid., 70.

27. Haedo, *Topografía*, vol. 1, 88.

28. Ellen G. Friedman, *Spanish Captives in North Africa in the Early Modern Age* (Madison: University of Wisconsin Press, 1983), 149. See also Luis Astrana Marín, *Vida ejemplar y heroica de Miguel Cervantes Saavedra*, vol. 3 (Madrid: Reus, 1948–1958), 89–91.

29. Manca, *Il modello di sviluppo*, 141.

30. Ibid., 152. My translation.

31. Friedman, *Spanish Captives*, 125.

32. Ibid., 163, 166.

33. Maravall, *Estado moderno*, vol. 2, 448.

34. "El padre de don Luis, . . . que pretendía hacer de título a su hijo." Cervantes, *Don Quijote*, vol. 1, ed. Luis Andrés Murillo (Madrid: Castalia, 1978), 538. My translation. Raffel translates "the father wanted his son to marry into a title" (I, 44, 308).

35. Felipe Ruiz Martín, *Pequeño capitalismo, gran capitalismo: Simón Ruiz y sus negocios en Florencia* (Barcelona: Crítica, 1990), 155, 93; see also 111, 157.

36. Márquez Villanueva, "Leandra, Zoraida y sus fuentes franco-italianas," 96.

37. Haedo, *Topografía*, vol. 1, 57.

38. See Inalcik, "Capital Formation in the Ottoman Empire," 102.

39. Francisco de Quevedo, *Sueños,* vol. 2, ed. Julio Cejador y Frauca (Madrid: Espasa-Calpe, 1960), 175. My translation.

40. Anne-Marie Perrin and Françoise Zmantar (PEZ), "Jardins d'amour," in *El Candil* (Clermont-Ferrand: Université de Clermont II, 1985), 149–50. My translation.

41. Gerli, "Rewriting Myth and History," 53.

42. Maria Caterina Ruta, "Zoraida: los signos de silencio en un personaje cervantino," *Anales Cervantinos* 21 (1983): 128.

43. Dr. Antonio Sosa, *Diálogo de los mártires de Argel,* ed. Emilio Sola and J. M. Parreño (Madrid: Hiperion, 1990), 90. My translation.

44. Alison Weber, "Padres e hijas: una lectura intertextual de *La historia del cautivo,*" *Actas del Segundo coloquio de la Asociación de Cervantistas (1989)* (Barcelona: Anthropos, 1991), 428.

45. Ruta, "Zoraida: los signos de silencio," 130. My translation.

46. Márquez Villanueva, "Leandra, Zoraida y sus fuentes franco-italianas," 133.

47. Luis A. Murillo, "Cervantes's Tale of the Captive Captain," in *Florilegium Hispanicum: Medieval and Golden Age Studies presented to Dorothy Clotelle Clarke* (Madison, Wis.: Hispanic Medieval Seminary, 1983), 235.

48. Alban K. Forcione, "Cervantes's Secularized Miracle: *La fuerza de la sangre,*" in *Cervantes and the Humanist Vision: A Study of Four "Exemplary Novels"* (Princeton, N.J.: Princeton University Press, 1982), 348.

49. Perrin and Zmantar, "Jardins d'amour," 150.

50. Weber, "Padres e hijas," 429.

51. Carroll B. Johnson, "La sexualidad en el *Quijote,*" *Edad de Oro* 9 (1990), 125–36.

52. Cited in Clavero, *Mayorazgo,* 77–78. My translation.

53. Paul Julian Smith, "'The Captive's Tale': Race, Text, Gender," in *Quixotic Desire: Psychoanalytic Perspectives on Cervantes,* ed. Ruth Anthony El Saffar and Diana de Armas Wilson (Ithaca, N.Y.: Cornell University Press, 1993), 234.

## Chapter 5: Women and Men, Aristocrats and Gypsies

1. I translate from Harry Sieber's edition of the *Novelas ejemplares,* vol. 1 (Madrid: Cátedra, 1980), 61. All further references will be parenthetical.

2. Cited in Juan de Dios Heredia, *Vida gitana* (Barcelona: Ediciones 29, 1973), 147. My translation.

3. Cited in José Monleón [tío], *Treinta años de teatro de la derecha* (Barcelona: Tusquets, 1971), 18. My translation.

4. Bernard Leblon, *Les Gitans d'Espagne* (Paris: Presses Universitaires de France, 1985), 26.

5. Leblon, *Les Gitans,* 31–34. This apparently draconian suggestion pales by comparison with the systematic castrations and forced sterilizations envisioned on more than one occasion for the recalcitrant and unassimilable morisco population (see chapter 3).

6. Georges Güntert, "Discurso social y discurso individual en *La Gitanilla,*" in *Cervantes: Novelar el mundo desintegrado* (Barcelona: Puvill, 1993), 119.

7. Leblon, *Les gitans*, 24.

8. Bernard Leblon, "Les parentés fictives chez les Gitans au siècle d'or," in *Las parentés fictives en Espagne (XVIe–XVIIe siècles)*, ed. Augustin Redondo, travaux du "Centre de Recherche sur l'Espagne des XVIe et XVIIe siècles," no. 4 (Paris: Publications de la Sorbonne, 1988), 93.

9. Leblon, *Les gitans*, 24. My translation.

10. Ter Horst, "'Une saison en enfer,'" 103.

11. Ibid., 112.

12. Ibid., 111.

13. William Clamurro, "Value and Identity in *La Gitanilla*," *Journal of Hispanic Philology* 14.1 (Autumn 1989): 43–60; Joan Ramon Resina, "Laissez-faire y reflexividad erótica en *La Gitanilla*," *MLN* 106 (1991): 257–78.

14. Vilar, "El tiempo del *Quijote*," 339–40.

15. Mateo Alemán, *Guzmán de Alfarache* II, iii, 4, ed. Francisco Rico (Barcelona: Planeta, 1967), 803. My translation.

16. Alban K. Forcione, afterword, in *Cervantes's "Exemplary Novels" and the Adventure of Writing*, eds. Michael Nerlich and Nicholas Spadaccini (Minneapolis: The Prisma Institute, 1989), 350.

17. Resina, "Laissez-faire y reflexividad erótica," 259.

18. Francisco Márquez Villanueva, "Bonifacio y Dorotea: Mateo Alemán y la novela burguesa," *Actas del VIII Congreso de la Asociación Internacional de Hispanistas (1986)* (Madrid: ISTMO, 1986), 76–79.

19. Alison Weber also interprets Preciosa's speech in economic terms, to mean that virginity lost to marriage is in fact an investment, but identifies the profit to be made specifically as "procreative fruitfulness." See "Pentimento: the Parodic Text of *La Gitanilla*," *Hispanic Review* 62 (1994): 69.

20. Raymond Williams, *Marxism and Literature* (Oxford: Oxford University Press, 1977), 93–94.

21. Alban K. Forcione, "Cervantes's *La Gitanilla* as Erasmian Romance," in *Cervantes and the Humanist Vision: A Study of Four "Exemplary Novels"* (Princeton, N.J.: Princeton University Press, 1982), 139.

22. Ibid., 138.

23. Francisco Márquez Villanueva, "La buenaventura de Preciosa," *Nueva Revista de Filología Hispánica* 34 (1985–86): 741–68.

24. Forcione, "Cervantes's *La Gitanilla* as Erasmian Romance," 138.

25. Casalduero, *Sentido y forma de las "Novelas Ejemplares,"* 69.

26. "Margarita, not in the sense of 'flower,' but with the meaning 'precious.' In Cervantes's time, large, perfectly formed pearls were called margaritas." Cervantes, *Don Quijote*, vol. 3, ed. Francisco Rodríguez Marín (Madrid: Atlas, 1948), 99n.3. My translation.

27. Alison Weber's sensitive study of *La Gitanilla* insists correctly on the link between Preciosa and the workforce but leaves the other gypsy women out. See "Pentimento," 67.

28. Clamurro, "Value and Identity in *La Gitanilla*," 60.

29. Theresa Ann Sears, *A Marriage of Convenience: Ideal and Ideology in the "Novelas Ejemplares"* (New York: Peter Lang, 1993), 122n.85.

30. Rodríguez Luis, *Novedad y ejemplo*, vol. 1, 138.

31. Weber, "Pentimento," 59–75.

32. Thomas R. Hart, *Cervantes's Exemplary Fictions: A Study of the "Novelas ejemplares"* (Lexington: University Press of Kentucky, 1993), 35.

33. E. Michael Gerli, "Romance and Novel: Idealism and Irony in *La Gitanilla*," *Cervantes* 6 (1986): 29–38; "A Novel Rewriting: Romance and Irony in *La Gitanilla*," in *Refiguring Authority: Reading, Writing, and Rewriting in Cervantes* (Lexington: University Press of Kentucky, 1995), 24–40. Francisco J. Sánchez has also commented perceptively on Cervantes's exploitation of generic convention and readers' expectations. See "Theater within the Novel: 'Mass' Audience and Individual Reader in *La Gitanilla* and *Rinconete y Cortadillo*," in *Cervantes's "Exemplary Novels" and the Adventure of Writing*, ed. Michael Nerlich and Nicholas Spadaccini (Minneapolis: The Prisma Institute, 1989), 73–98.

## Chapter 6: *El amante liberal* and the Ottoman Empire

1. The following are representative of this line of inquiry: Thomas R. Hart, "La ejemplaridad de *El amante liberal*," *Nueva Revista de Filología Hispánica* 36.1 (1988): 303–18; Rafael Lapesa, "En torno a *La española inglesa* y el *Persiles*," in *De la edad media a nuestros días* (Madrid: Gredos, 1967), 242–63; Stanislav Zimic, "El amante liberal," in *Las "Novelas ejemplares" de Cervantes* (Madrid: Siglo XXI, 1996), 47–83.

2. Jennings, *Christians and Muslims*, 132.

3. Ibid., 136.

4. Ibid., 140.

5. Ibid., 143.

6. Astrana Marín, *Vida ejemplar y heroica*, vol. 2, 275.

7. Ottmar Hegyi, *Cervantes and the Turks: Historical Reality versus Literary Fiction in "La Gran Sultana" and "El amante liberal"* (Newark, Del.: Juan de la Cuesta, 1992), 218.

8. Haedo, *Topografía*, vol. 1, 346–61, 374–88.

9. Ibid., 346.

10. Emilio Sola and José F. de la Peña, *Cervantes y la berbería: Cervantes, mundo turco-berberesco y servicios secretos en la época de Felipe II* (Madrid: Fondo de Cultura Económica, 1995), 74.

11. Haedo, *Topografía*, vol. 1, 346–47.

12. Ibid., 347.

13. Ibid., 374–75.

14. Smith, "'The Captive's Tale,'" 231. Cf. the thoughtful critique by Diane E. Sieber, "Mapping Identity in the Captive's Tale: Cervantes and Ethnographic Narrative," *Cervantes* 18.1 (1998): 115–33.

15. Haedo, *Topografía*, vol. 1, 377–78.

16. Sola and de la Peña, *Cervantes y la berbería*, 86, 136.

17. Ortiz, *Memorial*, 406–7.

18. Fray Juan de Mariana, *Discurso sobre la moneda de vellón* (1609), vol. 31 of Biblioteca de Autores Españoles (Madrid: Rivadaneyra, 1861), 592. My translation.

19. Cited in Augustin Redondo, *Otra manera de leer el Quijote* (Madrid: Castalia, 1997), 86. My translation. More examples cited in Francisco Tomás Valiente, *El derecho penal de la monarquía absoluta (siglos XVI–XVII)* (Madrid: Tecnos, 1969), 162; Pelorson, *Les "letrados,"* 155.

20. Francisco Rodríguez Marín, *Nuevos documentos cervantinos hasta ahora inéditas* (Madrid: Revista de Archivos, Bibliotecas y Museos, 1914), números 11 and 12.

21. Diego Galán, *Cautiverio y trabajos de Diego Galán*, ed. M. Serrano y Sanz (Madrid: Sociedad de Bibliófilos Españoles, 1913), 42.

22. I. Metin Kunt, *The Sultan's Servants: The Transformation of Ottoman Provincial Government, 1550–1650* (New York: Columbia University Press, 1983), 31.

23. Jennings, *Christians and Muslims*, 103.

24. Georges Güntert, "Las dos lecturas de *El amante liberal*," in *Cervantes: Novelar el mundo desintegrado* (Barcelona: Puvill, 1993), 140.

25. Anthony J. Cascardi, "Cervantes's Exemplary Subjects," in *Cervantes's "Exemplary Novels" and the Adventure of Writing*, ed. Michael Nerlich and Nicholas Spadaccini (Minneapolis: The Prisma Institute, 1989), 49–72.

26. Francisco J. Sánchez, "Theater within the Novel."

27. Fernand Braudel, *The Mediterranean and the Mediterranean World in the Age of Philip II*, vol. 2 (New York: Harper Colophon, 1976), 1161.

28. Ibid., 1146.

29. Ibid., 1150–51.

30. Ibid., 1152–65.

31. Sola and De la Peña, *Cervantes y la berbería*, 84. My translation.

32. Ibid., 116.

33. Ibid., 110.

34. Ibid., 176.

35. Braudel, *The Mediterranean*, 867.

36. Godfrey Fisher, *Barbary Legend: War, Trade and Piracy in North Africa* (Oxford: Clarendon Press, 1957), 163.

37. Braudel, *The Mediterranean*, 878.

38. Sola and de la Peña, *Cervantes y la berbería*, 116.

39. Miguel Herrero García, *Ideas de los españoles del siglo XVII*, 2d ed. (Madrid: Gredos, 1966), 530.

40. Cited in Herrero García, *Ideas de los españoles*, 532. My translation.

41. Salvatore Salomone Marino, "I siciliani nelle guerre contro gl'infedeli nel secolo XVI," *Archivio Storico Siciliano* 37 (1912): 5.

42. Ibid., 18–19. My translation.

43. Braudel, *The Mediterranean*, 874.

44. Bartolomé Bennassar and Lucille Bennassar, *Les Chrétiens d'Allah: L'histoire extraordinaire des renégats* (Paris: Perrin, 1989), 252.

45. Ibid., 208–10.

46. Ulloa, *La hacienda real de Castilla*, 380.

47. Antonio Domínguez Ortiz, "La conspiración del duque de Medina Sidonia y el marqués de Ayamonte," in *Crisis y decadencia de la España de los Austrias* (Barcelona: Ariel, 1969), 119–20.

48. Astrana Marín, *Vida ejemplar y heroica*, vol. 2, 418.

49. In Cervantes, *Don Quijote*, vol. 9, ed. Francisco Rodríguez Marín (Madrid: Atlas, 1949), 242–57, appendix 18.

50. Astrana Marín, *Vida ejemplar y heroica*, vol. 2, 414.

51. Ibid., vol. 3, 106.

52. Bartolomé Bennassar and Lucille Bennassar, *Las Chrétiens d'Allah*, 70.

53. Sosa, *Diálogo de los mártires*, 182.

54. Bartolomé Bennassar and Lucille Bennassar, *Les Chrétiens d'Allah*, 258, 266.

55. Cited in Braudel, *The Mediterranean*, 877.

56. Bono, *I corsari barbereschi*, 5–6.

57. Fisher, *Barbary Legend*, 154.

58. Bartolomé Bennassar and Lucille Bennassar, *Les Chrétiens d'Allah*, 260. My translation.

59. Manca, *Il modello di sviluppo*, 152.

60. Haedo, *Topografía*, vol. 1, 76.

61. *Viaje de turquía* (1557), ed. Fernando García Salinero (Madrid: Cátedra), 440. My translation.

62. Braudel, *The Mediterranean*, 1019; Jaime Salvá, *La orden de Malta y las acciones navales españolas contra turcos y berberiscos en los siglos XVI y XVII* (Madrid: Instituto Histórico de Marina, 1944), 250, 253.

63. Salvá, *La orden de Malta*, 261.

64. See also Adrienne Martín, "Rereading *El amante liberal* in the Age of Contrapuntal Sexualities," in *Cervantes and His Postmodern Constituencies*, ed. Anne J. Cruz and Carroll B. Johnson (New York: Garland Press, 1999), 151–69.

65. Paul Julian Smith, "Cervantes, Goytisolo and the Sodomitical Scene," in *Cervantes and the Modernists*, ed. Edwin Williamson (London: Támesis, 1994), 167.

66. "Diálogo entre Laín Calvo y Nuño Rasura" (1570), *Revue Hispanique* 10 (1903): 150–81.

67. Ibid., 177. My translation.

68. Hegyi, *Cervantes and the Turks*, 233.

69. Ruth El Saffar, *Novel to Romance: A Study of the "Novelas ejemplares" of Cervantes* (Baltimore: Johns Hopkins University Press, 1974), 149.

70. Bartolomé Bennassar and Lucille Bennassar, *Les Chrètiens d'Allah*, 330–31.

71. Ibid., 268.

72. Ibid., 120–40.

73. Ibid., 281–82.

74. Ibid., 294.

75. Ibid., 296.

76. Cited in Hegyi, *Cervantes and the Turks*, 243–44. My translation.

77. Ibid., 232.

78. Sears, *A Marriage of Convenience*, 93.

79. Braudel, *The Perspective of the World*, 22.

80. Manca, *Il modello di sviluppo*, 79.

81. Ibid., 123.

82. Ibid., 123.

83. Jean-Joseph Goux, *Symbolic Economies: After Marx and Freud* (Ithaca, N.Y.: Cornell University Press, 1990), 202.

84. Grice-Hutchinson, *Early Economic Thought in Spain*, 100.

85. Gonzalo Díaz Migoyo, "La ficción cordial de *El amante liberal*," *Nueva Revista de Filología Hispánica* 35.1 (1987): 129–50; Güntert, "Las dos lecturas," 142; Sears, *A Marriage of Convenience*, 101.

86. Pierre Bourdieu, *The Logic of Practice* (Stanford, Calif.: Stanford University Press, 1990), 126.

87. Díaz Migoyo, "La ficción cordial," 148; Sears, *A Marriage of Convenience*, 100–101.

88. Sears, *A Marriage of Convenience*, 140, 185.

## Chapter 7: *La española inglesa* and Protestant England

1. El Saffar, *Novel to Romance*, 140; Alban K. Forcione, *Cervantes and the Humanist Vision: A Study of Four "Exemplary Novels"* (Princeton, N.J.: Princeton University Press, 1982), 93.

2. Rafael Lapesa, "En torno a *La española inglesa*," 244; Stanislav Zimic, "El amante liberal," 50.

3. Manuel Durán, *Cervantes* (Boston: G. K. Hall, 1967), 124.

4. José María Asensio y Toledo, "Sobre *La española inglesa*," in *Cervantes y sus obras* (Barcelona: F. Seix, 1902), 265–66.

5. Norberto González Aurioles, *Monjas sevillanas parientes de Cervantes* (Madrid: Alvarez, 1915), 15–16.

6. Agustín González de Amezúa, *Cervantes creador de la novela corta española*, vol. 2 (Madrid: CSIC, 1956–58), 136. My translation.

7. Harry Sieber documents Lansac in the *Calendar of State Papers (foreign series) of the Reign of Elizabeth, 1566–1568* in his edition of *Novelas Ejemplares*, vol. I, 258n.39. See also Robert W. Kenny, *Elizabeth's Admiral: The Political Career of Charles Howard, Earl of Nottingham* (Baltimore: Johns Hopkins University Press, 1970), 25. Karl-Ludwig Selig, on the other hand, is impressed by what he considers the "ahistoricity" of these names. See "Nuevas consideraciones sobre la temática y estructura de las *Novelas ejemplares*," *Beiträge zur romanischen Philologie*, Sonderheft (1967): 46.

8. Kenny, *Elizabeth's Admiral*, 184.

9. Luis Cabrera de Córdoba, *Felipe II Rey de España* (1619?), vol. 4 (Madrid: Aribau, 1877), 204.

10. *A Declaration of the Causes moving the Queene's Maiestie of England to prepare and send a Navy to the Seas for the defence of her Realmes against the King of Spaine's Forces* . . . (London: Deputies of Christopher Barker, 1596).

11. Kenny, *Elizabeth's Admiral*, 167.

12. Cabrera de Córdoba, *Felipe II Rey de España*, vol. 4, 204. My translation.

13. Fr. Pedro de Abreu, *Historia del saqueo de Cádiz por los ingleses en 1596*, ed. Manuel Bustos Rodríguez (Cádiz: Universidad de Cádiz, 1996), 244. My translation.

14. Sir William Slingsby, *Relation of the Voyage to Cádiz, 1596*, in *The Naval Miscellany*, vol. 20, ed. J. K. Laughton (London: Navy Records Society, 1902), 78.

15. Abreu, *Historia*, 256.

16. Ibid., 211–12.

17. Francisco de Ariño, *Sucesos de Sevilla de 1592 a 1604*, ed. Antonio María Fabié (Sevilla: Tarascó, 1873), 35. My translation.

18. González de Amezúa, *Cervantes creador*, vol. 2, 149–50.

19. See Slingsby, *Relation of the Voyage*, 85–86; and Abreu, *Historia*, 291–93.

20. Abreu, *Historia*, 221.

21. Ariño, *Sucesos de Sevilla*, 34–35.

22. Slingsby, *Relation of the Voyage*, 87.

23. Cabrera de Córdoba, *Felipe II Rey de España*, 209.

24. Slingsby, *Relation of the Voyage*, 69.

25. Jacob van Klaveren, *Europäische Wirtschaftsgeschichte Spaniens im 16. und 17. Jahrhundert* (Stuttgart: Fischer, 1960), 116–17. My translation. A much abbreviated account of these events is available in Braudel, *The Mediterranean*, 640.

26. Fray Juan de Mariana, *Historia general de España* (1601), vol. 31 of Biblioteca de Autores Españoles (Madrid: Rivadaneyra, 1861), 407. My translation.

27. In Cervantes, *Viage del Parnaso: Poesías varias*, ed. Elias L. Rivers (Madrid: Espasa-Calpe, 1991), 269. My translation.

28. Pierre Chaunu, *Séville et l'Amérique*, 41–48.

29. Albert J. Loomie, S.J., "Religion and Elizabethan Commerce with Spain," *Catholic Historical Review* 50 (1964–65): 39.

30. Cited ibid., 47.

31. Klaveren, *Europäische Wirtschaftsgeschichte*, 69.

32. Albert Girard, *Le commerce français à Séville et Cadix au temps des Habsbourg* (Paris: Boccard/Bordeaux: Ferret, 1932), 183–84.

33. Jean Sentaurens, "Séville dans la seconde moitié du XVIe siècle," *Bulletin Hispanique* 77 (1975): 358.

34. Melveena McKendrick, *Cervantes* (Boston: Little, Brown, 1980), 169.

35. Ariño, *Sucesos de Sevilla*, 35.

36. Philip Hughes, *The Reformation in England*, revised ed. (London: Barnes and Noble, 1963). See also, *inter alia*: John Bossy, "The Character of English Catholicism," *Crisis in Europe 1550–1650: Essays from Past and Present*, ed. Trevor Aston (London:

Routledge and Kegan Paul, 1965), 223–46; Linda Levy Peck, *Northampton: Patronage and Policy at the Court of James I* (London: Allen and Unwin, 1982), 9 and *passim*. Still serviceable is Martin Hume, *Treason and Plot: Struggles for Catholic Supremacy in the Last Years of Queen Elizabeth* (London: Eveleigh Nash, 1908).

37. Manuel da Costa Fontes, "Love as an Equalizer in *La española inglesa*," *Romance Notes* 16 (1975): 9. Pablo Virumbales, "Aproximaciones a la visión de la sociedad española en las *Novelas ejemplares* de Cervantes," *Anales Cervantinos* 16 (1977): 194.

38. Cited in Albert J. Loomie, S.J., *Spain and the Jacobean Catholics* (London: Catholic Record Society, 1973), 28. My translation.

39. J. E. Neale, *Queen Elizabeth I* (1934; reprint, Garden City, N.Y.: Anchor-Doubleday, 1957), 191.

40. *A Declaration of the Causes which mooved the chief Commanders of the Navie of her most excellent Majestie the Queen of England . . . to take and arrest in the mouth of the River of Lisbonne certain Shippes . . . prepared for the King of Spaine . . . the 30th day of June . . . 1589* (London: Deputies of Christopher Barker, 1589).

41. E. Allison Peers, "Cervantes in England," *Bulletin of Spanish Studies* 24 (1947): 227.

42. Américo Castro, *El pensamiento de Cervantes* (1925; reprint, Barcelona: Noguer, 1972), 287. My translation.

43. El Saffar, *Novel to Romance*, 160.

44. Francisco Icaza, *Las "Novelas ejemplares" de Cervantes: Sus críticos. Sus modelos literarios. Sus modelos vivos* (Madrid: Ateneo de Madrid, 1916), 162–63.

45. Lapesa, "En torno a *La española inglesa*," 254.

46. Thomas Hanrahan, "History in *La española inglesa*," *MLN* 83 (1968): 268.

47. Lee Bliss, "'Don Quixote' in England: The Case for 'The Knight of the Burning Pestle,'" *Viator* 18 (1987): 369–73.

48. Astrana Marín, *Vida ejemplar y heroica*, vol. 7, 35.

49. Abreu, *Historia*, 270.

50. Albert J. Loomie, S.J., *The Spanish Elizabethans: English Exiles at the Court of Philip II* (New York: Fordham University Press, 1963), 182–229. The complete matriculation history of St. Albans from its founding to 1862 was published by Canon Edwin Henson, *The Registers of the English College at Valladolid, 1569–1862* (London: Catholic Record Society, 1930).

51. Kenny, *Elizabeth's Admiral*, 25–36.

52. On this complex topic see: Hume, *Treason and Plot;* Jack Hurstfield, "The Succession Struggle in Late Elizabethan England," in *Elizabethan Government and Society: Essays Presented to Sir John Neale*, ed. S. T. Bindoff, J. Hurstfield, and C. H. Williams (London: University of London, Athlone Press, 1961); Kenny, *Elizabeth's Admiral*, 248–49; and Peck, *Northampton*, 18–22.

53. Luis Cabrera de Córdoba, *Relaciones de las cosas sucedidas en la corte de España desde 1599 hasta 1614* (Madrid: J. M. Alegría, 1857), 238, 242. My translations.

54. *Relación de lo sucedido en la ciudad de Valladolid desde el felicísimo nacimiento del príncipe nuestro señor, hasta que se acabaron las fiestas y demostraciones de alegría*

*que por él se hicieron,* in Cervantes, *Obras completas,* vol. 2, ed. Cayetano Rosell (Madrid: Rivadeneyra, 1863–1864), 230. My translation.

55. Ibid., 239.

56. Robert W. Kenny, "Peace with Spain, 1605," *History Today,* March 1970, 206.

57. Cited ibid., 206.

58. Thomé Pinheiro da Veiga, *Fastigimia* (Porto: Biblioteca Municipal, 1911), 149. My translation.

59. Albert J. Loomie, S.J., *Toleration and Diplomacy: The Religious Issue in Anglo-Spanish Relations 1603–1605* (Philadelphia: American Philosophical Society, 1963), 31. Loomie's documentation of these bribes and favors contains lists of names and amounts in escudos.

60. *Relación de lo sucedido,* 106.

61. Cabrera de Córdoba, *Relaciones* (22 June 1605), 244–45.

62. Pinheiro da Veiga, *Fastigimia* (15 June 1605), 150.

63. *Relación de lo sucedido,* 217.

64. Astrana Marín, *Vida ejemplar y heroica,* vol. 6, 30–31; Kenny, "Peace with Spain," 203.

65. Pinheiro da Viega, *Fastigimia,* 162–63.

66. Robert Treswell, *A Relation of such Things as were observed to happen in the Journey of the Right Honourable Charles, Earl of Nottingham, Lord High Admiral, His Highness's Ambassador to the King of Spain* (1605), in *Harleian Miscellany,* vol. 2 (London: Dutton, 1819), 566.

67. Cabrera de Córdoba, *Relaciones,* 266.

68. Ibid., 468.

69. Narciso Alonso Cortés, "Cervantes y la *Relación* del bautismo de Felipe IV," *Boletín de la Academia Argentina de Letras* 16 (1947): 527–40; Astrana Marín, *Vida ejemplar y heroica,* vol. 6, 37.

70. E. C. Riley, *Cervantes's Theory of the Novel* (Oxford: The Clarendon Press, 1962), 125n.1; 171, 173.

71. Pinheiro da Veiga, *Fastigimia,* 119–20.

72. Astrana Marín, *Vida ejemplar y heroica,* vol. 6, 11, 60–61.

73. Cabrera de Córdoba, *Relaciones,* 277.

74. Herbert Norris, *Costume and Fashion,* vol. 3 (London: Dent, 1938), 507, 489.

75. Miguel Herrero García, "Cervantes y la moda," *Revista de Ideas Estéticas* 6 (1948): 191–92.

76. Pinheiro da Veiga, *Fastigimia,* 69.

77. Norris, *Costume and Fashion,* vol. 3, 554.

78. *Relación de lo sucedido,* 247.

79. Guillermo Díaz Plaja, "La técnica narrativa de Cervantes: Algunas observaciones," in *Conferencias desarrolladas con motivo del IV centenario del nacimiento de Cervantes* (Barcelona: n.p., 1949), 21–25.

80. Kenny, *Elizabeth's Admiral,* 76–78.

81. Ibid., 68. See also K. R. Andrews, *Elizabethan Privateering* (Cambridge: Cambridge

University Press, 1964); and Michael Oppenheim, *A History of the Administration of the Royal Navy and of Merchant Shipping in Relation to the Navy* (London: J. Lane, 1896).

82. Pinheiro da Veiga, *Fastigimia*, 147.

83. Emile Benveniste, *Vocabulaire des institutions indo-européens*, vol. 1 (Paris: Editions de Minuit, 1969), 171–79. See also Georges Dumézil, *Idées romaines* (Paris: Gallimard, 1969), 47–59.

84. Casalduero, *Sentido y forma de las "Novelas ejemplares,"* 131.

85. Abreu, *Historia*, 256.

86. Casalduero, *Sentido y forma de las "Novelas ejemplares,"* 133.

87. González de Amezúa, *Cervantes creador*, vol. 2, 136.

88. Bossy, "The Character of English Catholicism," 234–35.

89. Narciso Alonso Cortes, *Casos cervantinos que tocan a Valladolid* (Madrid: Centro de Estudios Históricos, 1916), 22; González de Amezúa, *Cervantes creador*, vol. 2, 148.

90. El Saffar, *Novel to Romance*, 158.

91. Ibid.

92. Michel Cavillac, *Gueux et marchands dans le Guzmán de Alfarache (1599–1604): Roman picaresque et mentalité bourgeoise dans l'Espagne du Siècle d'Or* (Bordeaux: Institut d'Etudes Ibériques et Ibero-américaines de l'Université de Bordeaux, 1983), 147. My translation.

93. Enrique Tierno Galván, *Sobre la novela picaresca* (Madrid: Tecnos, 1974), 37, 43, 53, 83. My translation.

94. Bartolomé Bennassar, *Valladolid au siècle d'or: Une ville de Castille et sa campagne au XVIe siècle* (Paris: Mouton, 1967), 462, 466–67.

95. Ibid., 268.

96. Abreu, *Historia*, 301–2; 215–16.

97. Ibid., 301.

98. Vilar, "El tiempo del *Quijote*," 339–40.

99. Virumbales, "Aproximaciones a la visión de la sociedad," 194. My translation.

100. Schevill and Bonilla report that one of the nuns in Santa Paula was the daughter of a certain Francisco Cifuentes. Cervantes, *Novelas ejemplares*, vol. 2, ed. Rudolph Schevill and Adolfo Bonilla (Madrid: Gráficas Reunidas, 1923), 360–1. González de Amezúa denied any association with Cervantes (*Cervantes creador*, vol. 2, 139–40). Julio Rodríguez Luis has recently revived the idea (*Novedad y ejemplo*, vol. 1, 47n.10). Astrana Marín reports that the second husband of Juana Gaitán, the widow of Cervantes's good friend Pedro Laínez, was a certain Diego de Hondaro, a Burgalés whose mother's name was Cifuentes (*Vida ejemplar y heroica*, vol. 3, 373). Enough.

# Bibliography

Abreu, Fr. Pedro de. *Historia del saqueo de Cádiz por los ingleses en 1596.* Ed. Manuel Bustos Rodríguez. Cádiz: Universidad de Cádiz, 1996.

Alemán, Mateo. *Guzmán de Alfarache.* Ed. Francisco Rico. Barcelona: Planeta, 1967.

Alonso Cortés, Narciso. *Casos cervantinos que tocan a Valladolid.* Madrid: Centro de Estudios Históricos, 1916.

———. "Cervantes y la *Relación* del bautismo de Felipe IV." *Boletín de la Academia Argentina de Letras* 16 (1947): 527–40.

Anderson, Ellen M. "Playing at Moslem and Christian: The Construction of Gender and the Representation of Faith in Cervantes' Captivity Plays." *Cervantes* 13.2 (1993): 37–60.

Andrews, K. R. *Elizabethan Privateering.* Cambridge: Cambridge University Press, 1964.

Ariño, Francisco de. *Sucesos de Sevilla de 1592 a 1604.* Ed. Antonio María Fabié. Sevilla: Tarascó, 1873.

Asensio y Toledo, José María. "Sobre *La española inglesa.*" In *Cervantes y sus obras.* Barcelona: F. Seix, 1902. 265–66.

Astrana Marín, Luis. *Vida ejemplar y heroica de Miguel Cervantes Saavedra.* 7 vols. Madrid: Reus, 1948–58.

Aubrun, Charles V. "Sancho Panza, paysan pour de rire, paysan de vrai." *Revista Canadiense de Estudios Hispánicos* 1.1 (1976): 1–26.

Avalle-Arce, Juan Bautista. "*La Gitanilla.*" *Cervantes* 1 (1981): 9–18.

Bennassar, Bartolomé. *Recherches sur les grandes épidémies dans le nord de l'Espagne à la fin du XVIe siècle.* Paris: SEVPEN, 1969.

———. *Valladolid au siècle d'or: Une ville de Castille et sa campagne au XVIe siècle.* Paris: Mouton, 1967.

Bennassar, Bartolomé and Lucille Bennassar. *Les Chrétiens d'Allah: L'histoire extraordinaire des renégats.* Paris: Perrin, 1989.

Benveniste, Emile. *Vocabulaire des institutions indo-européens.* 2 vols. Paris: Editions de Minuit, 1969.

Bliss, Lee. "'Don Quixote' in England: The Case for 'The Knight of the Burning Pestle.'" *Viator* 18 (1987): 361–80.

Bono, Salvatore. *I corsari barbereschi*. Torino: Edizioni RAI, 1964.

Bossy, John. "The Character of English Catholicism." In *Crisis in Europe 1550–1650: Essays from Past and Present*. Ed. Trevor Aston. London: Routledge and Kegan Paul, 1965. 223–46.

Bourdieu, Pierre. *The Logic of Practice*. Stanford, Calif.: Stanford University Press, 1990.

Braudel, Fernand. "Conflits et refus de civilisation: Espagnols et Morisques au XVIe siècle." *Annales: Economies, Sociétés, Civilisations* 2.4 (1947): 397–410.

———. *The Mediterranean and the Mediterranean World in the Age of Philip II*. 2 vols. New York: Harper Colophon, 1976.

———. *The Perspective of the World*. Vol. 3 of *Civilization and Capitalism*. Berkeley: University of California Press, 1992.

Cabrera de Córdoba, Luis. *Felipe II Rey de España*. 1619?. 5 vols. Madrid: Aribau, 1877.

———. *De historia: para entendarla y escribirla*. 1611. Ed. Santiago Montero Díaz. Madrid: Instituto de Estudios Políticos, 1948.

———. *Relaciones de las cosas sucedidas en la corte de España desde 1599 hasta 1614*. Madrid: J. M. Alegría, 1857.

Caja de Leruela, Miguel. *Restauración de la abundancia de España*. 1631. Ed. Jean-Paul Le Flem. Madrid: Instituto de Estudios Fiscales, 1975.

Camamis, George. *Estudios sobre el cautiverio en el siglo de oro*. Madrid: Gredos, 1977.

*The Captive Lady*. Ed. A. R. Braunmuller. Oxford: The Malone Society, 1982.

Cardillac, Louis. *Morisques et chrétiens: Un affrontement polémique (1492–1640)*. Paris: Klincksieck, 1977.

Caro Baroja, Julio. "Los moriscos aragoneses, según un autor del siglo XVII." In *Razas, pueblos y linajes*. Madrid: Revista de Occidente, 1957. 96–97.

———. *Los moriscos del reino de Granada*. Madrid: ISTMO, 1976.

Casalduero, Joaquín. *Sentido y forma de las "Novelas Ejemplares."* Madrid: Gredos, 1962.

———. *Sentido y forma del Quijote*. Madrid: Insula, 1966.

Cascardi, Anthony J. "Cervantes's Exemplary Subjects." In *Cervantes's "Exemplary Novels" and the Adventure of Writing*. Ed. Michael Nerlich and Nicholas Spadaccini. Minneapolis: The Prisma Institute, 1989. 49–72.

Castro, Américo. "Como veo ahora el *Quijote*." Estudio introducción a la edición de *Don Quijote*. Madrid: Magisterio Español, 1971.

———. "Erasmo en tiempos de Cervantes." In *Hacia Cervantes*. 3d ed. Madrid: Taurus, 1967.

———. "La palabra escrita y el *Quijote*." In *Hacia Cervantes*. 3d. ed. 359–419. Madrid: Taurus, 1967.

———. *El pensamiento de Cervantes*. 1925. Ampliada con notas del autor y de Julio Rodríguez Puértolas. Barcelona: Noguer, 1972.

Cavillac, Michel. *Gueux et marchands dans le Guzmán de Alfarache (1599–1604): Ro-*

*man picaresque et mentalité bourgeoise dans l'Espagne du Siècle d'Or*. Bordeaux: Institut d'Etudes Ibériques et Ibero-américaines de l'Université de Bordeaux, 1983.

———. *Pícaros y mercaderes en el "Guzmán de Alfarache."* Granada: Universidad de Granada, 1995.

Cervantes, Miguel de. *Don Quijote*. 10 vols. Ed. Francisco Rodríguez Marín. Madrid: Atlas, 1949.

———. *Don Quijote*. 3 vols. Ed. Luis Andrés Murillo. Madrid: Castalia, 1978.

———. *Don Quijote*. Trans. Burton Raffel. Ed. Diana de Armas Wilson. Norton Critical Edition. New York: W. W. Norton, 1999.

———. *Novelas ejemplares*. 3 vols. Ed. Juan Bautista Avalle-Arce. Madrid: Castalia, 1987.

———. *Novelas ejemplares*. 3 vols. Ed. Rudolph Schevill and Adolfo Bonilla. Madrid: Gráficas Reunidas, 1923.

———. *Novelas ejemplares*. 2 vols. Ed. Harry Sieber. Madrid: Cátedra, 1980.

———. *Viage del Parnaso: Poesías varias*. Ed. Elias L. Rivers. Madrid: Espasa-Calpe, 1991.

Chaunu, Pierre. *Séville et l'Amérique aux XVIe et XVIIe Siècles*. Paris: Flammarion, 1977.

———. *Séville et l'Atlantique*. 10 vols. Paris: Armand Colin, 1955.

Clamurro, William. "Value and Identity in *La Gitanilla*." *Journal of Hispanic Philology* 14.1 (Autumn 1989): 43–60.

Clavero, Bartolomé. *Mayorazgo: Propiedad feudal en Castilla, 1369–1836*. Madrid: Siglo XXI, 1989.

Covarrubias, Sebastián de. *Tesoro de la lengua castellana*. 1611. Madrid: Turner, 1978.

Criado de Val, Manuel. *Teoría de Castilla la Nueva*. Madrid: Gredos, 1960.

Cruz, Anne J., and Carroll B. Johnson, eds. *Cervantes and His Postmodern Constituencies*. New York: Garland Press, 1999.

Davis, Nina Cox. "The Tyranny of Love in *El amante liberal*." *Cervantes* 13.2 (1993): 105–24.

*A Declaration of the Causes moving the Queene's Maiestie of England to prepare and send a Navy to the Seas for the defence of her Realmes against the King of Spaine's Forces . . . .* London: Deputies of Christopher Barker, 1596.

*A Declaration of the Causes which mooved the chief Commanders of the Navie of her most excellent Majestie the Queen of England . . . to take and arrest in the mouth of the River of Lisbonne certain Shippes . . . prepared for the King of Spaine . . . the 30th day of June . . . 1589.* London: Deputies of Christopher Barker, 1589.

"Diálogo entre Laín Calvo y Nuño Rasura" 1570. *Revue Hispanique* 10 (1903): 150–81.

Díaz Migoyo, Gonzalo. "La ficción cordial de *El amante liberal*." *Nueva Revista de Filología Hispánica* 35.1 (1987): 129–50.

Díaz Plaja, Guillermo. "La técnica narrativa de Cervantes: Algunas observaciones." In *Conferencias desarrolladas con motivo del IV centenario del nacimiento de Cervantes*. Barcelona: n.p., 1949. 21–25.

Díez Borque, José María. *Sociología de la comedia española del siglo XVII*. Madrid: Gredos, 1976.

Domínguez Ortiz, Antonio. *Las clases privilegiadas en la España de los Austrias.* Madrid: ISTMO, 1973.

————. "La conspiración del duque de Medina Sidonia y el marqués de Ayamonte." In *Crisis y decadencia de la España de los Austrias.* Barcelona: Ariel, 1969. 113–54.

————. *Desde Carlos V a la paz de los Pirineos.* Barcelona: Grijalbo, 1974.

————. "Documentos sobre los gitanos españoles en el siglo XVII." *Homenaje a Julio Caro Baroja.* Madrid: n.p., 1978.

————. *Orto y ocaso de Sevilla.* 2d ed. Sevilla: Universidad de Sevilla, 1974.

Domínguez Ortiz, Antonio, and Bernard Vincent. *Historia de los moriscos: Vida y tragedia de una minoría.* Madrid: Revista de Occidente, 1978.

Dumézil, Georges. *Idées romaines.* Paris: Gallimard, 1969.

Durán, Manuel. *Cervantes.* Twayne World Author Series. Boston: G. K. Hall, 1967.

Elliott, John Huxtable. *Imperial Spain.* London: Penguin, 1972.

El Saffar, Ruth. *Novel to Romance: A Study of the "Novelas ejemplares" of Cervantes.* Baltimore: Johns Hopkins University Press, 1974.

El Saffar, Ruth Anthony, and Diana de Armas Wilson, eds. *Quixotic Desire: Psychoanalytic Perspectives on Cervantes.* Ithaca, N.Y.: Cornell University Press, 1993.

Fernández Navarrete, Pedro. *Conservación de monarquías y discursos políticos.* 1626. Ed. Michael D. Gordon. Madrid: Instituto de Estudios Fiscales, 1982.

Fisher, Godfrey. *Barbary Legend: War, Trade and Piracy in North Africa.* Oxford: Clarendon Press, 1957.

Flores, R. M. *Sancho Panza through 375 Years of Continuations, Imitations and Criticism, 1605–1980.* Newark, Del.: Juan de la Cuesta, 1982.

Fontes, Manuel da Costa. "Love as an Equalizer in *La española inglesa.*" *Romance Notes* 16 (1975): 1–9.

Forcione, Alban K. Afterword. In *Cervantes's "Exemplary Novels" and the Adventure of Writing.* Ed. Michael Nerlich and Nicholas Spadaccini. Minneapolis: The Prisma Institute, 1989. 331–52.

————. *Cervantes and the Humanist Vision: A Study of Four "Exemplary Novels."* Princeton, N.J.: Princeton University Press, 1982.

————. "Cervantes's *La Gitanilla* as Erasmian Romance." In *Cervantes and the Humanist Vision: A Study of Four "Exemplary Novels."* Princeton, N.J.: Princeton University Press, 1982. 93–224.

————. "Cervantes's Secularized Miracle: *La fuerza de la sangre.*" In *Cervantes and the Humanist Vision: A Study of Four "Exemplary Novels."* Princeton, N.J.: Princeton University Press, 1982. 317–98.

Friedman, Ellen G. *Spanish Captives in North Africa in the Early Modern Age.* Madison: University of Wisconsin Press, 1983.

Fuchs, Barbara. "Border Crossings: Transvestism and 'Passing' in *Don Quijote.*" *Cervantes* 16.2 (Fall 1996): 4–28.

Galán, Diego. *Cautiverio y trabajos de Diego Galán.* 1600. Ed. M. Serrano y Sanz. Madrid: Sociedad de Bibliófilos Españoles, 1913.

# Bibliography

Garcés, María Antonia. "Zoraida's Veil: The Other Scene in the Captive's Tale." *Revista de Estudios Hispánicos* 23 (1989): 65–98.

García Arenal, Mercedes. *Los moriscos*. Madrid: Editora Nacional, 1975.

Gerli, E. Michael. "A Novel Rewriting: Romance and Irony in *La Gitanilla*." In *Refiguring Authority: Reading, Writing, and Rewriting in Cervantes*. Lexington: University Press of Kentucky, 1995. 24–40.

———. "Rewriting Myth and History: Discourse of Race, Marginality and Resistance in the Captive's Tale (*Don Quijote* I, 37–42." In *Refiguring Authority: Reading, Writing, and Rewriting in Cervantes*. Lexington: University Press of Kentucky, 1995. 40–60.

———. "Romance and Novel: Idealism and Irony in *La Gitanilla*." *Cervantes* 6 (1986): 29–38.

Girard, Albert. *Le commerce français à Séville et Cadix au temps des Habsbourg*. Paris: Boccard/Bordeaux: Ferret, 1932.

González Aurioles, Norberto. *Monjas sevillanas parientes de Cervantes*. Madrid: Alvarez, 1915.

González de Amezúa, Agustín. *Cervantes creador de la novela corta española*. 2 vols. Madrid: CSIC, 1956–58.

González de Cellorigo, Martín. *Memorial de la política necesaria y útil restauración de la República de España y Estados de ella y del desempeño universal destos Reinos*. 1600. Ed. José L. Pérez de Ayala. Madrid: Instituto de Estudios Fiscales, 1991.

Goux, Jean-Joseph. *Symbolic Economies: After Marx and Freud*. Ithaca, N.Y.: Cornell University Press, 1990.

Grice-Hutchinson, Marjorie. *Early Economic Thought in Spain: 1177–1740*. London: Allen and Unwin, 1978.

Güntert, Georges. "Discurso social y discurso individual en *La Gitanilla*." In *Cervantes: Novelar el mundo desintegrado*. Barcelona: Puvill, 1993. 112–26.

———. "Las dos lecturas de *El amante liberal*." In *Cervantes: Novelar el mundo desintegrado*. Barcelona: Puvill, 1993. 126–42.

———. "*La Gitanilla* y la poética de Cervantes." *Boletín de la Real Academia Española* 52 (1972): 107–34.

Haedo, Fr. Diego de. *Topografía e historia general de Argel*. 1612. 3 vols. Ed. I. Bauer y Landauer. Madrid: Sociedad de Bibliófilos Españoles, 1927.

Hamilton, Earl J. *Tesoro americano y la revolución de los precios en España, 1501–1650*. Barcelona: Ariel, 1975.

Hanrahan, Thomas. "History in *La española inglesa*." *MLN* 83 (1968): 256–72.

Hart, Thomas R. *Cervantes's Exemplary Fictions: A Study of the "Novelas ejemplares."* Lexington: University Press of Kentucky, 1993.

———. "La ejemplaridad de *El amante liberal*." *Nueva Revista de Filología Hispánica* 36.1 (1988): 303–18.

Hegyi, Ottmar. *Cervantes and the Turks: Historical Reality versus Literary Fiction in "La Gran Sultana" and "El amante liberal."* Newark, Del.: Juan de la Cuesta, 1992.

Henson, Edwin ed. *The Registers of the English College at Valladolid, 1569–1862.* London: Catholic Records Society, 1930.

Heredia, Juan de Dios. *Vida gitana.* Barcelona: Ediciones 29, 1973.

Herrera Puga, Pedro. *Sociedad y delincuencia en el siglo de oro.* Granada: Universidad de Granada, 1976.

Herrero García, Miguel. "Cervantes y la moda." *Revista de Ideas Estéticas* 6 (1948): 181–202.

———. *Ideas de los españoles del siglo XVII.* 2d ed. Madrid: Gredos, 1966.

Hess, Andrew C. "La batalla de Lepanto y su lugar en la historia del Mediterráneo." In *Poder y sociedad en la España de los Austrias.* Ed. J. H. Elliott. Barcelona: Crítica, 1982. 90–114.

Huerga, A. ed. *Avisos para predicadores del Santo Evangelio.* Barcelona: Espirituales Españoles, 1959.

Hughes, Philip. *The Reformation in England.* Revised ed. London: Barnes and Noble, 1963.

Hume, Martin. *Treason and Plot: Struggles for Catholic Supremacy in the Last Years of Queen Elizabeth.* London: Eveleigh Nash, 1908.

Hurstfield, Jack. "The Succession Struggle in Late Elizabethan England." In *Elizabethan Government and Society: Essays Presented to Sir John Neale.* Ed. S. T. Bindoff, J. Hurstfield, and C. H. Williams. London: University of London, Athlone Press, 1961.

Icaza, Francisco. *Las "Novelas ejemplares" de Cervantes: Sus críticos. Sus modelos literarios. Sus modelos vivos.* Madrid: Ateneo de Madrid, 1916.

Inalcik, Halil. "Capital Formation in the Ottoman Empire." *Journal of Economic History* 29 (1969): 97–140.

Irigary, Luce. "Des marchandises entre elles." In *Speculum de l'autre femme.* Paris: Eds. de Minuit, 1974. Reprinted as "When the Goods Get Together." In *New French Feminisms: An Anthology.* Ed. Elaine Marks and Isabelle de Courtivron. Amherst: University of Massachusetts Press, 1980. 107–10.

Iser, Wolfgang. "The Reading Process: A Phenomenological Approach." In *The Implied Reader: Patterns of Communication in Prose Fiction from Bunyan to Beckett.* Baltimore: Johns Hopkins University Press, 1974. 274–94.

Jardine, Lisa. *Worldly Goods: A New History of the Renaissance.* New York: Nan A. Talese–Doubleday, 1996.

Jennings, Ronald C. *Christians and Muslims in Ottoman Cyprus and the Mediterranean World, 1571–1640.* New York: New York University Press, 1993.

Johnson, Carroll B. "De economías y linajes en *La Gitanilla.*" *Mester* 25.1 (Spring 1996): 31–48.

———. "*La española inglesa* and the Practice of Literary Production." *Viator* 19 (1988): 377–416.

———. *Madness and Lust: A Psychoanalytical Approach to Don Quixote.* Berkeley: University of California Press, 1983.

———. "The Old Order Passeth, or Does It? Some Thoughts on Community, Commerce and Alienation in *Rinconete y Cortadillo.*" In *On Cervantes: Essays for Luis Murillo.* Ed. James A. Parr. Newark, Del.: Juan de la Cuesta, 1991. 85–104.

———. "Organic Unity in Unlikely Places: *Don Quijote I,* 39–41." *Cervantes* 2 (1982): 133–54.

———. "Ortodoxia y anticapitalismo en el siglo XVII: el caso del morisco Ricote." In *Hispanic Studies in Honor of Joseph H. Silverman.* Ed. J. V. Ricapito. Newark, Del.: Juan de la Cuesta, 1988. 285–96.

———. "La sexualidad en el *Quijote.*" *Edad de Oro* 9 (1990): 125–36.

Joly, Monique. "Afición de los extranjeros al vino y al jamón." *Nueva Revista de Filología Hispánica* 22 (1973): 321–28.

Kenny, Robert W. *Elizabeth's Admiral: The Political Career of Charles Howard, Earl of Nottingham.* Baltimore: Johns Hopkins University Press, 1970.

———. "Peace with Spain, 1605." *History Today,* March 1970, 204–8.

Klaveren, Jacob van. *Europäische Wirtschaftsgeschichte Spaniens im 16. und 17. Jahrhundert.* Stuttgart: Fischer, 1960.

Kunt, I. Metin. *The Sultan's Servants: The Transformation of Ottoman Provincial Government, 1550–1650.* New York: Columbia University Press, 1983.

Labib, Subhi Y. "Capitalism in Medieval Islam." *Journal of Economic History* 29 (1969): 79–96.

Lapesa, Rafael. "En torno a *La española inglesa* y el *Persiles.*" In *De la edad media a nuestros días.* Madrid: Gredos, 1967. 242–63.

Lapeyre, Henri. *Une famille de marchands: les Ruiz.* Paris: SEVPEN, 1955.

Lassel, Adriana A. "Mundo musulmán en Miguel de Cervantes." *Langues et Littératures: Revue de l'Institut des Langues Etrangères de l'Université d'Alger* 1 (1986): 93–104.

*Lazarillo de Tormes.* 1554. Ed. Francisco Rico. Madrid: Cátedra, 1987.

Leblon, Bernard. *Les Gitans dans la littérature espagnole.* Toulouse: Institut d'Etudes Hispaniques et Hispano-américaines de l'Université de Toulouse-Le Mirail, 1982.

———. *Les Gitans d'Espagne.* Paris: Presses Universitaires de France, 1985.

———. "Les parentés fictives chez les Gitans au siècle d'or." In *Las parentés fictives en Espagne (XVIe et XVIIe siècles).* Ed. Augustin Redondo. Travaux de "Centre de Recherche sur l'Espagne des XVIe et XVIIe siècles," no. 4. Paris: Publications de la Sorbonne, 1988. 87–94.

Llorens, Vicente. "Don Quijote y la decadencia del hidalgo." In *Aspectos sociales de la literatura española.* Madrid: Castalia, 1974. 47–66.

Loomie, Albert J., S.J. "Religion and Elizabethan Commerce with Spain." *Catholic Historical Review* 50 (1964–65): 27–51.

———. *Spain and the Jacobean Catholics.* London: Catholic Record Society, 1973.

———. *The Spanish Elizabethans: English Exiles at the Court of Philip II.* New York: Fordham University Press, 1963.

———. *Toleration and Diplomacy: The Religious Issue in Anglo-Spanish Relations 1603–1605.* Philadelphia: American Philosophical Society, 1963.

López Estrada, Francisco. "Apuntes para una interpretación de *Rinconete y Cortadillo:* Una posible resonancia creadora." In *Lenguaje, ideología y organizacion textual en las "Novelas Ejemplares."* Ed. José Jesús Bustos Tovar. Madrid: Universidad Complutense, 1983. 59–68.

Manca, Ciro. *Il modello di sviluppo economico delle città maritime barbaresche dopo Lepanto.* Napoli: Istituto Universitario Navale, 1982.

Maravall, José Antonio. "La crisis económica de los siglos XVI y XVII interpretada por los escritores de la época." In *Estudios de historia del pensamiento español.* Madrid: Cultura Hispánica, 1984. 153–96.

———. *Estado moderno y mentalidad social.* 2 vols. Madrid: Alianza, 1986.

———. *La literatura picaresca desde la historia social: Siglos XVI y XVII.* Madrid: Taurus, 1986.

———. "Reformismo social-agragio en la crisis del siglo XVII: tierra, trabajo y salario según Pedro de Valencia." *Bulletin Hispanique* 72 (1970): 1–37.

———. *Utopia and Counterutopia in the "Quixote."* Detroit: Wayne State University Press, 1991.

Mariana, Fray Juan de. *Discurso sobre la moneda de vellón.* 1609. Vol. 31 of *Biblioteca de Autores Españoles.* Madrid: Rivadaneyra, 1861. 577–94.

———. *Historia general de España.* 1601. Vol. 30 and 31 of *Biblioteca de Autores Españoles.* Madrid: Rivadaneyra, 1861. 1–575.

Márquez Villanueva, Francisco. "Bonifacio y Dorotea: Mateo Alemán y la novela burguesa." *Actas del VIII Congreso de la Asociación Internacional de Hispanistas (1986).* Madrid: ISTMO, 1986. 59–88.

———. "La buenaventura de Preciosa." *Nueva Revista de Filología Hispánica* 34 (1985–86): 741–68.

———. "La génesis literaria de Sancho Panza." In *Fuentes literarias cervantinas.* Madrid: Gredos, 1973. 20–94.

———. "Leandra, Zoraida y sus fuentes franco-italianas." In *Personajes y temas del Quijote.* Madrid: Taurus, 1975. 77–146.

———. "El morisco Ricote o la hispana razón de estado." In *Personajes y temas del Quijote.* Madrid: Taurus, 1975. 229–35.

Martín, Adrienne. "Rereading *El amante liberal* in the Age of Contrapuntal Sexualities." In *Cervantes and his Postmodern Constituencies.* Ed. Anne J. Cruz and Carroll B. Johnson. New York: Garland Press, 1999. 151–69.

Marx, Karl. *Economic and Philosophical Manuscripts of 1844.* Moscow: Progress Publishers, 1977.

Mas, Albert. *Les turcs dans la littérature espagnole du siècle d'or.* 2 vols. Paris: Centre de Recherches Hispaniques, 1967.

Mathieu, Jean. "Trafic et prix de l'homme en Méditerranée aux XVIIe et XVIIIe siècles." *Annales (Economies, Sociétés, Civilisations)* 9.2 (1954): 157–64.

McKendrick, Melveena. *Cervantes.* Boston: Little, Brown, 1980.

Mercado, Fr. Tomás de. *Suma de tratos y contratos.* 1571. Ed Restituto Sierra Bravo. Madrid: Editora Nacional, 1975.

# Bibliography

Molho, Mauricio. "Raíz folklórica de Sancho Panza." In *Cervantes: raíces folklóricas.* Madrid: Gredos, 1976. 217–336.

Moner, Michel. "El problema morisco en los textos cervantinos." In *Las dos grandes minorías étnico-religiosas en la literatura española del Siglo de Oro: los judeoconversos y los moriscos.* Ed. Irene Andres-Suárez. Actas del "Grande Séminaire" de Neuchâtel (1994). Annales littéraires de l'Université de Besançon, no. 588. Paris: Diffusion Les Belles Lettres, 1995. 85–100.

Monleón, José [tío]. *Treinta años de teatro de la derecha.* Barcelona: Tusquets, 1971.

Moret, Michèle. *Aspects de la société marchande à Séville au débout du XVIIe siècle.* Paris: Marcel Rivière, 1967.

Murillo, Luis A. "Cervantes's Tale of the Captive Captain." In *Florilegium Hispanicum: Medieval and Golden Age Studies presented to Dorothy Clotelle Clarke.* Madison, Wis.: Hispanic Medieval Seminary, 1983. 231–43.

Neale, J. E. *Queen Elizabeth I.* 1934. Garden City, N.Y.: Anchor-Doubleday, 1957.

Nerlich, Michael and Nicholas Spadaccini, eds. *Cervantes's "Exemplary Novels" and the Adventure of Writing.* Minneapolis: The Prisma Institute, 1989.

Norris, Herbert. *Costume and Fashion.* 6 vols. London: Dent, 1938.

Oliver Asín, Jaime. "La hija de Agi Morato en la obra de Cervantes." *Boletín de la Real Academia Española* 27 (1948): 245–339.

Oppenheim, Michael. *A History of the Administration of the Royal Navy and of Merchant Shipping in Relation to the Navy.* London: J. Lane, 1896.

Ortiz, Luis de. *Memorial.* 1558. In *Economía, sociedad y corona.* Ed. Manuel Fernández Alvarez. Madrid: Cultura Hispánica, 1963. 375–462.

Pascual Buxó, José. "Estructura y lección de *Rinconete y Cortadillo.*" In *Las figuraciones del sentido: Ensayos de poética semiológica.* México: Fondo de Cultura Económica, 1984. 181–213.

Peck, Linda Levy. *Northampton: Patronage and Policy at the Court of James I.* London: Allen and Unwin, 1982.

Peers, E. Allison. "Cervantes in England." *Bulletin of Spanish Studies* 24 (1947): 221–39.

Pelorson, Jean-Marc. *Les "letrados": juristes castillans sous Philippe III. Recherches sur leur place dans la société, la culture, et l'Etat.* Poitiers: Université de Poitiers, 1980.

Percas de Ponseti, Helena. *Cervantes y su concepto del arte.* 2 vols. Madrid: Gredos, 1975.

Perrin Anne-Marie, and Françoise Zmantar (PEZ). "Jardins d'amour." In *El Candil.* Département d'etudes hispaniques. Clermont-Ferrand: Université de Clermont II, 1985. 143–59.

Perry, Mary Elizabeth. *Crime and Society in Early Modern Seville.* Hanover, N.H.: The University Press of New England, 1980.

Phillips, Carla and William Phillips. *Spain's Golden Fleece: Wool Production and the Wool Trade from the Middle Ages to the Nineteenth Century.* Baltimore: Johns Hopkins University Press, 1997.

Pierson, Peter O'M. *Commander of the Armada.* New Haven, Conn.: Yale University Press, 1989.

# Bibliography

Pinheiro da Veiga, Thomé. *Fastigimia*. Vol. 3 of *Coleçao de Manuscriptos ineditos agora dados à estampa*. Porto: Biblioteca Municipal, 1911.

Quevedo, Francisco de. *Sueños*. 2 vols. Ed. Julio Cejador y Frauca. Madrid: Espasa-Calpe, 1960.

Ramírez Araujo, A. "El morisco Ricote y la libertad de conciencia." *Hispanic Review* 24 (1956): 278–89.

Redondo, Augustin. "Acercamiento al *Quijote* desde una perspectiva histórico-social." In *Otra manera de leer el Quijote*. Madrid: Castalia, 1997. 55–100.

———. "La princesa Micomicona y Sancho negrero *(Don Quijote I, 29)*." In *Otra manera de leer el Quijote*. Madrid: Castalia, 1997. 363–82.

———. *Otra manera de leer el Quijote*. Madrid: Castalia, 1997.

——— ed. *Les parentés fictives en Espagne (XVIe–XVIIe siècles)*. Travaux du "Centre de Recherche sur l'Espagne des XVIe et XVIIe siècles," no. 4. Paris: Publications de la Sorbonne, 1988.

*Relación de la gran presa que hicieron cuatro galeras de la Religión de San Juan, de dos naves y seis caramuzales, y dos galeras turquescas, con el número de cautivos, y cristianos libertados*. 1617. In Ignacio Bauer Landauer, *Papeles de mi archivo*. Madrid: Editorial Ibero-Africano-Americana, n.d. 91–92.

*Relación de lo sucedido en la ciudad de Valladolid desde el felicísimo nacimiento del príncipe nuestro señor, hasta que se acabaron las fiestas y demostraciones de alegría que por él se hicieron*. In Cervantes, *Obras completas*. Vol. 2. Ed. Cayetano Rosell. Madrid: Rivadeneyra, 1863–64. 191–250.

Resina, Joan Ramon. "Laissez-faire y reflexividad erótica en La *Gitanilla*." *MLN* 106 (1991): 257–78.

Riley, E. C. *Cervantes's Theory of the Novel*. Oxford: The Clarendon Press, 1962.

Rodríguez Luis, Julio. *Novedad y ejemplo en las "Novelas Ejemplares" de Cervantes*. Madrid: José Porrúa Turanzas, 1980.

Rodríguez Marín, Francisco. *Nuevos documentos cervantinos hasta ahora inéditas*. 2 vols. Madrid: Revista de Archivos, Bibliotecas y Museos, 1914.

Rodríguez Sánchez, Angel. "El poder y la familia: Formas de control y consanguinidad en la Extremadura de los tiempos modernos." In *Poder, familia y consanguinidad en la España del Antiguo Régimen*. Ed. F. Chacón Jiménez and J. Hernández Franco. Barcelona: Anthropos, 1992. 15–34.

Ruiz Martín, Felipe. *Pequeño capitalismo, gran capitalismo: Simón Ruiz y sus negocios en Florencia*. Barcelona: Crítica, 1990.

Ruta, Maria Caterina. "Zoraida: los signos de silencio en un personaje cervantino." *Anales Cervantinos* 21 (1983): 119–33.

*El sacrosanto y ecuménico concilio de Trento*. Traducido al idioma castellano por D. Ignacio López de Ayala, con el texto latino corregido según la edición auténtica de Roma publicada en 1564. Barcelona: R. Martín Indar, 1847.

Salazar Rincón, Javier. *El mundo social del "Quijote."* Madrid: Gredos, 1986.

Salomon, Noël. *Recherches sur le thème paysan dans la "comedia" au temps de Lope de*

# Bibliography

*Vega*. Bordeaux: Institut d'Etudes Ibériques et Ibéro-américaines de la Université de Bordeaux, 1965.

———. *La vida rural castellana en tiempos de Felipe II.* Barcelona: Planeta, 1973.

Salomone Marino, Salvatore. "Una scena di pirateria in Sicilia nel 1573." *Archivio Storico Siciliano*, n.s., 22 (1897): 217–28.

———. "I siciliani nelle guerre contro gl'infedeli nel secolo XVI." *Archivio Storico Siciliano* 37 (1912): 1–29.

Salvá, Jaime. *La orden de Malta y las acciones navales españolas contra turcos y berberiscos en los siglos XVI y XVII.* Madrid: Instituto Histórico de Marina, 1944.

Sánchez, Alberto. "Revisión del cautiverio cervantino en Argel." *Cervantes* 17.1 (1997): 7–24.

Sánchez, Francisco J. "Theater within the Novel: 'Mass' Audience and Individual Reader in *La Gitanilla* and *Rinconete y Cortadillo*." In *Cervantes's "Exemplary Novels" and the Adventure of Writing.* Ed. Michael Nerlich and Nicholas Spadaccini. Minneapolis: The Prisma Institute, 1989. 73–98.

Sánchez Ortega, María Helena. *La Inquisición y los gitanos.* Madrid: Taurus, 1988

Sánchez Romeralo, Jaime. "Miguel de Cervantes y su cuñado Francisco de Palacios." In *Actas del Segundo Congreso de la Asociación Internacional de Hispanista.* Nijmegen: Instituto Español de la Universidad de Nimega, 1967. 563–72.

Saravia de la Calle, Luis. *Instrucción de mercaderes muy provechosa, en la cual se enseña cómo deben los mercaderes tratar.* 1544, 1547. Colección "Joyas Bibliográficas." Madrid: n.p., 1949.

Sears, Theresa Ann. *A Marriage of Convenience: Ideal and Ideology in the "Novelas Ejemplares."* New York: Peter Lang, 1993.

Selig, Karl-Ludwig. "Nuevas consideraciones sobre la temática y estructura de las *Novelas ejemplares*." *Beiträge zur romanischen Philologie.* Sonderheft, 1967. 45–51.

Sentaurens, Jean. "Séville dans la seconde moitié du XVIe siècle." *Bulletin Hispanique* 77 (1975): 321–90.

Shell, Marc. *The Economy of Literature.* Baltimore: Johns Hopkins University Press, 1978.

Shipley, George A. "Lazarillo and the Cathedral Chaplain: A Conspiratorial Reading of *Lazarillo de Tormes,* Tratado VI." *Symposium* 37 (1983): 216–41.

Sieber, Diane E. "Mapping Identity in the Captive's Tale: Cervantes and Ethnographic Narrative." *Cervantes* 18.1 (1998): 115–33.

Slingsby, Sir William. *Relation of the Voyage to Cádiz, 1596.* In *The Naval Miscellany.* Vol. 20. Ed. J. K. Laughton. London: Navy Records Society, 1902. 23–92.

Sola, Emilio. *Un Mediterraneo de piratas: corsarios, renegados y cautivos.* Madrid: Tecnos, 1988.

Sola, Emilio and José F. de la Peña. *Cervantes y la berbería: Cervantes, mundo turco-berberesco y servicios secretos en la época de Felipe II.* Madrid: Fondo de Cultura Económica, 1995.

Sosa, Dr. Antonio. *Diálogo de los mártires de Argel.* Ed. Emilio Sola y J. M. Parreño. Madrid: Hiperion, 1990.

Smith, Paul Julian. "'The Captive's Tale': Race, Text, Gender." In *Quixotic Desire: Psychoanalytic Perspectives on Cervantes*. Ed. Ruth Anthony El Saffar and Diana de Armas Wilson. Ithaca, N.Y.: Cornell University Press, 1993. 227–38.

———. "Cervantes, Goytisolo and the Sodomitical Scene." In *Cervantes and the Modernists*. Ed. Edwin Williamson. London: Támesis, 1994. 43–54.

Spieker, Joseph B. "Preciosa y Poesía: sobre el concepto cervantino de la poesía y estructura de *La Gitanilla*." *Explicación de Textos Literarios* 4 (1975–76): 213–20.

Spitzer, Leo. "Perspectivismo lingüístico en el *Quijote*." In *Lingüística e historia literaria*. Madrid: Gredos, 1961. 135–87.

Starkie, Walter. "Cervantes y los gitanos." *Anales Cervantinos* 4 (1954): 138–86.

Templin, Ernest H. "Labradores in the *Quijote*." *Hispanic Review* 30 (1962): 21–51.

ter Horst, Robert. "'Une saison en enfer': *La Gitanilla*." *Cervantes* 5 (1985): 87–128.

Thomson-Weightman, Sandi. "The Representation of Woman in *El amante liberal*: Goddess, Chattel and Peer." *Mester* 21.1 (1992): 61–71.

Tierno Galván, Enrique. *Sobre la novela picaresca*. Madrid: Tecnos, 1974.

Treswell, Robert. *A Relation of such Things as were observed to happen in the Journey of the Right Honourable Charles, Earl of Nottingham, Lord High Admiral, His Highness's Ambassador to the King of Spain*. 1605. In *Harleian Miscellany*. Vol. 2. London: Dutton, 1819. 535–66.

Ulloa, Modesto. *La hacienda real de Castilla en el reinado de Felipe II*. Madrid: Fundación Universitaria Española, 1977.

Urbina, Eduardo. *El sin par Sancho Panza: parodia y creación*. Barcelona: Anthropos, 1991.

Valencia, Pedro de. "Discurso contra la ociosidad." In *Obras completas*. Vol. 4, bk. 1. Dirección y coordinación Gaspar Morocho Gayo. Ed. Rafael González Cañal. León: Universidad de León, 1994. 159–73.

———. "Discurso sobre el acrecentamiento de la labor de la tierra." 1607. In *Obras completas*. Vol. 4, bk. 1. Dirección y coordinación Gaspar Morocho Gayo. Ed. Rafael González Cañal. León: Universidad de León, 1994. 137–58.

———. "Discurso sobre el precio del trigo." 1608. In *Obras completas*. Vol. 4, bk. 1. Dirección y coordinación Gaspar Morocho Gayo. Ed. Rafael González Cañal. León: Publicaciones de la Universidad de León, 1994. 29–97.

Valiente, Francisco Tomás. *El derecho penal de la monarquía absoluta (siglos XVI–XVII)*. Madrid: Tecnos, 1969.

Vassberg, David. *Land and Society in Golden-Age Castile*. Cambridge: Cambridge University Press, 1984.

*Viaje de Turquía*. 1557. Ed. Fernando García Salinero. Madrid: Cátedra, 1980.

Vidal, Jeanne. *Quand on brûlait les morisques (1544–1621)*. Nîmes: n.p., 1986.

Vilar, Pierre. "El tiempo del *Quijote*." 1956. In *Crecimiento y desarrollo*. Barcelona: Ariel, 1976. 332–46.

Viñas Mey, Carmelo. *El problema de la tierra en la España de los siglos XVI y XVII*. Madrid: CSIC, 1941.

# Bibliography

Vincent, Bernard. "Amor y matrimonio entre los moriscos." In *Minorías y marginados en la España del siglo XVI*. Granada: Diputación Provincial, 1987. 47–72.

———. "La familia morisca." In *Minorías y marginados en la España del siglo XVI*. Granada: Diputación Provincial, 1987. 7–30.

———. "La Inquisición y los moriscos granadinos." In *Minorías y marginados en la España del siglo XVI*. Granada: Diputación Provincial, 1987. 119–56.

———. "Jesuitas y moriscos (1545–1570)." In *Minorías y marginados en la España del siglo XVI*. Granada: Diputación Provincial, 1987. 101–18.

———. "Los moriscos y la circuncisión." In *Minorías y marginados en la España del siglo XVI*. Granada: Diputación Provincial, 1987. 83–100.

———. "El nombre cristiano de los moriscos." In *Minorías y marginados en la España del siglo XVI*. Granada: Diputación Provincial, 1987. 31–46.

———. "El padrinazgo y los moriscos." In *Minorías y marginados en la España del siglo XVI*. Granada: Diputación Provincial, 1987. 73–82.

Virumbales, Pablo. "Aproximaciones a la visión de la sociedad española en las *Novelas ejemplares* de Cervantes." *Anales Cervantinos* 16 (1977): 177–98.

Weber, Alison. "Padres e hijas: una lectura intertextual de *La historia del cautivo*." In *Actas del Segundo coloquio de la Asociación de Cervantistas (1989)*. Barcelona: Anthropos, 1991. 425–31.

———. "Pentimento: the Parodic Text of *La Gitanilla*." *Hispanic Review* 62 (1994): 59–75.

Williams, Michael E. *St. Alban's College Valladolid: Four Centuries of English Catholic Presence in Spain*. New York: St. Martin's Press, 1986.

Williams, Raymond. *Marxism and Literature*. Oxford: Oxford University Press, 1977.

Williamson, Edwin. "Hacia la conciencia ideológica de Cervantes: idealización y violencia en *El amante liberal*." In *Cervantes: Estudios en la víspera de su centenario*. Vol. 2. Kassel: Editorial Reichenberger, 1994. 519–33.

Ynduráin, Domingo. "*Rinconete y Cortadillo*: De entremés a novela." *Boletín de la Real Academia Española* 46 (1966): 321–33.

Zimic, Stanislav. "El amante liberal." In *Las "Novelas ejemplares" de Cervantes*. Madrid: Siglo XXI, 1996. 47–83.

Zmantar, Françoise. "Qui es-tu, Hazan, òu es-tu?" In *Le personnage en question: IV Colloque du S.E.L. Travaux de l'Université Toulouse-Le Mirail*. Série A, tome 29. Toulouse: Université Toulouse-Le Mirail, 1984. 165–73.

# Index

'Abd al-Malik (king of Morocco), 83, 127
Abreu, Fray Pedro (chronicler), 156, 157, 161, 166,
181, 188–89, 190, 191, 213 nn. 13, 15, 16, and 20,
216 n. 49, 218 nn. 85, 96, and 97
Aceite, Fernando (morisco spice merchant), 58
Acuña, Don Martín de (diplomat), 126
Alemán, Mateo (novelist), 64, 210 n. 15
Algiers (city): and captives, 64, 65, 84, 130, 137,
185; Cervantes in, 120, 123, 127–28, 178, 184,
208 n. 20; corsair economy in, 78–79, 177; European merchant-bankers in, 79–80, 132, 143,
182–83; homosexuality in, 133; languages spoken in, 139; mercantile economy in, 77, 122–23; and new order, 71, 83, 84, 92; and religion,
87, 88, 174; and *residencia*, 124
Alicante (city), 82, 138
Alí Pasha or Ochalí (king of Algiers), 120–22,
126, 128, 132
Alí Pasha or Ochalí (character), 91, 120, 123, 125,
134, 136, 140, 146, 149
Almería (city), 56
*Almojarifazgo*, 46
Alonso Cortés, Narciso, 184, 217 n. 69, 218 n. 89
Alpujarra, 7, 53, 59, 118
Amabile family (Sicilian merchants), 137
Amadís de Gaula (character), 16
*Amante liberal, El*, 11, 99, 153, 177, 192
Amsterdam (city), 59, 60, 74
Ana Félix (character), 65–68
Andrés/Don Juan (character), 100–114
Andrés-Suárez, Irene, 207 n. 37
Andrews, K. B., 217 n. 81
Antwerp (city), 60, 75, 181

Ariño, Francisco de (chronicler), 157, 161, 162,
215 nn. 17, 21, and 35
Aristocracy, 97, 156, 180; and bourgeoisie, 41,
98–99, 188–89, 190, 193; and gypsies, 96–99,
101–7, 113; lifestyle of, 187–89; order, 99–101,
113; values of, 153. *See also* Feudalism; *Hidalgos*; Old order
Asensio y Toledo, José María, 154, 214 n. 4
Astrana Marín, Luis, 119, 165, 171, 172, 173, 211 n.
6, 213 nn. 48, 50, and 51, 216 n. 48, 217 nn. 64,
69, and 72, 218 n. 100
Aubrun, Charles V., 22, 23, 24, 25, 201 nn. 7 and
8, 203 nn. 27, 28, and 29
Augsburg (city), 54, 55; Diet of, 54; as financial
center, 63–64
Augsburg Confession, 55
Austria, Don Juan de, 91, 127, 131
Avalle-Arce, Juan Bautista, 37, 204 n. 11
Aznar Cardona, Pedro (political-religious writer), 54, 62, 206 n. 13
Azpilcueta, Martín de (economist, theologian),
106

Baeza, Jerónimo de (jurist), 208 n. 11
Bazán, Don Alvaro de (naval commander), 91
Bennassar, Bartolomé, 187, 188, 203 n. 12, 218 nn.
94 and 95; and Lucile Bennassar, 130, 132, 136,
137–38, 213 nn. 44, 45, 52, 54, 58, 70, 71, 72, and
73, 214 nn. 74 and 75
Benveniste, Emile, 179, 218 n. 83
Bleda, Fray Jaime (political-religious writer),
60, 206 n. 18, 207 n. 30
Bliss, Lee, 165, 216 n. 47

# Index

Bono, Salvatore, 78, 84, 132, 213 n. 56
Booth, Wayne, 95
Borgal, Guillaume (French merchant in Algiers), 132
Bossy, John, 181, 215 n. 36, 218 n. 88
Bourdieu, Pierre, 2, 150, 214 n. 86
Bourgeoisie, 67; and aristocracy, 186, 191–93; assimilated to aristocratic lifestyle, 25, 187–88, 189–90; bourgeois order, 97; and capitalism, 42, 50, 61, 189; institutions of, 2; lifestyle of, 186; mentality of, 98, 136; professions among *moriscos*, 56–59; values of, 104, 153. *See also* New order
Braudel, Fernand, 3, 26, 53, 59, 60, 74, 126, 128, 129, 130, 142, 199, 203 n. 38, 205 n. 5, 206 nn. 28 and 29, 212 nn. 27, 28, 29, 30, 35, 37, and 43, 213 nn. 55 and 62, 214 n. 79, 215 n. 25
Bustos Tovar, José Jesús, 204 n. 7

*Caballeros*, 3, 15, 23; and merchants, 41, 49
Cabrera de Córdoba, Luis (historian, chronicler), 155, 156, 157, 158, 161, 166–67, 170, 171, 172, 173, 187, 215 nn. 9, 12, and 23, 216 n. 53, 217 nn. 61, 67, 68, and 73
Cádiz (city), 128, 154, 164, 166, 168; commercial rivalry with Sevilla-Sanlúcar, 159–61, 189; sack of, 155–62, 177, 179, 181, 184, 188
Caja de Leruela, Miguel (economist), 19, 20
Calderón de la Barca, Pedro (dramatist), 103
Calmette, Joseph, 73
Capital, 20, 48, 61, 62, 63, 64, 65, 75, 78, 84, 88, 92, 105, 180, 181, 183, 184; flight of, 62–63; formation of, 10, 56, 64
Capitalism, 26, 27, 42, 49, 50, 61, 63, 74, 76, 78, 82, 85, 101, 106, 107, 108, 143, 195; in Algiers, 77–80; in Ottoman Empire, 75–77; vs. feudalism, 2, 7, 11, 36, 48, 92, 104, 113, 189, 190, 193, 199. *See also* Commerce; Money; Profit
Captives: classes of, 83; ransom of, 79–80, 84–85, 143, 177, 184
Cardillac, Louis, 53, 206 n. 8
Cardona, Don Sancho de (admiral of Aragón), 60
Caro Baroja, Julio, 53, 59, 62, 206 nn. 19 and 21, 207 nn. 33 and 34
Carranza, Don Luis de (politician), 47
Carrasco, Sansón (character), 10, 22, 30
Carrasco, Tomé (character), 22, 23, 26, 31
Casalduero, Joaquín, 54, 109, 180, 204 n. 2, 206 n. 11, 210 n. 25, 218 nn. 84 and 86
Cascardi, Anthony J., 126, 212 n. 25
Castellar, Conde de (politician), 55

Castro, Américo, 3, 6, 15, 52, 95, 98, 164, 199, 202 n. 2, 205 n. 3, 206 n. 12, 216 n. 42
Cavillac, Michel, 186–87, 202 n. 14, 218 n. 92
*Censos*, 17, 18, 27
Cervantes, Miguel de (novelist), 2, 5, 8, 17, 20, 26, 36, 37, 40, 41, 43, 44, 45, 50, 51, 52, 55, 64, 71, 76, 79, 88, 94–96, 118, 119, 120, 121, 122, 124, 126, 127–28, 131, 134, 145, 152, 153, 154, 161–62, 164, 166, 168, 169, 171–73, 175, 181, 184, 186, 189–93, 197, 200
Chaunu, Pierre, 44, 205 nn. 17 and 20, 215 n. 28
Chivalry, 11, 40–42
Chomsky, Noam, 87
Cid, El, 42
Clamurro, William H., 99, 113, 210 n. 13, 211 n. 28
Clavero, Bartolomé, 73, 207 nn. 6, 7, and 8, 208 nn. 9, 10, 11, 12, and 13, 209 n. 52
Clemente/Don Sancho (character), 100–101, 107–8
Clothing: as commodity, 140, 146–47; as investment, 5; as marker of identity, 5, 119, 135, 136, 138, 141–42, 173–74, 176; and sex appeal, 140, 144, 146
*Coloquio de los perros, El*, 22, 188
*Comedia* (genre), 42, 102
*Comentario resolutorio de cambios* (1566), 106
Commerce, 6, 7, 19, 28, 44, 48–49, 56, 75, 76, 77, 143, 154, 174, 176, 177, 178, 182
Commodification, 11; of humans, 7, 22, 25, 27, 79, 80, 83, 117, 128–29, 130, 138, 143–48, 150, 152, 177, 180, 184
Commodity, 6, 34, 77, 79, 83, 102, 107, 113, 142; book as, 10; poetry as, 106, 107; virginity as, 103; women as, 103
Constantinople (city), 122, 124, 126, 138, 139, 149, 150; vs. Madrid, 117, 120, 124
*Conversos*, 4, 10, 25, 64, 67, 109, 135, 154, 162, 191. *See also* New Christians
Córdoba (city), 58
Cornelio (character), 134–35, 150, 152
Cornwallis, Sir Charles (diplomat), 167, 168, 170
Corsair economy, 78–80, 121, 132, 143, 177, 178
Cortado, Diego "Cortadillo" (character), 37–39
Cortes (parliament), 9, 20, 56, 57, 58
Covarrubias, Sebastián de (lexicographer), 9, 17, 21, 44, 72, 109, 123, 180, 202 n. 13
Credit, 48, 75, 79, 84, 106, 107, 159, 179, 183, 184, 185, 188
Criado de Val, Manuel, 40, 204 n. 9
Cruz, Anne J., 9, 213 n. 64
Cyprus, 76, 117–19, 125, 138, 142, 143, 144, 147, 148, 149, 150

# Index

# Index

# Index

# Index

CARROLL B. JOHNSON, president of the Cervantes Society of America, has been a member of the Department of Spanish and Portuguese at the University of California at Los Angeles since 1964 and was for thirteen years its chairman. In this post he "learned to have patience in adversity." He is the author of four books on Spanish Golden Age narrative fiction, including *Inside Guzmán de Alfarache* (1978) and *Madness and Lust: A Psychoanalytical Approach to "Don Quixote"* (1983).

Typeset in 10.5/13 Minion
with Minion display
Designed by Dennis Roberts
Composed by Jim Proefrock
at the University of Illinois Press
Manufactured by Maple-Vail
Book Manufacturing Group

University of Illinois Press
1325 South Oak Street
Champaign, IL 61820-6903
www.press.uillinois.edu